Vision for God

Vision for God

The Story of Dr. Margaret Brand

DR. MARGARET BRAND
with DR. JAMES L. JOST

Discovery House Publishers

Books, music, and videos that feed the soul with the Word of God

Box 3566 Grand Rapids, MI 49501

Discovery House Publishers is affiliated with RBC Ministries, Grand Rapids, Michigan.

Discovery House books are distributed to the trade exclusively by Barbour Publishing, Inc., Uhrichsville, Ohio.

Requests for permission to quote from this book should be directed to: Permissions Department, Discovery House Publishers, P.O. Box 3566, Grand Rapids, MI 49501.

Lyrics of "Find Us Faithful" by Jon Mohr, published by Birdwing Music, are used by permission of EMI Music.

Library of Congress Cataloging-in-Publication Data
Brand, Margaret, 1919–
    Vision for God: the story of Dr. Margaret Brand / Margaret Brand with James Jost.
        p.   cm.
ISBN 1-57293-138-8
1. Missionaries, Medical—India—Biography. 2. Leprosy—
India—Treatment. 3. Physicians—India—Biography.
4. Brand, Margaret, 1919– I. Jost, James. II. Title. [DNLM:
1. Brand, Margaret, 1919– 2. Physicians—England—
Personal Narratives. 3. Physicians—India—Personal
Narratives. 4. Physicians—South Africa—Personal
Narratives. 5. Leprosy—England—Personal Narratives.
6. Leprosy—India—Personal Narratives. 7. Leprosy—
South Africa—Personal Narratives. WZ 100 B8171v 2006]
R722.32.B73B732   2006
610.92—dc22   2006018949
[B]

*This book is dedicated to
my beloved husband Paul
and
To my dear children—
Christopher, Jean, Mary, Estelle,
Trish, and Pauline*

We're pilgrims on the journey of the narrow road,
And those who've gone before us line the way.
Cheering on the faithful, encouraging the weary,
Their lives a stirring testament to God's sustaining grace.

Surrounded by so great a cloud of witnesses,
Let us run the race not only for the prize,
But as those who've gone before us, let us leave to those behind us,
The heritage of faithfulness passed on through godly lives.

After all our hopes and dreams have come and gone
And our children sift through all we've left behind,
May the clues that they discover and the memories they uncover
Become the light that leads them to the road we each must find.

Oh may all who come behind us find us faithful.
May the fire of our devotion light their way.
May the footprints that we leave lead them to believe,
And the lives we live inspire them to obey.
Oh may all who come behind us find us faithful.

—Jon Mohr

Contents

Foreword

For nearly a decade I followed Dr. Paul Brand around the world, retracing the steps of his youth in England and observing him with patients at leprosariums in Louisiana and India. Sitting under a tamarind tree, bouncing along in a Land Rover, screeching through the London "tube" (subway), we explored together his remarkable life. I had never met anyone so wise, and as a young writer I greedily absorbed that wisdom. I spent most of a decade working with Dr. Brand, a collaboration that resulted in three books. Meanwhile, all this time my wife kept saying, "When are you going to write about Margaret? She's the real story!"

As you will see, it would be difficult to invent a life more full of adventure than Margaret Brand's. Born in England but raised in South Africa, she went away to boarding school in England, took medical training in London during the Luftwaffe Blitz, then moved to India where she reared six accomplished children and became a world expert on leprosy's effects on the eye. On eye camps in rural India Dr. Margaret would perform more cataract surgeries in one day (sometimes a hundred) than many American ophthalmologists perform in a month.

Three of the Brands' children followed their parents into careers in medicine and two daughters married doctors. One of these sons-in-law, Jim Jost, finally accepted the challenge of trying to compress this life into one book. He told me that one scene from the family lore convinced him: eight-year-old Margaret and her sister wandering the streets of London wrapped in leopard skins while carrying bags full of gold coins. Her family had sailed from South Africa, their luggage inadvertently left behind, and arrived in England with no warm clothes and no money other than gold, which was virtually worthless as England had just abandoned the gold standard.

Reading this memoir, you find other colorful scenes: fermented marmalade exploding in the family luggage, Margaret frantically hemming an uneven dress en route to meet the queen of England. You will learn the challenges of being a mother to six rambunctious children in a foreign country. One of the Brand youngsters was always hanging from a tree, battling malaria or a tropical virus, getting her head caught in the jaws of a leopard. You will learn too of the unexpected and providential way Dr. Margaret found herself drawn into the unexplored field of leprosy ophthalmology, and of her consulting trips to places like Turkey, Ethiopia, and China.

You will not, however, encounter the three-dimensional person that is Margaret Brand. You will miss the twinkle in her eye, the ready laugh and good humor, the boundless devotion to her beloved husband and family, the esteem in which her profession holds her. No book could capture that fullness, and if it could she would never allow it to be published. If I had to choose one adjective to describe Dr. Margaret, I would choose humility. She downplays her accomplishments, storing awards in closets and decorating her walls instead with family photos. About her adventuresome life, she simply shrugs and gives God the credit for protection and safety.

When I interviewed Paul Brand, we would inhabit the world of ideas, exploring such issues as the problem of pain and design features of the human body. Margaret could hold her own in such discussions too. I remember asking her a single question, "When you look into a person's eye, what do you see?" and sitting enraptured as she talked for half an hour. There was a difference between the two interviewees, however. Both had uncanny memories of their patients (many of them "nobodies" from the Untouchable caste), but whereas Paul tended to remember best the surgical procedures and rehabilitation, Dr. Margaret would flesh out personal details and family backgrounds. As she talked, resurrecting these details, Paul's eyes would often fill with tears. This unique couple had accomplished the rare medical feat of treating and loving patients simultaneously.

As I spent more time in the Brands' home, I felt drawn into their orbit of love as well, made almost a part of their family. We would dine together on their fresh-picked vegetables and homemade bread, or perhaps Margaret's famous chicken curry. Sometimes, as we discussed personal or family issues, Dr. Margaret would softly interrupt. "Can we just pray about that?" she would say, and go on to express her compassion in a beautiful and simple prayer.

Paul Brand died in 2003. Margaret lives on in the modest little cottage she shared with him in retirement overlooking Puget Sound in West Seattle. She still travels internationally, serves on the boards of global charities, plays the violin, and remains active in her local church. All who have visited the Brands come away amazed at their simple lifestyle. They have made a tiny footprint on the planet in terms of accumulating resources and consumer goods. But they have left a very large imprint in other ways, by devoting themselves in service to some of the most neglected people on the planet. Having spent many hours with them both, I cannot help but think this was the vision God had for humanity: talented people serving others with cheer and compassion while embracing life—all of it—with contentment and gratitude.

It is one of the great privileges of my life to have spent such intimate time with Paul and Margaret Brand. I rejoice that now other readers can get to know what my wife has always called "the real story." Maybe you too will get a renewed glimpse of what God had in mind.

Philip Yancey

Preface

Margaret Elizabeth Berry Brand—known affectionately to many as "Dr. Margaret"—spent her childhood in South Africa and returned to England as an expatriate child of the British Empire. She went on to be one of only a few young women studying medicine in London in the midst of World War II. She married a dashing fellow student, Paul Brand, who became a world-famous surgeon, and together they pioneered practices in the treatment of leprosy in India and throughout the world. Without benefit of formal training in eye diseases, Dr. Margaret became an ophthalmologist and one of the foremost authorities on the problems of ocular leprosy. Her contributions to the field extend from America to Ethiopia, Brazil to China.

Most importantly to her and to her husband Paul, Margaret became the mother to six children, raising them in an atmosphere of deep and abiding Christian faith. Her life has been spent as wife, mother, teacher, and doctor, serving the Lord cheerfully in whatever capacity He has required of her.

This, then, is Dr. Margaret's story, told as much as possible in her own words (in the boldface type), as no one can equal her skill at storytelling. She, however, agreed to the project reluctantly.

It is the grace of God, which is available to everyone, that has enabled me to accomplish what I have done, and His grace that has overruled many of my foolish mistakes.

Dr. Margaret does not believe that her life or her achievements merit special mention. But her husband Paul, who died in 2003, had always hoped that her life story would be told.

Dr. Paul W. Brand was internationally known as a twentieth-century pioneer in orthopedic reconstructive surgery and rehabilitation, a researcher into the mysteries of leprosy, an innovative theorist on the sensation of pain as a gift, an author who wrote of his own theological insights, and a lecturer on Christian subjects. Of Margaret, the love of his life, he would want it said that his success was in great measure due to the Lord giving him such an extraordinary wife and companion for over sixty years. He wanted it known that he could not have accomplished what he had achieved were it not for Margaret.

This book, in the end, then, is a gift from Margaret to Paul, the love of her life.

Acknowledgments

This book is drawn from taped interviews conducted by Dr. Margaret's son-in-law and daughter, Jim and Mary Brand Jost. The Brands' personal assistant, Molly Coyner Cozens, performed the heroic task of transcribing hours of audiotapes to paper—strange names and words and all—giving the Josts a body of written material from which to work.

Margaret and Jim would like to thank Carol Holquist of Discovery House Publishers for her loving offer to publish this book and for committing the considerable resources of Discovery to this endeavor. And we cannot begin to express our gratitude to Judith Markham, master editor, who spent untold hours applying her expert skills to this project. On behalf of our beloved Paul Brand and the Brand family, we thank these two special people for the heartfelt gift they have given us.

Also instrumental in this biography/autobiography were the works of biographer Dorothy Clarke Wilson, including *Ten Fingers for God* (Paul Brand Publishing, 1989), a biography of Paul; *Granny Brand* (Paul Brand Publishing, 1976), a biography of Paul's missionary parents; and *Dr. Ida* (Hodder and Stoughton, 1959), a biography of Dr. Ida Scudder, the founder of Vellore Christian Medical College.

Please note that we have protected the identity of certain people by using either initials or pseudonyms.

In this book the following are used interchangeably:

Vellore for the Christian Medical College (CMC) located in Vellore, South India.

Karigiri for the Schieffelin Leprosy Research and Treatment Centre located in Karigiri, South India.

Carville for the United States Public Health National Hansen's Disease Center located near Carville, Louisiana, USA.

Chapter 1

Margaret's Irish Heritage

"If you just work hard enough, you can get there."

It was a Friday afternoon, early in November 1948. We were living on the campus of the Christian Medical College in the city of Vellore, India. I was home with the children. Christopher was four years old, Jean was two, and baby Mary just two weeks old. The weather in Vellore at that time of year is delightful, and I was savoring the enjoyment of being at home as a mother, without any additional responsibilities, when a messenger came to the door and handed me a chit (a note). We had no phones on the campus, so to communicate around the college we would send a messenger by bike, who would then return with the reply. This message was from the acting director of the hospital, Dr. Carol Jameson:

> Dear Margaret,
>   We don't wish to hurry you, but we must have more help in the Eye Department as soon as possible.
>   Carol

The Eye Department! I thought. She has to be joking! I turned the piece of paper over and wrote:

Dear Carol,
    I don't mind being hurried but I know nothing about eyes. You'll have to look for someone else. Sorry.
    Margaret

I assumed that was the end of the matter. But one hour later the messenger returned with another chit. It simply said:

You'll learn. Please start on Monday.
Carol

So six words on a little slip of paper changed my life!

Changed her life, indeed. And what a remarkable life it has been, characterized by the confidence that she can accomplish whatever is required because of her trust in the Lord. This remarkable life began in a small Irish village with two young people who had a tremendous sense of adventure and a drive to succeed.

Margaret's parents were born in Ireland. Both came from Protestant families in areas that were predominately Catholic, and their family loyalties were as much with England as with Ireland. Her father, William Arthur Berry, was the son of parents of modest means who owned a draper shop in the village of Bundoran, located on Donegal Bay on the western coast of Northern Ireland. He was the middle child of the family, born in 1879, with an older sister, Matilda Jane, and a younger brother, Fred. His parents' church background was that of the legalistic Scottish Presbyterians and was associated with a more restrictive attitude toward behavior, which did not appeal to William, who had an adventurous spirit and reveled in taking on challenges. William's character also was marked by an intense drive to master any subject put before him and a desire to explore the world beyond Ireland. He would later impart this same intensity of purpose to his three daughters.

    One memory that echoes across the years was my father saying, "If you just work hard enough, you can get there." He had disciplined himself, so not surprisingly he encouraged us to do the same.

William worked hard at his studies and did exceptionally well, but there was no money available to send him to the better schools. His only hope was to win scholarships, and at about age eleven or twelve he did just that. He sat for an open examination and won a scholarship to the famous Portora Royal High School in the small city of Enniskillen, County Fermanagh. While there he found that he enjoyed the sciences and began somewhat ambitiously considering a career in medicine. Practically speaking, the possibility of his pursuing this dream was slim, given his lack of funds and his modest background.

After finishing high school Will apprenticed himself to a chemist (pharmacist) in Ireland. This work confirmed his interest in the medical sciences, but the position did not satisfy his ambitions. He was determined to see something of the larger world, to pursue his love of learning languages, and to continue with preparations toward an eventual career as a physician. He had done well studying French in high school, so when the opportunity arose to apprentice himself to an apothecary in Paris, he did not hesitate.

In Paris his days were spent mixing stock medicines, ointments, and pills in the apothecary shop. At the end of the workday he would retire to his garret room above the shop, wrap himself in his blanket, and study a correspondence course from London through which he hoped to qualify for the London Matriculation, a pre-university qualification. Will's room had no heat and no running water, and his daily food rations were little more than a loaf of bread, a piece of cheese, and a few apples. His most prized possessions were a woolen blanket, a candle, and his books. On the colder nights he kept warm and awake by walking the floor, candle in one hand and book in the other.

After two years he sat for the London Matriculation examination and received a "first-class pass," which was a remarkable achievement for a correspondence course student. In fact it was remarkable enough to win him a scholarship at Queen's College, Belfast, in Northern Ireland, where he began the next phase of his medical education. In typical fashion, he excelled at Queen's College, and on the strength of his grades he next won a scholarship to St. Mary's Hospital Medical College in London.

St. Mary's had a good reputation as a medical school, but its reputation as a soccer-playing school was better known! My father had no idea how to play soccer. He didn't even know where the sports field was. He was absolutely focused on studying, and he later expected us to do the same— that was the hardship of growing up with a father such as he!

> At St. Mary's my father won nearly every prize for which he competed.
> He could not afford to buy the expensive textbooks, but he won most of
> his library as prizes.

William Berry attained his MB degree (comparable to the MD degree
in the United States), qualifying him to enter medical practice as a general
practitioner, which would have been enough for most students. There were
few medical specialty-training programs at the turn of the century, and most
doctors went no further than the MB degree. But William chose to continue
onward and obtained the British "Doctor of Medicine" degree (comparable
to a PhD in the United States), with his specialty interest being communica-
ble diseases and public health, both major fields at the turn of the century.

During one of his clinical rotations, William met a nurse at Trinity
College Hospital in Dublin. Margaret Muriel Johnston, known as "Peggy"
to her family, was also from the Donegal Bay area and was also Protestant,
although her family were members of the Church of Ireland, a bit less strict
than the Presbyterians. Peggy grew up in a large and happy farming family of seven girls and two boys. Her daring spirit must have been refreshing
to William—"Will" to her. Here was a girl who rode horses bareback and
climbed trees, who could work outdoors on a farm or indoors on a sick ward.
What better person to share William's sense of adventure and his desire to
explore new worlds?

Peggy Johnston went on to take a position at a hospital in London, and
she and Will married in 1912 in Paddington Presbyterian Church in London.
Although Peggy changed her last name from Johnston to Berry, Will wanted,
for unclear reasons, to change her first name as well:

> She was generally called Peggy as she was growing up, but when she
> married my father he said he wanted her to be called Greta, like Gretchen,
> which was the equivalent of Margaret in German. For some reason my
> father loved German names. I never heard her called anything else.

Will's first position as a qualified doctor was in public health in the
London area. Neither Will nor Greta had any relatives in England, so they
relied upon each other for comfort and support—a situation that would assume even greater importance in the near future and would remain true for
the rest of their lives.

The Berry's first daughter, Anna, was born in 1914. That same year also saw the start of World War I, and Will enlisted, as did most young physicians of his day. He was commissioned as a captain in the Royal Army Medical Corps but remained in England at the beginning of the war, during which time, in 1915, the Berrys' second daughter, Frieda, was born. As the war in Europe intensified, however, Will was sent to a military base on Bere Island in Bantry Bay off the Irish coast for a year, where Greta and the girls were able to accompany him. When his next assignment sent him to the war front in Belgium, however, his family returned to London, where they lived through the terror of the German Zeppelin dirigibles flying overhead and dropping bombs.

Will never forgot the images from the trenches, not only of the injured but also those sick from pestilence and disease. As many soldiers succumbed to infectious diseases as to wounds. His knowledge of public health issues, such as clean water and safe food supplies, was as important on the battlefield as it had been in London. He not only dealt with war casualties but also with more mundane problems such as lice and fleas, bedbugs and rats.

When Will was given the opportunity to transfer to a different theater of the war, the war zone in East Africa where the Germans controlled the region of Tanzania and Kenya, he accepted—as much to escape the mud of Europe as to see more of the world. To reach East Africa, troop ships from Europe had to travel down the West African coast and around the Cape of Good Hope off Cape Town, South Africa. The Suez Canal, opened in 1869 to connect the Mediterranean Sea with the Red Sea, would have been the most direct route but was under threat of attack from Turkish forces under German command. On the way to East Africa the ship stopped at Cape Town, and when shore leave was granted Will explored the area as much as he could. He was enthralled with the climate and the landscape, vowing that if he ever had the chance he would return to this enchanting place with his family.

When the war ended in 1918, Will returned to London and took a job as Medical Officer of Health in Kingston-on-Thames, involved once again with the health of the general public rather than a typical medical practice. The Berrys' third daughter, Margaret Elizabeth Berry, was born on June 19, 1919.

Margaret was my mother's name, Elizabeth my grandmother's. Nothing wrong with those, but Mother knew of children with those

names who were called Maggie Liz. She did not like the sound of that, so early on she decided to call me Pearl (one of the meanings of Margaret). Pearl was the name I went by until I was in college, when I chose to use my given name Margaret.[1]

⌒

In 1921, Will saw an advertisement for a position as Medical Officer of Health in the town of Bloemfontein, South Africa, and he considered this an exciting opportunity. The government was seeking a district medical officer in the area of public health who would be based in Bloemfontein but responsible for a large territory surrounding the city. South Africa was divided into four provinces: Cape Province, the Orange Free State, the Transvaal, and Natal. Bloemfontein, which means "fountain of flowers" in the Afrikaans language, was the capital of the Orange Free State and was located on the Highveld, where the landscape was rolling grasslands with scattered trees.

A few miles outside of Bloemfontein was an abandoned British military compound with houses available for those government employees in need of a residence. It was here that Will brought his young family, thousands of miles from England. They traveled first by ship to Cape Town and then by train some six hundred miles to their new home located amid a somewhat flat and arid landscape, where the primary industry of the area was sheep farming. Yet they were not totally isolated from civilization or from their English heritage. The town of Bloemfontein had several shops that sold imported goods from England and Europe, and any number of materials and foodstuffs could be ordered from England. There were also plenty of British expatriates living in the area, including other families with small children.

Will looked forward to the challenge of public health issues that would encompass everything from cities to farms to native villages. The weather, the diseases, even the pests were new to him, and he was pleased with the opportunity to learn new languages, both the Boers' Afrikaans as well as native dialects. For Greta, it was a chance to leave the grime and dreariness of London and return to the countryside.

Despite the unusual terrain and climate and dangers that were very real,

---

1. To this day Margaret is still called Pearl by some Berry family members and old friends.

South Africa was an exciting place—a blend of foreign cultures that encouraged self-reliance and innovation. Both Will and Greta possessed the kind of spirit such an endeavor required, and they embraced this new adventure with gusto.

Chapter 2

Growing Up in South Africa

"Whatever happens, be loyal to one another."

The Berry family soon adjusted to life in the rural countryside of Africa, and the girls, ages six-and-a-half, five, and eighteen months, thrived in this new environment. Their garden produced a wide variety of vegetables, hens provided the family with eggs, and their cows gave them milk, cream, and butter. Greta made traditional Irish breads and created a variety of unusual jams from the fruits that were available. She was constantly busy. If not baking she was working with the young man who helped with the family garden. If not helping the girls with their lessons, she was sewing new clothes for them from fabric obtained in Bloemfontein.

The Berry home was filled with books and music. Will and Greta loved music, especially Mozart, who was one of their favorites, and the sounds from the records on their gramophone filled the house. Will sometimes played the harmonica, and he was good at whistling with a beautiful trill.

Religion was largely confined to whatever religious instruction the girls received at school and occasional attendance at church services. Will did not allow the girls to do schoolwork on Sundays, perhaps as a holdover from his own strict upbringing. And Greta did teach the children to recite the Lord's Prayer, which became a bedtime ritual throughout their childhood.

Will also took advantage of their exotic locale to provide the children with memorable and unusual family holidays. In the 1920s, a family motoring holiday would have been difficult enough in England, given the quality of automobiles and roadways in that most civilized of countries. Only parents with an unusual degree of self-confidence would have attempted the daunt-ing effort of a motoring holiday from Bloemfontein north to Bulawayo in Rhodesia, a trek of some seven hundred miles.

We were some of the first people in Bloemfontein to have a car. I first remember going to school in a pony trap (a type of two-wheeled cart). We must have got our first car somewhere around 1924 or 1925. Later on we had a posh sedan car with a permanent roof, but our first was an open-sided one with a fairly wide running board on which we could stack our luggage or the dog carrier.

I remember vividly a long trip we made from Bloemfontein all the way up to the northern part of the Transvaal, which was in the next state north of us. We covered hundreds of miles and had to take our own petrol (gas), drinking water, and, most essential, the wherewithal for repairing tire punctures. There were many days when we seemed to do nothing but sit beside the road while my father mended yet another puncture. This was not simply a matter of putting on a spare tire. He had to remove the inner tube, patch the hole, put the inner tube back into the tire, pump it up with a hand pump, and then put the tire back on the car.

I especially remember crossing the Limpopo River on our journey. The Limpopo separates the Transvaal of South Africa from Rhodesia (now Zimbabwe) to the north. Rudyard Kipling made this river famous in his story "How the Elephant Got His Trunk." (Kipling was special to the folk of Bloemfontein because he started and was the first editor of *The Friend,* the one English newspaper available in Bloemfontein.) In his story Kipling described the Limpopo as "the great, green, greasy Limpopo River, all set about by fever trees."

In Kipling's day the river was famous for its crocodiles, and there were still plenty in our day as well. Since there was no bridge across the river, the car had to be towed through the water by a team of donkeys at a crossing where the river was shallow. The carburetor was removed and carried across in a boat, along with other belongings, by my mother and us girls. My father stayed in the car, with the water rising to the level of the axles.

A poor little donkey was tethered upstream in the water to attract any crocodiles away from the travelers who were fording the river. I was as relieved to see that he was still alive and well when we safely got across as I was to see our car coming out of the river on the other side.

The Berry girls attended St. Michael's school in Bloemfontein, some four miles from their home. St. Michael's was "the English school," an Anglican-based institution with lessons and texts in English and a curriculum based upon the British school system. Anna, the oldest, excelled at school, enjoying her studies and seeming to do everything well. Frieda displayed something of a rebellious spirit and was famous more for her antics than for her academic performance. Margaret seemed to be a mixture of her two older sisters.

School activities included sports such as netball, field hockey, and track. During the summer months (October to March) swimming was available, but the public swimming pool was nearly three miles from the school, and travel to the pool meant a long, hot walk. After school there were Girl Guides activities, just like those available in England. And then there was music. All the girls were enrolled in music lessons. Piano was mandatory, but all three began studying second instruments as well. Frieda took cello lessons, while Anna and Margaret took violin instruction. Anna and Frieda eventually gave up their study of stringed instruments, despite encouragement from their parents, but Margaret continued with the violin into adulthood.

The city of Bloemfontein contained two main business streets and a network of residential streets. As it was the judiciary center of the Orange Free State, courthouses and law offices were prominent, and the town center offered butcher shops for meat, greengrocers for vegetables, and shops in which to purchase other foodstuffs as well as fabric or ready-to-wear clothing. The paved streets were lined with brick and stone buildings, and electric streetcars provided transport. Bloemfontein boasted a library, a natural history museum, a post office, and a cinema, which went from showing silent films to "talkies" during Margaret's childhood there. Telephones were just becoming available, although radio (known as "the wireless") did not appear until 1930.

Despite the civility offered by Bloemfontein, the veld could be a hostile place. The weather could change rapidly, with thunderstorms bringing high winds, fierce lightning (one neighbor was killed during such a storm), and flash floods. An unusual rodent, the meerkat, harbored fleas which carried the organisms that caused bubonic or pneumonic plague. Wild animals threatened the chickens and cows, and there was always the danger of venomous snakes, poisonous spiders, and stinging scorpions. Animals, reptiles, and insects were not the only danger. Angry native Africans posed their own threat.

On one occasion a native man had a vendetta against Dr. Berry, for some unknown reason. The man was scared off the premises one night by the barking of the family dog but returned some nights later and fed the dog poisoned meat, causing the animal to go into convulsions and die at Mrs. Berry's feet.

Although the Berrys and their servants lived near other British families within a defined area, it was not a gated compound, and there wasn't any type of police protection. Their residence had a fence around it, but the iron bars primarily served as a visible boundary for the children rather than a bulwark against potential surrounding dangers. There was a policeman living a few miles away, but he himself had been the victim of native unrest.

There was a time when the African natives in the nearby township got hold of some potent illicit liquor and were just going crazy on it. They decided to get rid of all the "whites" that lived on the far side of the township, which included us. We had no police protection out that far. There was one police officer, who lived about two miles from us, and his children played with us. But one of his daughters was ambushed and her throat slashed. That and other incidents did little for our peace of mind. We children were told not to go outside our fence.

I can remember one day standing on a fence bar looking anxiously down the road just outside. Our house was on a bit of a hill, and we could see down the dirt road for a few miles. Our parents had gone into town, and we were watching for their return. The waiting was tense and I was scared. Anna and Frieda told me, "Well, if the natives come, they will come with knobkerries." A knobkerrie is a heavy stick with a big knob on the end that was used to club an enemy to death—quite a vicious weapon!

Rather fearfully I asked, "What if they do? And what do we do?" And I remember the comfort of Anna saying to me, "Well, don't worry. Even if they kill us we'll be with Jesus. We'll be alive again." Oh, my! For the first time in my young life (I was barely five years old) I was quite confident that whatever happened, death wasn't necessarily the end and that Jesus had something better for us. I was at peace. But I surely was glad to see my parents return.

Another frightening experience occurred when the Berry girls decided, against all parental admonitions, to explore the deserted military hospital outside the security of their compound. This was always a favorite site, a wonderful place to hunt for untold "treasure." But it was close to the area where Africans roamed and was considered to be especially dangerous at that time because of the natives' rebellion against a government attempt at prohibiting liquor.

We enjoyed playing "let's pretend" games in the old buildings of an abandoned military hospital, which was about four hundred yards from our house, outside our boundary fence. Off limits to us! But there was an old operating room and a morgue, and we just loved to explore there. It offered all kinds of imaginary adventures.

So on one rather hot afternoon when we were playing with the children of a family that was visiting us, while the four parents were talking in the living room we five girls slipped out of the house, through the fence, and over to the hospital. We went to the room that had padded walls, high windows out of reach, and a door that could be opened only from outside. It would have been used to house mentally disturbed patients. A small opening, about eight square inches, in the upper part of the door would have allowed staff to look in to monitor the patient. We thought it was a wonderful place to play!

We went in and Frieda shut the door. At first we didn't realize the significance of this, but we soon found that we were prisoners. The door could be opened only from the outside. It was a hot afternoon, and we got hotter and hotter and so thirsty. The dust was terrible. We tried to climb up to the windows, but the walls were padded with horsehair that was filled with the dust of many years. The dust that came out of those pads as we tried to climb was more suffocating than the hot air. We examined each other's tongues to see whose was the driest and therefore which one of us was the most likely to die first. We decided that whoever died first was to tell God to please send some help! Since Anna's tongue was the driest, she probably would be the first to go.

We took turns climbing on each other's backs to get a fresh breath of air through the little peephole (to this day I still have a phobia about being closed in a room unless I know I can get out again). We knelt and recited the Lord's Prayer.

We had reached the point where we thought our parents would never find us, when we heard a low whistle. But we were afraid to make too much noise because we knew there were hostile natives in the vicinity and if they heard us they might set the building on fire. So one of us, standing on someone's back, looked out the peephole.

The person whistling was our garden boy who was outside in the hallway. We called to him, and he let us out. By this time we had shed our clothing because of the heat, but we didn't care. Five naked little girls ran through that door and across the veld to our home.

The boy who had rescued us said that he wouldn't have known we were there except that our dog was lying outside the door. The dog hadn't made a sound. He was just lying there, and the garden boy guessed that we might be somewhere nearby.

We deserved and got a serious lecture, but the relief of being alive made any sort of punishment seem trivial.

By early 1931, Anna, now sixteen, had completed her South African matriculation (the equivalent of a high school education) and had decided to become a physician. This was as remarkable and as daunting a goal for her as it had been for her father, although for different reasons. Women physicians were exceedingly rare, and there were few training opportunities for women in any country. Only three medical colleges in London accepted women, and they had but a handful of openings. Anna was from a Commonwealth country, had no connections or sponsors in England, and could not be certain that her education in South Africa had been adequate. Yet she did have the full support of her parents, especially her father, who felt that she and her sisters could achieve any goal.

Anna could pursue her dream only by returning to England. On a family vacation in 1927 the Berrys had investigated several boarding schools in preparation for just such a future need. They had chosen Malvern Girls College (MGC) in the town of Malvern, in the west of England near the Welsh border. Despite its name, the school was not a college in the American sense but rather had grades equivalent to high school along with two years of pre-university preparation.

Given Anna's serious intent, enrolling her at Malvern was the best decision. A more difficult decision, however, was whether Frieda and Margaret should go with her. After much consideration, Will and Greta decided that all of their girls should enroll at Malvern. This was not an easy decision—how heart wrenching it would be to have all three daughters leave home at the same time—but it was logical to keep the sisters together and allow them to continue their education. It also helped that Anna had already assumed the role of the responsible young adult and would be able to serve as surrogate mother to her younger sisters.

Plans were made for Greta and the girls to depart Cape Town by ship and sail to England via Antwerp, Belgium, leaving just before Christmas 1931. Trunks had to be packed not only for the three girls, who would not be returning to Bloemfontein for several years, but also for Greta, who planned to stay in England for a few months, helping her daughters adjust to their new lifestyle in what would be something of a foreign country to them.

Young Margaret had scant recollections of England other than those of the one family trip there in 1927 when she was eight years old, along with the stories she had heard from her family and their English friends. While she was excited about the chance to go to England with her sisters and start at a new school, she felt she belonged in South Africa. She knew more South African history than British history, and she even had acquired what would be recognized as a South African accent in the UK. She could not imagine life without the veld: the open spaces to roam, the animals, the many domestic pets, the games in the trees and rooftops, the joy of lying on the stoop on a hot afternoon, shaded by grapevines and enjoying the fruit they offered. She was by no means wild and uncivilized. She had had a taste of the expected standards of decorum and behavior from her experience at St. Michael's. But the closer the time came for departure, the more she sensed that she was leaving a world she loved and perhaps might not see again. What might the future hold?

Finally the morning came for one last painful goodbye. We hugged our servants who had taken good care of us. We hugged our dogs, the numerous cats and kittens, and silently, nearly in tears, we circled our home. It was so hard letting go.

As Will drove his family to the train that would start them on their journey to England, knowing he might not actually see them for several years and would only be able to communicate by slow sea mail, he surprised Margaret with words she never forgot.

My father, even with his intense interest in our academic progress, gave us one last memorable gift. As he drove us to the station to catch our train to Cape Town, he said, "Whatever happens, be loyal to one another. You are a family. Support each other." He said nothing about grades or scholarships, no admonitions to study harder, no lectures about proper behavior. Just loyalty.

My father later told us that when he returned to his office after saying goodbye to us, he put his head down on his hands and cried. He hadn't realized just how empty his life was going to be without his girls.

Chapter 3

England and Boarding School

"I see now how good God was to me!"

The three-week voyage from Cape Town to London was not without incident, and one episode in particular haunted Margaret for the rest of her life, especially when she traveled by ship years later with her own small children.

> Our ship was a Dutch freighter with just a few passengers. One of the passengers had a nine-month-old baby, the cutest little fellow. One day the mother said to me, "Would you like to take care of him for just a little while? I just need to go down to our cabin." I was delighted.
>
> I thought he would enjoy watching the ocean, so I took him to the deck railing where he could look down at the waves. And I thought I had a secure hold on him, but suddenly he pushed back and was in danger of falling into the ocean. I didn't have time to think but instinctively grabbed his clothing and was able to pull him back to safety.
>
> Afterward, I was in shock and shaking. When his mother came back to get him, I went to our cabin and simply cried and cried. The thought of what nearly had happened was so appalling I couldn't speak of it for a long time. I used to have nightmares about it.

Another difficulty was not as traumatic but certainly made for an uncomfortable voyage. As Greta Berry and her daughters sailed northward into the cold winter weather of the North Atlantic, they needed to take out their winter clothing, which was packed in their trunks in the hold of the ship.

We left South Africa in the heat of summer in the Southern Hemisphere, but by the time we were halfway to England, we were getting quite cold. My mother went down to the hold to get warmer clothes and coats for us, but our trunks were not there! A telegram was sent and we learned that our trunks had been left on the wharf in Cape Town. Poor Mother was in despair. We would be without any warm clothing now and for weeks after we arrived in England. Fortunately some "karosses" (large rectangular shawls made from wild cat skins sewn together) were packed in our cabin luggage. Mother had planned to give these as gifts to family and friends. They were warm and would make attractive bed covers or wall decorations. While not intended as garments, they now became a godsend to us. There were three shawls, one for each of us girls. But what about Mother? The captain, who felt responsible for the situation, was very concerned. The best he could do was to offer Mother the winter coat of one of his smallest officers. It was warm even if much too large.

So that's how we arrived in England on January 14, 1932—with animal skins draped around us girls and Mother in a naval officer's oversized coat—and we couldn't get a taxi. Nobody would pick us up! Finally a cab driver took pity on us and drove us to the hotel where we would be staying. Thereupon Mother ordered us to bed to keep warm while she, still dressed as a Dutch naval officer, went shopping for some winter clothing.

But now we faced an even more serious difficulty—a lack of money.

Upon our arrival in England, Mother was shocked to discover that the monetary value of gold had plummeted due to the country having gone off the gold standard. I didn't understand what that meant, but I did realize that it meant trouble for us. Dad had given Mother a quantity of gold coins. He assumed, based on their value, that we would have plenty of cash for all our needs. But no one wanted gold. It was almost worthless. We trudged from bank to bank, trying to sell those coins. We had bags of them! And nobody was interested.

With all kinds of expenses ahead—school uniforms, fees, non-uniform items, hotels, and travel—it was a nightmare, especially for Mother. All she could do was send telegrams back to South Africa and trust that Dad would advise her. We never got thrown out of our little bed and breakfast hotel, so I assume he found a way to resolve that situation. But it was a difficult time and contributed to a tremendous homesickness for the land we'd left behind.

Despite arriving in one of the largest cities in the world in midwinter without possessions or adequate funds, Greta was able to work through each difficulty and to continue with the plans she and Will had made. It may have helped that, being in the middle of the Great Depression, she and her girls were not the only ones struggling to make do. And once their trunks arrived, life looked a little brighter.

By the end of January Greta and her daughters left London for the town of Malvern, where they checked into a small hotel. This would be their residence until classes began and the girls moved into their rooms at the school and where Greta would stay for the next few weeks until the girls had adjusted to their new surroundings. Before they could begin classes, the girls had to take examinations to determine the grades appropriate for their abilities. Their mother had to purchase their school uniforms, including the correct shoes and stockings, from prescribed stores. This amounted to a considerable list of items.

> The first term that we went to MGC (1932) we all wore black stockings and black shoes. We had to have six pairs of stockings at the start of each term. We had to have Sunday shoes as well as everyday shoes, which included one pair for indoors—specific for the house (dormitory) we were assigned to—and another for outdoors. We had to have Wellington boots for wet weather (we wore those a lot!), sneakers for gym classes, hockey boots if we played field hockey, and lacrosse boots for that sport. Outfitting three girls with all that was quite an expense, and I remember how anxious we felt about it. Then, the very next term, the school changed the color of stockings and shoes from black to brown! At least those of us who had just purchased the black items were allowed to wear them until they wore out.

The school buildings housed classrooms, art studios, science labs, a library, an assembly hall, and sports facilities. The senior girls lived in the dormitories on the top floors of the main building, while middle school girls were housed in converted private homes in the surrounding district, all within walking distance from the main school building. The majority of the students were boarders whose parents lived elsewhere in the British Isles or, like the Berry girls, were expatriates whose parents lived abroad. Anna was placed in a senior house. Frieda and Margaret were placed in the same middle school house at first, according to grade level rather than age.

The transition to this strange place and its demands was not at all easy for Margaret. She was twelve years old and a new girl in a group that had already been together for the first half of the school year. Then there was the climate. She was not used to damp cold, and would, in fact, never become accustomed to it. She missed the colors, sights, smells, and warm sun of South Africa. She even developed chilblains, sore, itchy reddened nodules on the toes caused by exposure to cold.

> I was so miserable with the chilblains. With that extra swelling my shoes were always too tight. I would spend the nights with severe itching and the days with intense aching pain in my feet. That did nothing to make me love England!
>
> On Sunday mornings the whole school attended Malvern Priory, a beautiful old church dating back to the fourteenth century. But I cannot say I ever appreciated it. To get there required about a two-mile walk, after which my hands and feet would be frozen. The thin leather of my gloves and shoes didn't keep out the cold. And the thawing out process was so painful. I would sit through the service, rocking back and forth with my aching, burning hands and feet, longing to get out.
>
> But it wasn't just the climate change that was so difficult. Initially, I hated everything about the school. I was put into classes too advanced for me. The French, Latin, and science classes were far beyond what I had studied in South Africa. I was fairly good with math, but overall school was not easy for me. I tried to get out of it any time I could, so I made the most of any health problem.
>
> I had had rheumatic fever when I was about eight years old, and in the cold damp climate of England, I started to have joint pains. The school doctor was afraid that, with my health history, I was getting another attack of rheumatic fever and put me in the school sanatorium. The nurse in charge was a kind, motherly woman, and she gave me books to read,

jigsaw puzzles to do, and no schoolwork. I thought this was just fine, even though I was there for several weeks. Also, my mother was still in England and would drop in often.

I missed so much schoolwork that after the spring break they moved me to a lower class, where I was much more comfortable and no longer had to struggle to keep up with the lessons and homework. My confidence returned, and I started to enjoy school and even became quite a model student. In time I was appointed head of our house, Avenue House, and eventually head of the entire middle school. I didn't know what that appointment really meant, and I don't suppose it made a whole lot of difference to those whom I was supposed to represent. I was the gym captain and the golf captain for middle school, and I did well on the swimming and field hockey teams. I was quite good in ballet and was chosen for some nice solo parts in the ballets that we performed. I enjoyed art but did not excel. Needlework was encouraged, and I did manage to finish a camisole for my mother.

Looking back I can see that I received plenty of recognition for whatever talent I may have had and that my ego was boosted, perhaps more than it deserved. But no matter what honors and accolades I was fortunate enough to receive, I treasured even more the friendships I made. Living so closely together, as one does in boarding school, gives one a unique opportunity to get to know others. And I am so grateful for those dear friends who still count me a friend some seventy years later.

Mrs. Berry stayed in England from January until the spring. But in May she received a sad letter from Will. Politically the climate was worsening. The entire country was feeling the tension between British and Afrikaans people, and Margaret's father was feeling pressure to resign from a number of Afrikaans administrators with whom he worked. His job was in jeopardy. He also admitted that he was lonely, missing Greta and his girls. She decided to return to South Africa. The worst of the difficult transition for the girls had been completed. Margaret was doing better in the warmer weather of the English spring, the girls had made friends at school, and they had become accustomed to their new surroundings and to the schoolwork required of them.

The school summer holidays were six to eight weeks long, and children whose parents were out of the country had to find somewhere to go for this period. Fortunately for the Berry girls, their parents had a friend, Miss Freshney, who had been a nurse in Bloemfontein. She and her sister owned a small farm in Lincolnshire on the east coast of England. At their invitation, the girls spent the holidays on the farm. This was a wonderful arrangement. Miss Freshney knew Bloemfontein and its homesteads, knew and loved their parents, and understood the girls' homesickness. Her farm was fully stocked with horses, cows, pigs, chickens, and everything else the girls had left behind in Africa. Their first summer holidays away from their parents could not have been at a better place, and the time passed all too quickly. But England now looked much better than it had during the first months after their arrival.

During the autumn term (September to December) of 1932, the girls supported and encouraged each other, just as their father had hoped. They spent the Christmas holidays with family friends, and, happily for them, Greta was able to return from South Africa for a few weeks at Easter in 1933.

By now Margaret was doing well at Malvern and was beginning to demonstrate a new sense of responsibility. In 1933 she applied to take a scholarship exam that could help cover about 30 percent of her school fees. When she won the scholarship, her father was overjoyed. He was grateful to see his daughter showing the same drive he had demonstrated in taking on academic challenges and in trying to help pay her own way. For Margaret, it gave her new confidence and an incentive to stay near the top of her class.

Even with this success, however, she still struggled to catch up in some areas. For example, despite attending "the English school" in Bloemfontein, Margaret knew more about South Africa than she did about England, the country of her birth, and she sounded more South African than English.

> I had to take elocution lessons because I had such a strong South African accent. They said, "Child, you can't speak like that here in England." The South African accent, with its rather flat sound, was offensive to the English—not at all "the Queen's English."
>
> Also, while I was quite knowledgeable about South African history, I didn't know British history. When we went to see a production of a satire about British history, "1066 and All That," I didn't have a clue as to what was true and what was tongue-in-cheek, so I didn't know when to laugh

or why. Ashamed of my ignorance, I made a great effort to correct it, and my newly acquired knowledge came in handy in the scholarship exam.

That same year the concept of "pen pals" became popular. One day our geography teacher announced that she had made contact with somebody in South Africa. My ears perked up. She went on and said that we could be pen pals with girls in a school in Bloemfontein. Was I dreaming? Could she really be talking about the town, thousands of miles away, where I'd gone to school? The teacher explained that we were to be given the names of girls in a school called St. Michael's. Then she read out the names of girls who had been my classmates, some of my best friends. And one of them was assigned to me as my new pen pal. What a connection! All my feelings of being uprooted just vanished. I didn't realize it at the time, but I see now how good God was to me.

Other than expensive telegrams, the only means of communication between boarding school children in England and their parents scattered throughout the British Empire was letters. It would have been unimaginable, if not impossible, to phone England from India or Africa. For months, and sometimes years, the only contact parents had with their children was written correspondence. The Berry girls were no exception, but it took time for them to learn the significance of this communication and how to do it well. One incident with her father was in part responsible for Margaret's later dedication to exhaustive letter writing.

I was a poor letter writer. Our parents wrote lovely letters, telling us what the animals were doing and all the kinds of things they knew would interest us. I would write, "Dear Daddy, We're doing fine. I'm sorry. I've got to go now. I've got to get my sweets out." (Twice a week we could have four ounces of candy from our "tuck" supplies. Candy days were very significant to us boarders!) Such letters must have served only to emphasize the distance between Dad and his girls. Later, when our own girls were in boarding school and we received letters from them, I deserved to get some of my own medicine dished up to me, but my children were much better than I had been!

My dad finally wrote telling me what my letters to him were like, and I realized what a cad I was. After that I began writing him in great detail,

telling him what a typical day was like and all the other stuff he was yearning to know. Was he ever happy!

By the end of 1933, with Dr. Berry's public health government post becoming ever more difficult as prejudice against non-Afrikaner whites intensified, he decided that he and Greta should leave Bloemfontein. He had spent twenty-two years in public health, and although his most recent work chiefly pertained to a tropical country with somewhat unique problems, he did have impressive accumulated experience, which might help him as he sought new employment. England was still mired in the heart of the Great Depression, and he might have done better to seek a job elsewhere in Africa, perhaps Kenya or Rhodesia, or some other Commonwealth country such as India. But his children were settled in England, and Anna was about to leave Malvern and begin university. His daughters were going to be in England for at least the next several years, and the most important thing for him to do was to reunite the family.

Will was now fifty-four years old, and it would not be easy for him to start a new medical career. But, as he had demonstrated from childhood, his nature was to trust that he could do whatever was necessary to succeed. And in his wife he had a companion with great strength of character. Job or not, Depression or not, he and Greta sorted and packed their possessions, said their goodbyes, and, in 1934, returned to England to create a new future for themselves and their girls.

Chapter 4

At Home in London

"Now Pearl would be Margaret."

Will and Greta Berry rented a house in Northwood, a lovely neighborhood about fifteen miles northwest of London center. Their new home was some seventy miles from Frieda and Margaret at Malvern, but Anna, who was about to start her studies as a medical student at University College, London, would live at home and commute by train. These new beginnings for the family looked promising, save for the fact that Will could not find any permanent posts available and there was a limit as to how long their savings would last, especially with school fees for the girls. Even as the family gathered to celebrate their first holiday together in three years, Will's concern for their future somewhat muted their joy.

> We were told not to expect much for Christmas, not even a tree. My father said, "No turkey. Nothing special. No frills." My mother was able to find a turkey on sale, though once we tasted it we knew why it was on sale. She also managed to make a traditional type Christmas cake. She was determined to do that. Anna was always creative in thinking up and making little gifts, so even though we didn't have a Christmas tree to put them under, we at least had a few wrapped presents.

Failing to find a position in the public health field, Will decided he would try to establish a general family practice, seeing patients in his home. This would not be an easy undertaking. It had been over twenty years since he was directly involved in the multifaceted aspects of clinical medicine, and what current clinical knowledge he did possess pertained to the tropical illnesses of southern Africa. Being a general practitioner (GP) in 1930s London was demanding. General practitioners delivered babies, provided gynecological care, treated toddlers and children, set fractures, managed a variety of adult diseases from pneumonia to high blood pressure to heart disease, and had to be available seven days a week, twenty-four hours a day. Specialists in medicine and surgery were few and only worked within hospitals. Thus, care for all types of medical problems fell to the neighborhood GP.

The typical GP worked out of his own home, meaning that part of the house was set aside as clinic rooms (usually called "the surgery"). This took the form of either a dedicated downstairs area or an addition built on to the house, which included a waiting room, an examination room, and, in Dr. Berry's case, a small pharmacy for mixing medications for patients. House calls were done on a daily basis, and emergency house calls could be required day, night, or weekends. Almost all physicians and surgeons were in solo practice, and group practice was rare. Advertising was by word of mouth. Payment was in cash only. Some employed people had health insurance, but such patients were rare. (The British National Health Service, which provides health care coverage to all citizens, would not come into existence until the late 1940s.)

Logistically, it was not difficult for a British-trained physician to start a practice. One had only, literally, to hang up a "shingle" (a sign) on one's door. The obstacles for Will Berry were that he was unknown in the area and unknown to the local medical community; also, because of the Depression people had trouble finding money for food, let alone medical care. The odds against his succeeding were considerable. He did not, however, have other options, so with borrowed money he built a house that included a surgery, hung his sign, and waited.

> **Patient referral depended solely on word of mouth, and in the beginning, patients were slow in coming. Dad became very depressed. We had a lot of expenses and not much money coming in. And then when patients did come but couldn't pay, Dad often cancelled their bills. We were not the only ones who didn't have any money!**

One important service that Dr. Berry could offer, which set him apart from other physicians, was his ability to make up the patients' medications himself. This not only saved the patients a trip to the chemist (the pharmacist), but also gave Dr. Berry an important additional source of income. His earlier efforts in learning pharmacology had been time well spent.

Slowly, ever so slowly, his practice began to grow, and after a few years the family was able to enjoy a more comfortable lifestyle. But those first few years back in England were lean and stressful, with the entire family feeling the pressures.

We felt poor. The other girls at school went to movies. We didn't. They would go on vacations, and we wouldn't go anywhere. There was no way my dad would spend or "waste" our money on unnecessary things. But he did take us to the Old Vic Theatre in London to see excellent performances of Shakespeare's plays and other classics, and we saw one ballet. Since he considered this high quality and educational, and not entertainment, it was a legitimate expense. But nobody at school wanted to talk about ballet or Shakespeare. Most girls wanted to talk about the latest movie stars, and I knew little about them.

In the 1930s women were expected to learn domestic skills and to plan their future in terms of marriage and children. The only careers for women were teaching and nursing. Thus, it was both remarkable and radical for Dr. Berry to feel so strongly that his daughters should consider becoming professionals. The reason for his attitude is unclear, as nothing in his background or in his family tradition explains such a philosophy. Certainly nothing in English society at the time supported such a conviction. His own wife happily lived the traditional role of mother and homemaker and clearly enjoyed her status. Yet the career successes his daughters would achieve were directly related to his nontraditional ambition for them. He wanted them to be as resolute about their pursuit of a professional career as he was, and he discouraged anything that might be a distraction.

I wanted to learn something about cooking. My mother was an excellent cook, and I was enjoying watching her in the kitchen one day when my father said, "This isn't your place. You get back to your books." Also, we had very little social life. Dad was so anxious for us to do well enough to have a proper career. He would often say, "What would

happen if you didn't marry, or if you married and your husband became disabled or died? What would you do?" Most women didn't have careers, and he was keen that we would not be caught in such a situation—not if he could help it.

Anna was proceeding with her medical studies, and Frieda had decided upon a career in the nursing profession. This especially pleased Mrs. Berry, who had been a nurse and was still practicing some nursing by helping her husband with his clinical work at the home surgery. Margaret, at age sixteen, was also leaning toward the medical sciences, but her father thought she should consider entering the diplomatic service—influenced in part by his own love of languages. Unfortunately Margaret's chief academic weakness happened to be languages.

Even before I left South Africa I had been interested in medical work. I wanted to be a veterinarian. Watching my father work with the cows and our other animals, I couldn't believe there could be a more wonderful life. But things changed. I think it was perhaps during my last year at Malvern that I decided I would be a doctor. When my father realized he wasn't going to change my mind about the diplomatic service, he was entirely supportive of my medical interests.

Margaret had done sufficiently well in the School Leaving Certificate that she gained matriculation exemption. This enabled her to apply for entrance into almost any university in the country, with the exception of Oxford and Cambridge. (The system has changed now and involves two more years of high school study before most British universities will accept students.) Margaret applied to University College, London, in the premedical course. But when she went to London in 1936 for the admissions interview, she was disappointed to be advised to wait another year because of her young age. They did promise to save a place for her in the 1937 admissions group. The staff at Malvern assumed she would spend that extra year at their school, studying premedical sciences and trying for a scholarship or at least an entry into an Oxford or Cambridge college. Her father, however, had other plans. He had contacted a London school, the Chelsea Polytechnic, which he thought would be a better place for her next set of preparatory courses for university. Young Margaret learned about his decision in a difficult manner.

One day the principal came to me when I was in the swimming pool. Miss Brooks was an imposing figure in more ways than one, and she looked stern as she said, "Get out of the pool. I want to talk with you." I got out and stood at the edge of the pool dripping and shivering as she went on. "Just why do you want to leave Malvern? Just think of what you have here. Why do your parents want to take you away? You don't have any say in this, do you? You don't want to go away, do you?"

That's the first I realized that a decision had been made and that my father had sent a letter of intent to withdraw me from Malvern. I didn't know how to answer Miss Brooks, and I guess she could see I was embarrassed. She turned and left me, still dripping and wondering to myself what lay ahead.

By this time, Anna had completed her premedical course work, the first two years of a six-year program leading from basic medical sciences courses through clinical courses. Anna's achievements cannot be overstated. Not many women even got that far. At that time the number of women in the starting classes was only twenty-five percent of the total class size, and this dropped to less than ten percent by the time the class moved into clinical courses later in the curriculum. Dr. Berry was determined that Margaret should have whatever special help was available in order for her to succeed as Anna had.

Women in medicine were not common during the 1930s, and competition for places was fierce. Most of the major London hospitals had a medical school, but only three accepted women students. One of the three was The London School of Medicine for Women, which accepted only women and was extremely difficult to get into. Two others, Kings College and University College, would take twenty women into the pre-clinical program, but would accept only the top eight women (versus sixty men) into the final clinical medicine years. In addition, my father was hoping that I could earn a scholarship, as he had done some thirty-five years earlier, by taking yet another exam, and he feared I would not achieve all this by staying another year at Malvern. He was probably right.

In 1936 Margaret left Malvern Girl's College and spent the next year living at home and commuting into London to take courses at Chelsea Polytechnic (now called the Chelsea College of Science), where she took courses in physics, botany, zoology, chemistry, and German and French science vocabulary. In addition, her father enrolled her in University Correspondence College to take the same four sciences by correspondence as well as an English composition course. Besides providing a different means of learning the same material, the correspondence course work largely involved essay work, with test booklets in each subject completed and returned weekly. Such composition skills were crucial, as the scholarship examination was in essay format. Winning the scholarship prize would not only be a significant honor but would also help with the fees once Margaret started university.

I'm sure I agreed to this plan, but it was my dad's idea. He was a very persuasive man. Every week I would have a test, a paper, which I had to write for the correspondence courses. I was also taking violin lessons. The only social life I had was when I went once a week to play with the London Junior Symphony. I didn't question any of this. I thought I was a typical, normal girl.

My daily travel, six days a week, involved a long commute: two trains and a twenty-five minute walk each way. Despite our lack of funds, my father insisted on purchasing a seasonal first-class train ticket for my protection and comfort. I spent a good deal of my daily two hours on the trains reading works of English literature of which I had heard but had not read. I never got through the whole reading list, but it was a wonderful extension of my education just to read the ones I did.

My main purpose for being at the polytechnic was to take classes that would prepare me to sit for the scholarship I hoped to win. It was a tough course. Most of my fellow students were planning to go into pure science, not medical school. They would need to know more chemistry, physics, and biology than I did at that stage.

To mark this new phase in her life, Margaret, who was still known as Pearl to family and friends, decided that she would begin using her given name.

I wanted to change my name when I went to Malvern, but the headmistress said, "Oh, we have dozens of Margarets here. We don't have any Pearls. You will be Pearl." So there I was, stuck with Pearl, which I considered to be my little-girl name. Now I could be Margaret. (My parents continued to call me Pearl, as did all of the people with whom I had grown up. And in later years my husband would sometimes call me Pearl with a little twinkle in his eye. Some of my nieces and nephews still call me Auntie Pearl, and I get letters addressed to "Dr. Pearl Brand.")

Margaret was only seventeen years old, and most girls that age would not spend a year preparing to take a formidable, fiercely competitive scholarship examination. But she was an unusual young woman and the daughter of a father who was ambitious for her professional success.

Early in 1937 I sat for the scholarship examination. The theory portion, which occupied us for about a week, was held in the hall of one of London's ancient trade guilds, the Haberdasher's Hall, appropriately located on Threadneedle Street. About two hundred of us filed in to take our places at our assigned desks. Upon completing this first part we returned with much trepidation to see the results. No marks were listed, but if your name was on the list for the next phase, which was the practical exam, you knew that you had successfully passed the first part. To my great relief my name was listed in all four subjects—chemistry, physics, botany, and zoology. On to the next round!

The practicals were tough. The zoology section required the dissection of a rabbit, a procedure I had seen demonstrated but never actually done myself. I made a mess of that! Fortunately this accounted for only 50 percent of the zoology grade. I was better prepared, thanks to my training at the polytechnic, for a long set of questions involving taxonomy (the identification and classification of organisms). I had no problem with botany or physics, but did not do well with chemistry. I had not allowed for a train delay, which made me thirty minutes late, and I had to work very fast to complete the assignments. But finally that hurdle, too, was behind me.

Once again the successful candidates were listed, and I went on to the last hurdle, an interview.

Following my interview I sat in the hall outside the room and waited. I don't remember, but I guess I prayed. (At that stage in my pilgrimage most of my prayers were pleas for help to get me out of trouble.) Aside from the achievement, which itself would be a reward, the financial benefits would help with my university fees for the next three years.

It seemed as if I waited forever. Finally the door opened and I was called into the room. There I saw smiles on the faces of the selection committee as they came forward to shake my hand and congratulate me. I had won the scholarship!

I started University College in September of 1937.

Chapter 5

A New Life Begins

"It may be the most important thing you ever do."

Margaret's next academic challenge was the first year of the six-year medical program at University College. Like Anna, she would live at home and commute to London daily. She assumed that besides studying, her only other activity would be violin practice. But her first year at University College would be a new beginning in ways she could never have imagined. For it was during this first year that Margaret began two new relationships. The first of these was when she came to know Christ.

As I look back on my days before I encountered Christ in a new way, I realize how satisfied I had been with myself. I had finished well at Malvern, and added to that I had won a prestigious scholarship. My parents could hardly praise me enough. Spiritually I was also satisfied with myself. I had been confirmed, taken communion several times, usually prayed once a day, occasionally read the Bible, and more or less kept the Ten Commandments. Surely God would be satisfied with that, would He not?

I think that God had tried to break through my smug satisfaction many times, but those experiences I had very quickly put behind me. Then something happened.

It began one morning just before I was to start at University College when I received in the mail an invitation to attend the "Freshers' Squash" (a freshman social gathering where people tended to get "squashed" together), hosted by the University College Christian Union, a branch of the Intervarsity Student Christian Fellowship. I read the invitation and with a smirk laid it aside, saying, "Fancy going to a religious tea party. Who on earth would want to go to that?" My sister Anna was at the table. She was a rather private person, so I did not know that she had an interest in the Christian Union. She took up the invitation, read it, and quietly said, "I would go to it if I were you. It may be the most important thing you ever do."

I did respect Anna. During the years we were separated from our parents, it was Anna who looked after us. She did our packing for us; she saw to it that our clothes were properly marked with our nametags sewn in; she made certain we behaved. And she had blazed some of the trail I was now following. She was a wonderful big sister. Anna said, "Go to it," and so I went.

The speaker at this social event was a young surgeon at University College, a Mr. Arnold Aldis. His message did intrigue Margaret but not enough to change her attitude dramatically. Yet this experience and the significance of Anna's endorsement planted a seed. About five weeks later, thanks to another person close to Margaret, her fellow student and biology lab partner Olive Gray, Margaret made a life-changing decision.

Olive was a seriously committed Christian. In addition to our immediate interests of zoology and botany labs, we discussed many things, including what Christ meant to her. She would invite me to the midweek, noon-hour evangelistic meetings of the Christian Union. I went with her because I enjoyed her company and thought she was a wonderful friend.

At one particular meeting the speaker read a passage from the fifth chapter of the gospel of St. Luke. It was about the disciples fishing in the Sea of Galilee. They were tired and disappointed, but Jesus told them to go back out into the deep water and let down their nets again. Peter, the experienced fisherman, perhaps feeling a bit exasperated with such advice since he knew his job so well, responded by saying, "We've been working all night and have taken nothing." Then he added, as he looked at Jesus, "We'll do as you say." So out they went and caught so many fish they could hardly bring the boats ashore.

The speaker applied the message to the audience, but actually I felt he was speaking directly to me. He said, "You think you're doing pretty well. Perhaps you go to church." I thought, *Yes, I'm okay on that point.* He mentioned a few other things, which I smugly checked off, then he paused to give us time to think before he continued. "But if you had to meet God now and tell Him what you have done with your life, what would you say? Do you feel, like Peter, that you have taken nothing? Are you empty?" For the rest of the day I pondered those words.

That night I could not sleep. Finally I went on my knees. I tearfully confessed to my emptiness and asked Jesus to come in and take control. I was feeling so miserable, so desolate at that moment that I wanted to surrender unconditionally. He could send me into "deep water" if He chose, just as long as He would be in charge.

My commitment made, an astonishing thing happened. I don't have words to describe the emotion. The closest I can come is to quote these lyrics by John W. Peterson:

> Heaven came down and glory filled my soul,
> When at the cross the Savior made me whole.
> My sins were washed away and my night was turned to day,
> When Heaven came down and glory filled my soul.[1]

Those words would have meant little to me before my encounter with God that night. But after that encounter my whole perspective on life changed. I bought a small paperback New Testament and read, longing to learn all I could. I went to the Christian Union Bible studies, which helped tremendously.

But not everyone was happy about my new passion. My parents, in fact, were quite worried. "What do you mean, 'you're going to Bible study'?" they asked. They warned me not to go overboard. "Religious mania" was mentioned many times.

As a family we had not stayed in close contact with our grandparents (I very much regret that now!). Grandpa Berry lived alone in Dublin, and occasionally he wrote to us and would conclude with a Scripture verse.

---

1. Lines from "Heaven Came Down and Glory Filled My Soul" by John W. Peterson © 1961, renewed 1989 by John W. Peterson Company. All rights reserved. Used by permission.

This had meant little to me until after my own experience. Then I wrote and told him about it. I knew he would understand, and he did. He was delighted. He told me he had long prayed for us all and was overjoyed to live long enough to see some answers! It was a great encouragement to him.

My friend Olive was helpful in directing me to other Christian study aids that were of great assistance as I began my spiritual journey. For example, I was uncertain about what to do during my daily personal time with the Lord. I needed help, someone to show me, and Olive did that. She told me to start with Scripture Union study guide materials for devotions, and I did so from the time I first became a Christian.[2] Scripture Union taught me to start by praying just a short prayer: "Lord, help me see what is in this passage for me." After reading the short passage one was to meditate and ask two or three questions: "What does this passage mean to me? Did I learn something about God or Jesus or the Holy Spirit that I didn't know? Is this passage telling me about something that I should be doing, or something that I shouldn't be doing?"

There were then several short questions to answer regarding the details of the passage. I could do that. Then the study guide said to pray again. Well, I never knew what to pray for, but I would start off with "Lord, help me today." That might be all that I would say. Gradually, over the years, I found myself becoming more conversational with God. But I also learned that it is important to sometimes simply be quiet and listen. Just say, "Lord, if you're trying to say something to me, just let me hear." Sometimes when I am worried, it is during the quiet times that I best realize that I don't need to be worried. That God is taking care of things.

Margaret felt more fulfilled than ever before, but she began to see that self-fulfillment was only a part of her new joy. She now knew that all she could achieve or become was for the sake of a much grander purpose than she had imagined.

⟶

---

2. Scripture Union is an organization in England, which now has a branch in the United States.

Margaret's first year in medical college also marked the beginning of another significant relationship when she met a fellow student named Paul Wilson Brand.

Margaret and Paul first met in the chemistry laboratory when bench places were assigned alphabetically. She was Berry; he was Brand. They shared the same lab bench, the same sink, and the same laboratory equipment. While Paul, with his dashing good looks and maturity, stood out from the other male students, for Margaret there was something even more impressive. He was also a strong Christian.

I was attracted to Paul from the first moment I saw him. To find him also at Christian Union meetings, where obviously he carried a lot of responsibility, was almost too good to be true!

As Margaret and Paul worked together in the laboratory, she began to learn more about this appealing fellow. Besides sharing the same intellectual curiosity, the same pursuit of academic excellence, and the same commitment to Christ, they also shared unusual backgrounds. She had come to England from a childhood in South Africa; he had spent his childhood in India.

Paul was born in India in 1914 to British missionaries Jesse and Evelyn Harris Brand. When Paul was nine years old, the family returned to England for a one-year furlough. His parents decided, reluctantly, that Paul should remain in England to begin traditional schooling under the guardianship of his Grandmother Harris and two of the unmarried Harris aunts, Auntie Eunice and Auntie Hope, his mother's older sisters. His younger sister, Connie, would return to India with their parents. When it came time for departure, however, Connie convinced her parents that she should stay with her brother. Tragically neither Paul nor Connie ever saw their father again. Paul was still in England at the age of fifteen when his father, Jesse, died of Blackwater Fever, a deadly complication of malaria. His mother, Evelyn, returned to her children and her relatives, heartbroken and grieving. But after a year she felt compelled to return to southern India to continue, for Jesse's sake and for the Lord, the work that the two of them had started.

Jesse Brand had been a remarkable missionary, sharing his many different skills with the hill people whom he dearly loved. But although a good deal of his work involved medical care, he had never trained as a doctor. He hoped that one day his son might return to India as a physician.

Paul finished high school but was not interested in further academic study, least of all in pursuing a career in medicine. His interest was in building things, as he remembered his dear father doing in India—huts and roads, perhaps someday churches and schools. After high school Paul entered the building trades, doing manual construction labor during the day and taking classes in civil engineering in his free time. He decided that he would return to India to help his mother, and to that end he enrolled in a one-year missionary preparation program. The training included everything from digging latrines and learning how to survive in the wilderness to evangelizing on English village street corners.

Part of this training included basic medical care skills, and he found himself captivated enough to expand on this by spending time learning homeopathic medicine as his mother had done. It was while he was observing in a hospital that Paul Brand realized that his calling was to train as a physician. He would become a medical missionary, and he would go to India or wherever God chose to send him.

Now in 1937, this twenty-three-year-old fellow was in one of the best medical colleges in Britain with plans to return to India as a doctor rather than as a carpenter. Such a remarkable personal history and such meaningful goals impressed his chemistry bench partner.

Paul Brand's appeal to Margaret was obvious, but the similarities in their histories and hopes did not add up to certain romance. Margaret noticed that several other fine girls considered him a "great catch" and that she was not "the only pebble on the beach." She didn't know that the attraction was mutual. She only knew that Paul Brand was a bigger prize than any scholarship she had gone after and that she had no previous experience to guide her in trying for such a prize.

Neither of them were schooled in the ways of courtship, and their first "date" went on to become a highlight of the family history.

One day Paul asked me if I would like to go with him to a "PM." Well, I knew what a PM was; my father was always doing PMs—post-mortem autopsies. But I didn't expect to be attending such things so early in my medical training. So although surprised, I was excited to be doing this and even more excited to be going with Paul. I was soon to discover that he meant something quite different.

The room we went to did not look at all like a morgue—more like a

meeting room. And I was surprised that such an odd collection of people would be interested in an autopsy in this strange setting. Most confusing of all, there was no sign of a body, and everyone was down on their knees! I soon realized what it was all about. To Paul, raised in a missionary family, PM meant "prayer meeting." It was only after the meeting that I told Paul what I was expecting, and it became a standing joke for us. And a lesson that one should be very careful about acronyms!

Paul may have been senior in age and in Christian experience, but he felt far behind in knowledge of the sciences such as chemistry, physics, and biology, which he and Margaret were studying during that first year as bench partners. Margaret was an excellent student and had won scholarships, while Paul had never enjoyed school. He had been learning the building trades and jungle survival skills while she had been at her desk. So Paul was glad to have such a superb tutor to help him with the chemistry material they were trying to master—and appreciative that this tutor happened to be such an attractive girl.

At the end of the first year at University College, Margaret finished first in the class of eighty students. Paul finished second.

Chapter 6

The War Years

"You will keep him in perfect peace whose mind is stayed on you"
(Isaiah 26:3).

Although the young medical students were busy with the exhaustive work of academics and oppressive workloads, they were well aware of what was happening in the world around them, and in 1938 their country was preparing for the possibility of war.

On September 1, 1939, Hitler's troops invaded Poland. In response, France and Britain issued an ultimatum demanding that Germany withdraw; if Germany did not comply, the two allies would declare war against Germany. On Sunday morning, September 3, 1939, Prime Minister Chamberlain solemnly announced to the nation that the ultimatum had been ignored and that England was now at war with Germany. Within a few hours the ominous wailing of air raid sirens permeated London and the surrounding districts.

> **We had had air raid drills before, but somehow coming right after the declaration of war that Sunday morning we thought, *This is no practice drill. This is the real thing.* And it was a chilling thought. It proved to be a false alarm, but my mother, who had experienced the Zeppelin raids during World War I, was not easily reassured.**

Margaret's first challenge in medical college had been to pass the first MB (Bachelor of Medicine) examination, which was on basic premedical science. Then followed eighteen months of human anatomy and physiology, preparing for the second MB exam. Margaret was halfway through that eighteen-month period when the war began.

Because of thorough planning, by the time war was declared, the medical colleges were ready to continue training medical personnel even though London itself might be threatened. Plans had been made to evacuate medical students, as well as children, pregnant women, and others at risk, from the London area to presumably safer cities and towns throughout Britain. The plan for the medical students was to send the men to the port city of Cardiff in Wales and the women to the city of Sheffield in north central England.

The evacuation was an upheaval, but it was not as bad for us students as it was for the thousands of children, pregnant women, and others at risk in bomb-threatened cities such as London. Host homes throughout Britain, chosen beforehand in the planning stage, hastily prepared to receive two, three, or more evacuees who arrived carrying only an overnight bag and a change of clothing. It was a stressful time for everyone. The host home, referred to as "the billet," had to make huge adjustments. Temporary schools and hospitals sprouted overnight. Uncertainty and fear of never getting back to their own families again took a heavy emotional toll on the children.

Margaret went with the other women students to Sheffield, and Paul went to Cardiff. Their separation was not a hardship since at this time they were just friends. Yet Paul was apparently interested enough to visit her when he had the opportunity to hitch a ride on a friend's motorcycle.

A friend of Paul's was going to come up to Sheffield to see his girlfriend, so he asked Paul if he wanted to go along on the back of the bike. Of course I was tickled pink that he came all that way to see me, although it was a miserable trip for him—195 miles in the cold and over difficult countryside.

In March of 1940, in the midst of dealing with the stress of course work and the threat of German invasion, Margaret's class took their second MB exam. This was a critical milestone since, regardless of getting passing grades in the exam, only the top eight women would be accepted for the clinical course at University College in London. The others would have to apply to provincial medical schools elsewhere in the country. The men students were required only to pass their exams. Margaret finished in the select group of eight.

To be one of the successful eight women admitted to the clinical studies would have been considered enough of an achievement, but Dr. Berry had more in mind for his daughter. He urged Margaret to try for Part One of the Fellowship of the Royal College of Surgeons (FRCS). At that time this was largely an examination in the subjects she had just been studying, but at a more advanced level, so it was logical to do it at this juncture while they were fresh in her mind. Were she to pass that exam, she would then, after completing her university qualifying exam, be able to study for the Part Two FRCS and thus qualify as a surgeon. Women surgeons were quite an anomaly at that time, and Margaret was not sure she was keen to go that way. She did not yet know what path she might choose after she graduated, but certainly if she decided to follow a surgical career it made sense to have her Primary Fellowship behind her. She decided to attempt the FRCS, accepting the fact that, in doing so, she would fall behind her class. So while the other students who had passed the second MB returned to London, where the threat of invasion had lessened for awhile, Margaret remained in Sheffield for three months to concentrate on further anatomy and physiology review.

In mid-June 1940 Margaret returned to London to take the Primary FRCS exam. Despite all her efforts and special preparation, however, she did not pass the examination. She did very well on the anatomy but not well enough on the physiology.

> **My father was keen for me to be a surgeon. He didn't force me in that direction, but he strongly encouraged me to consider it, at times being rather manipulative in his methods as he persistently but gently tried to get me to go his way. When I didn't pass the Primary FRCS, however, he went into a real clinical depression.**
>
> **I have to admit that I was rather discouraged myself, having taken those months to prepare for the examination and then not passing. Yet I am sure I would have done something very different with my life had I been successful. It was one of those instances where our disappointments are God's appointments.**

After failing the Primary FRCS exam, Margaret resumed her original goal of working for the final MBBS degree. The possibility of achieving any personal dreams, however, was contingent on how the war progressed. And she was surrounded by the realities of that war.

Rationing of food, clothing, and fuel was mandatory, and our ration books became one of our most valued possessions. Attacks of poison gas were expected, so we were issued gas masks early on and ordered to carry them at all times. Then, as days passed without sign of an air raid, we became somewhat complacent, which we were about many aspects of the war initially.

Strict blackout laws were enforced. Air-raid wardens patrolled the streets at night and checked each home to see that no light escaped from some unguarded window. Even travel became difficult. At night, streetlights and vehicle headlights had to be reduced to a mere glimmer. Road signs and railway station signs had been removed to make it harder for invading enemy paratroops to find their way into and around our cities. Unfortunately, it also made it hard for us to find our own way in an unfamiliar area, something I soon found out when I had graduated and was doing a "locum" for a doctor in north London. Without street signs, responding to a house call at night was no easy matter.

Based on experience from World War I, air raids were expected from the start, so the provision of bomb-proof shelters and practice drills for getting to them became a priority. My father immediately arranged for the construction of a concrete shelter in our back yard, and in the house we had a Morrison shelter. This was like a heavy steel table with space under it for a mattress that could sleep several people (since most air raids were at night). The rest of the time it served as a table. It would not save us from a direct hit but would spare us if the house were partially destroyed.

Throughout Britain there was mandatory registration for all adults. Subsequently everyone's role was contingent on what the various war committees needed of us. Obviously many went into the armed service, and others were assigned to work in the munitions factories. We medical students were considered important enough as potential doctors to be allowed to continue our training. Still others were assigned to till the land and produce food. Everyone who could was urged to create a vegetable garden and was instructed on how to use every square inch for growing food.

Once all this was established, life settled down to a fairly routine matter. Most of us felt that the war would never really touch us. We were confident that our troops, together with the French and Belgians, would contain Hitler's army. It was quite inconceivable that we could actually be defeated.

On May 10, 1940, Hitler's forces overran Belgium, Luxembourg, and The Netherlands. Within a few days, tens of thousands of British, French, and Belgian troops were huddled at Dunkirk, the only escape port on the northern French coast. An armada of small boats, fishing boats, and pleasure craft scurried across the English Channel to pick up all who could wade out to them. In all, more than 164,000 troops were evacuated. The months of complacency experienced by Margaret and her colleagues were over.

We, the ordinary public, had to depend on the nightly radio broadcasts from the British Broadcasting Corporation (BBC) to get some idea of what was happening. No one dared to express optimism, but our resolve was high: We would not capitulate. That resolve was tested when the news came that France had made its peace with Germany and that Italy had joined the war, allied to Germany. Now we had to fight on alone against a more formidable enemy. We were loyally supported by contingents from most of the Commonwealth countries, but it would be another eighteen months before the United States would join us. An invasion of our homeland now seemed inevitable. It wasn't a matter of "if" but "when."

Each evening, before the nightly BBC news bulletin at 9:00 p.m., we heard the chimes of Big Ben, the famous clock above the Houses of Parliament. In many homes this solemn sound evoked a moment of silence as we prayed for our nation. To this day, whenever I hear Big Ben, I remember those moments of prayer.

In July 1940, Germany began daylight raids over southern England. Waves of German bombers from various airfields in France, Belgium, and Holland invaded Britain's airspace, attempting to destroy British air defenses and open the way for invasion by German army units that were massing in France to cross the Channel. Although the British fighter planes were far outnumbered, they were manned by pilots and gunners fiercely determined to protect their homeland. The British Air Force was augmented by volunteers from the United States, from other countries in the British Commonwealth, and by experienced personnel from several European countries. As their own countries fell, these pilots had flown their planes to England. The Polish airmen especially were known for their outstanding bravery and boldness. Their country had been the first to fall, and they had a personal account to settle with the Nazis.

Day after day, air battles raged in the skies over Britain. Margaret, now a twenty-one-year-old medical student, quickly became involved in caring for the casualties that arrived at her hospital in London, where she was doing a surgery rotation. She was serving on the wards as a "dresser," whose responsibility was to change the dressings of the wounded and the surgical patients.

I was preparing to change the dressing on a rather foul-smelling wound when I noticed a young, attractive woman standing a little way off. She wore a nurse's uniform, but not one from our hospital, so I reckoned she was one of the many nurses who volunteered time to help the war effort. She looked as though she would like to help, but no one had assigned her a job. Having completed my task, I asked her if she'd like one. She answered in a rather refined European accent that "yes she would, very much." So I handed her a tray loaded with dirty instruments, bowls, and soiled dressings. I told her where to dispose of the dressings and instructed her to wash the bowls and instruments and return them to the sterilizer. She said "sure" and, holding the tray as far from her nose as she could, started walking off with it.

Then I saw the ward supervisor rush after her and take the tray from her, and I sensed I was in trouble. The supervisor came storming toward me. "Do you know who you gave that tray of disgusting dressings to?" she asked angrily. Well, no, I had no idea. "That was the Duchess of Kent!"

The duchess was a lovely person and wanted to help in whatever way she could. But as the sister-in-law of King George, King of England, she probably deserved a nicer job than I had given her. My education thus far really had not covered things like this!

After a series of surprising losses, the Luftwaffe Command changed its strategy and began night bombing instead of daylight raids. The major cities, especially those with heavy industry and ports, continued to be their prime targets, but now London center and the British populace were included.

In mid-September 1940, a group of medical students from our hospital went to a retreat sponsored by the Intervarsity Christian Fellowship at Sunbury-on-Thames, a bit west of London. Times were tense. We were feeling the stress and needed to get away, relax, and be quiet in God's presence. Paul Brand was the chairman of our College Christian Union. He and others had been told privately that if an invasion occurred, they should destroy all the records of membership. Reports out of Holland said that committed Christians had been targeted early as potential troublemakers (such as offering safe haven to Jewish refugees). I don't remember the speaker's name or the main topic, but I do remember that we were greatly strengthened and spiritually refreshed by what we heard and shared with one another.

The news on the radio that Sunday evening was bad. Heavy raids were in progress over most of southern England, and especially over the dock area of London. Incendiary bombs had started widespread fires, and then high explosives demolished huge areas of buildings. As we looked east toward London we could see a bright orange glow in the sky. In those days of strict blackout regulations it could mean only one thing . . . fire!

None of us knew what lay ahead. But we knew we could trust God to be in charge. So we sang as we walked to the train station: "You will keep him in perfect peace whose mind is stayed on You" (Isaiah 26:3).

As the train carried us back to London, we said little, but we were shocked to see the devastation on the way in. What more was to come?

On arriving back at the hospital we were assigned to Casualty Clearing teams. Senior and junior doctors, as well as medical students, were part of each team. No team would take two consecutive nights on duty.

I was on duty the night the first land mine was dropped on London. It fell about one-half mile from our hospital, right outside a large YMCA hostel. By that time most buildings had been prepared for bomb damage by taping the windows with heavy-duty adhesive tape so that even if the glass shattered, the shards would not become dangerous missiles. Somehow, though, the YMCA had not been adequately prepared. The land mine shattered almost every window in the building, and about thirty young men were rushed to our hospital, their condition critical. Many were bleeding profusely from multiple wounds caused by the flying glass.

Our blood bank was soon exhausted. We simply had to try and stop the bleeding, suturing the wounds as fast as we could. We took out obvious bits of glass, but there was no time to go after each piece, and many of those men carried fragments of glass in their bodies for months. If we students didn't learn all we should have during the war, we at least learned a lot about suturing.

I was not on duty the night several incendiary bombs were dropped near the hospital. Some of them penetrated a tunnel under the road, which connected the hospital buildings, where people had taken shelter, hoping to be safe. Instead, they were trapped there by fires. Many were barely alive when they were brought to the Casualty Clearing Station, and many died within days. Back then there was little we could do for them, and nothing left me feeling quite so helpless as those terrible burn injuries.

The air raids over London substantially disrupted the medical school curriculum. For eight months, from September of 1940 to May of 1941, there were almost nightly bombings of the London area as well as other cities. As the result of her FRCS exam preparations, Margaret had missed courses in basic pathology and pharmacology. With the intensity of the war increasing, the courses could not be offered in London, but Cardiff University was willing to host another group of London students as well as some of the London faculty. So Margaret set off for Cardiff, hoping for "a quiet place to study."

Her first few weeks were quiet, which gave her time to settle in and learn her way around the city.

For travel within the city we would rely on buses and trams. In Cardiff my residence was quite a distance from the hospital, and I decided that a bicycle would be very practical. I searched through second-hand stores and found just what I needed and could afford. It was not the latest model and was very heavy, most notably when it had to be walked up some of the steep hills. But it was sturdy and priced at ten shillings. (In those days that amount would buy lunches for two weeks in the school cafeteria.) I probably rode about fifteen to twenty miles every day, from my room to one hospital, back to my room, and then off again to another hospital.

In Cardiff, Margaret stayed, upon Paul's recommendation, at the home of Jenny Morgan, a widow who took in evacuees. Paul had stayed there when he and the other male medical students had been evacuated to Cardiff in 1939.

"Granny M," as they called her, was a devout Christian, and Margaret's move into Granny Morgan's household could not have come at a more opportune time for this new young Christian. At University College in London, a good deal of Margaret's free time was involved with Christian Union activities, where she had other Christian youth to commune with on her journey of faith. But at home with her parents, loving though they were, she did not enjoy the same spirit of belief. Granny Morgan's home was a vibrant, living example of what a Christian home could be like.

Granny deserves to have a whole book written about her. She was the elderly widow of a coalmine owner in South Wales and lived in a nice house in Llandaff, near Cardiff. She was rather petite with a generous head of white hair, a lined face, and a twinkle in her bright eyes. She was very deaf but managed to hear with the help of an old-fashioned ear trumpet.

One of Granny's joys was the weekly prayer meeting in her home. Those who came were people who took seriously the privilege of prayer, and I was glad to be with them when possible. Because of her deafness, Granny couldn't tell who was praying and what they were saying, as we would be on our knees, our heads bowed. But her sight was keen, so as we prayed she would look round to see whose lips were moving. Then, as quietly as she could, she would shuffle across the room on her knees and bring the bowl of her ear trumpet up under the chin of the speaker. Until one got used to it, it could be a bit disconcerting!

Granny would attend court cases involving young women who had been found guilty of some minor felony such as shoplifting or prostitution. If the magistrate sentenced them to imprisonment, she would plead to have the sentence reduced and would take such women into her home to help them get straightened out. They would do housework for her, and she shared her love with them and led many to accept Jesus. That little old lady with shining bright eyes and a long-handled ear trumpet became a familiar figure to the Cardiff magistrates. When friends warned her that she might get robbed or hurt because of these associations, she responded, "I may be a fool, but let me at least be a fool for Christ's sake."

As the war went on, Cardiff got its share of bombing. One of Granny's close friends was bombed out of her home with nothing but the nightdress she was wearing, and Granny realized this might happen to her too. So she made a practice of wearing everything she could put on, one layer over another, day and night. She stitched an enormous pocket onto one of her many petticoats, and in it she carried her Bible, her purse, her spare ear trumpet, and all the household's ration books. She would walk down the hill to the stores accompanied by her faithful dog, an elderly black retriever, who also was rather deaf. The neighbors loved her and delighted in watching her dive into her famous pocket in search of a ration book or other object.

Granny Morgan's home was in the old village of Llandaff, where an ancient cathedral was located less than a half mile from her house. The first night that Cardiff was attacked, an aerial land mine hit the cathedral. Granny's next-door neighbors received a tombstone from the church graveyard through their roof and into their bathtub. Granny lost every pane of glass in her house.

We knew from the sound of high explosive bombs, from the barrage of anti-aircraft guns, and from the large numbers of buildings on fire that we should prepare for trouble. But we had no air-raid shelter to run to, no safe place to hide. So we crouched under the dining room table and waited prayerfully.

We had not waited long when the whole house shook, and the wall near us bulged, as though it would cave in on top of us. Every window shattered.

But we were alive! We praised the Lord and set about trying to make the best of it. We normally depended on a small coal fire in the grate to keep us warm, but it was a cold winter night, and with the windows shattered, the wind blew our blackout curtains open. We had been so drilled in complying with blackout regulations that we didn't dare maintain our fire. What a great relief when finally the "all clear" siren sounded! With the help of flashlights we collected blankets and coats and returned to the table in the dining room, shaken but alive, uninjured, and thankful. Next morning, with the help of kind neighbors, we boarded up our windows (replacement glass panes were unavailable).

This raid did nothing for Granny's confidence. From that night on, she slept downstairs with all her clothing on.

The hospital to which the London medical students were assigned for most of their teaching sessions was on a hill a little way outside of Cardiff. Unfortunately the smokestack from the hospital laundry building made it look like a factory. So the German bombers, possibly thinking it a munitions factory, gave it particular attention that night. Happily their aim was not so good, and none of the nine high explosives that were dropped hit the buildings themselves.

So much for studying in peace and quiet!

There were a lot of inconveniences, not to mention the stress of trying to cope with the injuries, especially the burns, a lot of disruption, of uncertainties, of loss of friends and neighbors, but I don't remember ever feeling that we medical students couldn't deal with those. I think we all grew up quickly. Echoing what Churchill had said, we were going to fight back . . . we refused to let "them" get us down and became quite belligerent in our determination to make it through all these situations.

While in Cardiff, Margaret had one encounter that could have changed the course of her life.

Granny Morgan let the WEC (World Evangelical Crusade) use her home as their Welsh headquarters and as a home for missionaries on furlough. While I was staying there, a single man from South Africa moved in. He tried to get me to give up my medical studies and join the mission. "God can heal," he said. "He doesn't need doctors." I agreed that God could heal, but I was noncommittal about giving up my medical career, so he continued to try and persuade me. There was no hint of any romantic motive in his argument or his pursuit. He genuinely thought I was wasting my life studying for a medical degree when I could simply be sharing the "Good News" of Jesus. He almost persuaded me.

The thought of returning to Africa held great appeal, and I felt very burdened about it. I searched my heart. I prayed. I agonized. I was a young Christian and was living with people who had much more experience than I and were very persuasive. I talked with Kitty Flint, Granny Morgan's daughter, who was my confidante in many ways. She helped me keep things in perspective. I kept thinking of the fifth commandment, "Honor thy father and thy mother," struggling to balance that with Jesus' words, "He who loves father or mother more than me is not worthy of me"(Matthew 10:37). God surely didn't mean those to be irreconcilable.

As I prayed and pondered and talked, I began to see things a bit from my parents' perspective. They had sacrificed a lot for my education. To give up at that stage would seem to them as if I didn't care, didn't appreciate them, certainly didn't respect them. Was that honoring them? They wouldn't have understood. They would have been hurt and angry. And I could not see how that would draw them to a closer relationship to God. So He would not have been honored. Finally my mind was made up. I would finish my medical course. If it then seemed right, I would go into missionary work and use my medical knowledge—or not—as God would choose. That seemed to settle the issue, and I felt at peace.

Another spiritual matter that confronted me while I was in Cardiff was the subject of baptism. I had been baptized as an infant in a Presbyterian church. Until then that had been fine with me. Granny Morgan, however, was a Baptist, and for her baptism was a witness to the fact that the individual was choosing to trust and follow Jesus. Granny and I argued about infant baptism versus believer's baptism, and she challenged me to find Scriptures supporting my views. I could not. So after much thought and prayer, I presented myself to a Baptist minister and asked to be immersed as a witness to my belief.

❧

The people of Britain were, as Margaret says, "belligerent in our determination to make it through" the war. One evidence of this resolve was the average citizen's acceptance of the rationing system, which affected every individual and every profession, every activity and every celebration. In 1940 Britain the challenge of "making do" became a way of life.

When the rationing system began, each person was entitled each week to one shell egg plus three substitute egg powders, four ounces of meat, two rashers of bacon, two ounces of butter, four ounces of margarine, one half pound of sugar, and a half pound of jam. As the war progressed other items were restricted, specifically milk and bread. An adult could get ten ounces of milk per day, a child twenty. We could get three slices of bread daily, but flour was not rationed, so those people who knew how to bake bread fared better. My mother made a nourishing bread from whole wheat and soy flour.

Occasionally items that were not rationed became available, but we had to stand in line a long time to get them. Fresh fish, a great treat, was one. If you saw a line anywhere near the fishmonger, you would hurry to join it. The principle was, "Get in line first, then ask 'what is this line for?'" But paper also was scarce, so if you found yourself in line but without paper to wrap your prize in, you might just be disappointed. Newspaper was a precious commodity, something difficult to imagine now.

My father had shortages of medicines, but with his pharmaceutical background he could usually substitute effectively. The hardest thing was the rationing of petrol, which forced everyone to use the limited public transportation. Doctors, however, were allowed a greater petrol ration due to the nature of their work.

Somehow we coped, and studies after the war by the British Medical Research Council showed that the general health of the populace was better during the war than it was in the 1950s! We got the essentials.

Despite what might now be perceived as a time of deprivation for the British populace, many who lived through it look back at that experience with some fondness. They believe that their mettle was thoroughly tested; and like "the boys"—the soldiers, sailors, and pilots in direct battle with the enemy—the citizenry at home showed the world how strong their spirit truly was. Under this siege mentality, an unusual camaraderie developed, especially in the larger cities such as London. Yet some of the same dangers still existed in the big city, war or no war.

I always took a commuter train from our home in Northwood to Euston Square, the station on the London Underground system nearest to University College Hospital. It was an old train with numerous small compartments, each with its own door to the platform. Like all trains, the window glass was covered with shatter-resistant black netting. Since the train would run above ground part of the way, blackout restrictions had to be observed, so each compartment was lit by only a small blue bulb. At night or when the train went through a tunnel, it was rather dark inside, with just enough light for a new passenger to find an empty seat.

One day I boarded the train as usual. Two stops later another passenger got on. He sat opposite me, and very soon I began to feel uneasy about him. But since there were several other passengers in the compartment I tried to ignore the man's odd behavior and planned to change to another compartment at Baker Street Station, a major junction, when we reached it. At the station everyone in my compartment got up to leave, including the "problem" passenger. So I sat back down, thinking I had the place to myself. Then, just as the train moved out of the station and into a long tunnel, the fellow quickly jumped aboard again. So there I was, in this almost blacked-out compartment with this guy who was behaving strangely. He stood up, and I didn't know what he was going to do. I tried to stay calm and just pray. I thought of pulling the emergency cord if he really threatened me. But before I could move, he came over and tried to sit on my lap. I pushed him away and said, "I will report you at the next station!" By that time I was shaking like jelly, and I doubt that my voice carried much conviction. Happily, at that moment the train pulled into a lighted station and stopped. He didn't waste any time getting out and away. I felt so horrible I just wanted to throw up. I was still in shock when I encountered Paul in the hospital corridor some fifteen minutes later. He took one look at me and asked, "Is there anything wrong?" and I told him about the incident.

The only other bad experience I remember happened toward the end of the war when I was helping Dad in his practice. Not only was he allowed the use of a car because he was a doctor, but also he received an extra petrol allowance in order to use it. City buses ran on a very limited schedule so people expected they could get a lift if they saw someone with a car.

One day on my way to a woman in labor I saw a man desperately trying to thumb a ride. I pulled up and let him in. I realized my mistake when I told him how far I could take him and he said, "You'll go where I tell you to go!" That was a shock, and I wondered what I could do. For all I knew, he might be armed. I drove on, saying nothing, while keeping a watch for some help and praying. Then I saw the answer to that prayer.

I drove to the curb and stopped the car right in front of a policeman and calmly said to my passenger, "I think this is as far as I can take you." He was out of that car and gone in a second. I should have reported the incident, but I was in a hurry. I made it to the delivery on time.

By the middle of 1941 Margaret was back in London, as was Paul Brand, both rotating as students through a variety of assignments in different locales. Their paths would cross in classes and on hospital duty, and they saw each other at Christian Union activities. Margaret was still captivated by this fellow, but she wasn't certain if the attraction was mutual.

I had been in love—maybe the better word is "infatuated"—with Paul ever since our first meeting across the chemistry bench in 1937. But it seemed presumptuous of me to think that I would be his choice of life mate when so many other girls were also longing for that role. Paul seemed not to notice their flirting with him, although he seemed to enjoy the shoulder hugging and attention he received from them, and he sought their company in the lecture halls and the cafeteria. I felt chilled by all this, and I needed to resolve the matter. So I took it to the Lord. I confessed before Him that I really, from my heart, wanted Paul to have a joyful life, and that if someone other than myself would be better for him, then "so be it." I also told the Lord that even if I never got married, I just wanted to be all He had in mind for me to be. It was a precious moment of recommitment, and I got up from my knees with a new sense of freedom. From then on, I no longer suffered pangs of jealousy when I saw Paul enjoying the attention of other girls. I was free to let Paul be Paul.

Chapter 7

A Pivotal Year

"So, will you marry me?"

aul Brand was unaware of how his behavior around his female admirers was perceived by Margaret. She was, in fact, the only girl whose admiration he sought. During one of his visits to Granny Morgan, he had discussed with her whom he might marry. By this time, Granny M. had come to know Margaret quite well and was one of the first to see that these two young people were right for each other. She told Paul as much, and made a strong case for his choosing Margaret as his wife. Margaret, of course, knew nothing about this.

Paul viewed his demeanor toward his female colleagues as simply being friendly and polite to other students who were being so friendly with him. Margaret saw it otherwise and kept her distance. Then, about six months after Margaret had turned her future and Paul's over to God, Paul revealed his true feelings for her.

Paul and I had been at a meeting of the Medical Students Christian Union, a branch of the London Inter Faculty Christian Union, for which I was the organizing secretary. Afterward a group of us walked back to the hospital, and as we walked along the dark quiet streets (no air raids that night!), Paul came alongside me and took my hand. Much as I enjoyed that moment, I reacted negatively and tried to pull away. But he persisted, and finally I said, "I don't know if this is going to work. I thought I was your girl some time ago, but apparently I wasn't, so I don't want to get hurt a second time."

Once back in the hospital area we found a quiet place and had a long, open talk. We each learned a few things about men and women and how they perceive one another's behavior. Once he realized how his demeanor toward the other girls had affected me, he was very apologetic and reassured me that he cared for no one as he did for me. And after that he was polite to the other girls but careful to avoid any conduct that might be misconstrued.

The blossoming of the relationship between Margaret and Paul began in the midst of absolute uncertainty about the future of the world. Although the United States had declared war on Japan and Germany in December 1941, the threat to England was as great as ever. The one certainty for Margaret was that she had found someone who could be her companion for life, someone who trusted God's will as much as she did.

Two other marriages had recently taken place in the Berry household. Anna, now serving as a civilian doctor in an ear, nose and throat clinic, had married one of her former classmates in early 1941. Her husband, Anthony Hargreaves, was a medical officer in the Royal Air Force. Frieda, a qualified nurse, was also in the RAF, where she had met Jim Ross who was serving as a dental officer in the same unit. They married late in 1941.

The Berry home into which Paul came as a suitor to Margaret would become an important as well as comforting addition to his life. He had not been part of a traditional household with mother and father since he left India at age nine. His primary home in London was with his two aunts while his mother remained in India. His sister, Connie, had always been nearby, and one uncle, Bertie Harris, had served somewhat as Paul's surrogate father. As part of the Berry family he would once again be a son who could enjoy the presence of parents as well as two new "sisters" and two new "brothers."

With their lives fully committed to Christ, Paul and Margaret talked more and more about future plans, being optimistic that in spite of the global conflict, God would grant them and the rest of the world a future for which to plan. They frequently discussed what they might do if they did marry, if they did graduate successfully, and if there was a safe end to the war. Both were interested in going into medical missionary work, either in Africa or India.

During our very first conversations when I was getting to know him across the chemistry bench, Paul had told me about his father dying from malaria when Paul was only fifteen. He could have been angry and bitter about losing his dad when he was still so young, but clearly he was not. Instead he intended to offer himself as a medical missionary. His attitude deeply impressed me. Later on he came to know that I, too, wanted to be a missionary, and that I thought I'd go to Africa because that was the place I knew. From the beginning, my commitment to Christ meant I would go wherever He sent me, and from the start I considered overseas missionary work.

Paul proposed to Margaret in the spring of 1942, some five years after they had first met at the lab bench. The air was warm and fresh, flowers were in bloom all around, and the war seemed a distant nuisance.

It was a lovely spring Saturday in 1942—a day when the war seemed far away. We had walked up into some beautiful bluebell woods near our Northwood home. We climbed up on a gate and sat quietly, relishing all the glory of spring and the closeness of each other. For Paul it seemed the right moment to ask the crucial question. No, he did not fall on one knee (difficult on the top of a gate!). He simply said, "Assuming one or the other of us gets called by God to serve Him in some other country, we shall go together. So, will you marry me?" I was too happy to say anything profound. I just said, "Of course!" And that was our engagement ceremony.

At home, Paul formally asked for my hand, and Dad tried to say all the things a dad should say, ask the appropriate questions, and seem very serious. But in his heart he was rejoicing, as was Mum. Paul was already very special to them.

They set their wedding date for May 29 of the following year, 1943. By then Margaret would be twenty-three and Paul twenty-eight. The next twelve months would be their final year in medical college, with their attention focused primarily on completing their studies. Fortunately they would have the help of the Berry family, Paul's sister Connie, and his cousin Dr. Nancy Robbins with the wedding preparations. Connie and Nancy would be

Margaret's attendants, and Paul's best man would be Farnham St. John, one of his dearest friends.[1] The wedding ceremony would take place at Emmanuel Church in Northwood, an Anglican church that the Berry family had attended, somewhat intermittently, for eighteen years. Anna and Frieda had also been married there.

Planning a wedding is difficult enough in the best of times but especially challenging in the middle of a war.

My mother wanted to make my wedding dress, but fabric and other clothing items, including shoes, were all stringently rationed. We reviewed our ration books and realized there was no way that we had enough to obtain the material for a wedding dress. Then one of my father's patients said, "I'm not going to need any new clothes this year. I would like to give my coupons to Margaret. It will be my wedding gift to her." So she gave me all her coupons, and we were able to buy enough material to make a wedding dress. Some gift!

For other items we made do very nicely. Frieda had offered me her wedding dress, but we were not nearly the same size and it just didn't look right; however, I was glad to use her veil and other accessories. One of Connie's friends had recently had a wedding in her family, and she offered two bridesmaids' dresses that fitted Connie and Nancy just fine. They were gold-colored and not exactly what I had in mind, but who cared? They matched each other, and that was more important than the color.

In those days only the bride received a wedding ring, as most English men didn't wear jewelry. But during the war it was impossible to buy gold items of more than fourteen karats, and Paul was unhappy buying a ring of only fourteen karat gold for his bride. Then we were given another incredible gift. The twenty-four-karat wedding ring that had belonged to Paul's grandmother, Grandma Harris, had been lovingly put away for decades. Paul's aunties said that it was ours if we wanted to use it. What an honor to inherit such a treasure! Since it wasn't my size, Paul sent it to a cousin, a jeweler in Bristol, and asked him to alter it for me.

---

1. Farnham's sister, Patricia St. John, became famous for her children's books, all of which were a great blessing for our young family. She was also a teacher at our girls' boarding school in Wales (Clarendon).

Paul and Margaret's final year of medical college was indeed arduous. Due to the time constraints imposed by the war, both had chosen to combine their final year of medical college studies with six months of clinical internship. This would qualify them to go directly into practice after graduation. At the end of the academic year, they also faced the university final exams, which they had to pass to receive the degrees they had worked toward over the previous six years.

Only one week prior to the wedding, they received what they considered to be one of the best wedding presents they could have imagined. Both received notification from London University that they had passed their exams and had attained the London MB, BS degree, equivalent to the MD degree in the United States. War or no war, Dr. Paul Brand and Dr. Margaret Berry could proceed with their wedding.

The great day arrived, but one important item did not.

By the day of the wedding, Grandma Harris's ring hadn't come back from the jeweler in Bristol. Paul, attired in a traditional morning suit, set out from his home, along with his two aunts, to catch the train to the church in Northwood. They happened to pass a small jewelry shop on the way to the station. Paul dashed into the shop and said he wanted to buy a wedding ring. The jeweler, probably surprised at this last minute shopping by the young groom standing in front of him, asked for the size. Paul had no idea, but guessed that it would be about right if it fit his own little finger. Only when he had solemnly slipped the ring onto my finger during the wedding ceremony did he realize how far off his guess had been. I had to keep my hand clenched to prevent the ring dropping off! It was a little disconcerting, but the ceremony went ahead beautifully in every other way.

When the proper ring eventually came from Bristol, Paul and I privately repeated that part of the service as we asked the Lord's blessing on the ring and all that it symbolized. I still wear Grandma Harris's ring today.

The Anglican (Episcopal) order of service for marriage is quite long, really very challenging and solemn. There is plenty of music, and every time I hear or sing the hymn "Praise My Soul the King of Heaven" I am reminded of the wonderful moment when my father and I processed up the aisle behind our church choir and the vicar, as we all were singing those words to the rousing melody by John Goss. And that was just the beginning of a grand ceremony and the grand adventure of my life as Mrs. Paul Brand.

Paul's beloved aunts, his sister, and members of his mother's extended family who lived in the vicinity of London were there to celebrate the event. But his mother was in India and could not return for the wedding of her only son. Understandably she was concerned about the young woman he had chosen to marry and had to trust what her daughter, Connie, as well as her other relatives thought of Paul's betrothed. Fortunately Margaret passed muster, and in a letter Paul let his mother know that this was the woman for him. In Paul's words:

> "Mother had never met Margaret until well after we were married and had only seen one photograph of her. She was worried that, since Margaret was so attractive, I had fallen for the wiles of a 'worldly' woman. Margaret had naturally wavy hair, and when Mother saw this in a photo, she thought Margaret had had a 'permanent,' thereby making her worldly. There had been an agreement in the Brand family that whomever Connie or I considered marrying had to get the 'okay' from the other sibling so that neither would be swayed by the ploys of the opposite sex. However, everyone who met Margaret liked her so much that by the time we were actually married, Mother was feeling much more comfortable and had decided that Margaret would actually be good for me.
>
> "My letter to Mother said, 'The one thing that is different is that I've got Margaret! It all happened one day when I went over to Northwood to spend an evening with the Berrys. Margaret and I went for a walk. There was a gate and we sat on it and talked over serious matters. And then I said, 'Will you?' and she said, 'Yes!' Well, I never have been so really happy before as I was from then on, and still am.'"

The newlyweds spent a one-week honeymoon in the Wye Valley area, a brief respite after their grueling final academic year in the shadow of the war. During this time alone together, Margaret began learning new things about her husband, such as his love of adventure.

Paul delighted in trying new "short-cuts" in the course of the walks we took. I nearly went for an unplanned swim in the river as I attempted to follow him through one of his short-cuts. I could see there would be plenty of surprises ahead!

Margaret and Paul had already decided that, upon their return to London, she would live with her parents in Northwood while he was at the hospital in the city. She would not pursue postgraduate training but would join her father in his practice. As her one attempt at moving into an advanced program—trying to qualify for the FRCS position—had ended unsuccessfully, she did not want to take on the demands that further study in a postgraduate program would require. The choices for women were extremely limited, and the competition for these few posts would be even more intense than some of the struggles she had already conquered. She wanted her attention to go to her new career, that of being wife to Paul and, hopefully, one day becoming mother to his children. Meantime, she enjoyed working with her own father while at the same time helping her husband with his further training.

As a medical student, Paul had been given a deferment from military duty. Having graduated, he was now expected to enter military service, unless he continued his medical training. Paul clearly enjoyed the challenges he had faced in the past two years, seeing and managing more difficult casualty cases than he would have had it not been for the war, since students had assumed more responsibilities given the manpower shortages. He was drawn toward the surgical fields that had occupied so much of his time in the past few months and especially enjoyed orthopedic work, which fit with his past study of mechanical problems in the building trade.

Dr. Berry, who had encouraged Margaret to consider surgery, now urged his new son-in-law to consider the same. Margaret concurred with Paul's decision to enter an FRCS program, but first he had to face the same qualifying examination that had stopped her. It was not unusual for candidates to take the exam several times before passing, but to his amazement Paul was successful on his first attempt. It helped that he was older, more experienced, and had a wife to encourage him.

The Central Medical War Committee granted him an extension on his deferment, and Paul became a surgical officer, working at various hospitals around London. He would do this for the next two years, after which he would face the final FRCS qualifying examination. If he passed that, he would be considered a surgeon and would go by the title Mister Brand, as in England only nonsurgical physicians are called doctor.

Margaret and her father had no doubt that Paul would qualify. Meanwhile, father and daughter began a new phase in their relationship as they started practicing medicine together. They were in a position to teach one another, he sharing his years of experience and she sharing the newer procedures for diagnosing and treating illnesses. Margaret herself was especially interested in pediatrics and brought this expertise to their practice.

Paul and Margaret hadn't made any specific plans to start a family. They chose to leave this in the Lord's hands, trusting that they would be ready whenever the time came. But it came somewhat sooner than they had expected. A few months after their marriage, Margaret became pregnant, with the baby due in March of 1944.

Margaret continued working with her father, seeing patients in the attached surgery and making house calls. Then, as her due date approached, she began lightening her workload. Plans were made for her to go the Royal Northern Hospital in London once she went into labor. In such strange times, they had to hope that the blessed event would not coincide with an air raid.

I went into labor late in the day on March 8. Paul was with me at the hospital until he got called away on the evening of March 9. That was fine, since it seemed unlikely that I would deliver before the following day. The doctor gave me some morphine, assured me that I would sleep quietly, and that next day I would have proper contractions and ultimately deliver. (I was not too excited about the "proper contractions" and "the next day" part, since I had been in labor for more than twenty-four hours!) Labor, I had read and believed, was not that painful if you relaxed and had the right attitude. Simple. By this time, however, I was getting disillusioned about my attitude! But I did sleep for about an hour.

Meanwhile the enemy launched one of their usual night attacks. Paul, on the other side of London at Great Ormond Street Hospital where he worked, could see the fires and explosions occurring in the neighborhoods around the Royal Northern. No bombs hit the building that night, but there were a lot of fires in the area.

When I woke after my one hour of sleep, things were moving quite fast. But the baby's head was not in a good position, so the next three or four hours were hard work. Finally, around five in the morning, I managed to deliver. What joy and what relief! Later that day I was reading *Daily Light,* a collection of Bible verses for each day of the year. I had always found it a helpful little devotional book, and particularly so that day. The first verse for the morning of March 10 was from Psalm 30:5. "Weeping may endure for a night but joy cometh in the morning." It surely did! Christopher Brand arrived safely on March 10, 1944.

When Paul finally got to bed the night before, he had slept heavily and did not hear the nurse knock on his door to give him the message about the arrival of his new little son. She hadn't the heart to wake him, as she knew how exhausted he was. So she just left a note by his bed, telling him that his wife had been delivered of a bonny bouncing baby and all was well. When he woke and read the note, he bounced out of bed, hurriedly dressed, and made his way across the city. There he discovered that Royal Northern Hospital had been cordoned off because of several unexploded bombs. After they had been cleared away and the burning buildings gotten under control, he was allowed to cross the lines.

My appearance gave him a bit of a start. In the course of a rather long labor, I had developed massive subconjunctival hemorrhages. I looked like I had been in a fight, with the whites of my eyes colored deep red! But we laughed that off and shared our joy and thanksgiving for a beautiful, healthy son.

The Berry household in Northwood now consisted of Dr. and Mrs. Berry, Margaret and baby Christopher, and Anna and her fourteen-month-old daughter, Ruth. Paul, busy with his surgical training, returned to Northwood as often as possible, while Anna's husband, Anthony, came around whenever his military duties allowed.

When Christopher was about three months old, Margaret and Paul were able to take a brief holiday at the home of Paul's Aunt Lillie and Uncle Arthur in Bromley, south of London, some distance from the worst of the air raids. The young family went there early in June when the beauty of summer in England was at its best. It was a world away from the noise and confusion of London, with no air raid sirens destroying their sleep at night. They not only enjoyed the peace and relative safety, but also had much needed time to bond with their baby son.

At the time the young Brand family was enjoying their brief holiday, Allied forces were preparing to launch the invasion of Normandy from secret staging areas along England's southern coast, not far from Bromley. It was hoped that this would be the beginning of the end of the war in Europe, but such a conclusion was several months away.

In May 1944 Paul experienced a setback in his progress toward obtaining his Fellowship of the Royal College of Surgeons. He had attempted his final qualification only one year after passing Part One and had failed, but only just. His only option appeared to be proceeding with the military duty that was awaiting him. He applied for a medical post with the RAF, since there was a rumor that they might be expanding their medical corps in India.

It seemed unlikely that the Central Medical War Committee, which decided the need and distribution of medical personnel, would allow him a further deferral, yet it did so based upon an unexpected invitation that Paul received: to sign on for one year as an assistant on the surgical unit at his medical college alma mater, University College Hospital. Thanks to the head of the surgical unit, Professor Pilcher, Paul was to remain in training for his fellowship, despite failing his first attempt at the final examination.

This was wonderful news since it would give Paul a second chance at the FRCS while being able to remain near Margaret and Christopher. Margaret could continue helping her father in his practice, with her mother assisting Margaret by babysitting Christopher. This was a splendid arrangement for Margaret, who could practice medicine part-time and raise her son as well.

Raising children, of course, always involves the unexpected.

Christopher had gone down for his late-morning nap. The weather was cold and the room was chilly, so I left a small electric heater on the other side of the room, safely away from his crib.[2] Mother was downstairs in the kitchen and would hear him if he cried, so I took off to do some house calls. When I returned, the house was quiet. Presumably Christopher

---

2. As in most houses in England in that era there was no central heating. If we were using a room we would warm it by an electric heater or keep a coal fire in the grate.

was still asleep, but I wanted to check on him. As I opened the door of his room, I was met by a cloud of acrid smoke. It smelled like burning feathers—and it was burning feathers!

After waking from his nap and (we concluded) having nothing better to do, Christopher had thrown his little pillow at the heater. The pillow had caught fire and was smoldering, about to blaze. Christopher was sitting quietly in his crib, coughing but not crying. It was providential that I got home when I did.

Christopher was an adventurous little fellow. When he was a little over two years old, his venturesome nature gave us quite a scare. Anna's daughter, Ruth, was staying with us, and she had not been used to a bed, only a crib. So she had Christopher's crib and he, delighted with the sudden promotion, was to sleep in Anna's old room, in her bed.

It was one of those long, light summer evenings. We had had our usual story, good night prayer, and kiss, and I had left him, confident that he would soon be asleep. But Christopher had other ideas. Why not explore his surroundings and check out drawers?

Sometime later when I went to check on him, I heard the scurry of little feet as he hopped back into bed. But evidence of his crime was all over the floor. As I started to clear it up, I saw an open bottle of sodium barbiturate (sleeping pills) and some tablets scattered around. Anna must have left this medication in one of the drawers, and he had found it.

Alarmed, I asked Christopher if he had swallowed any of the pills. He cheerfully answered that he had and that they were nice. (Barbiturates are very bitter, but children often have unusual tastes, so I could not reassure myself by his response.) One or two pills might not have mattered, but I had no idea how many he might have swallowed, and alarm bells were ringing in my mind.

I scooped him up and took him downstairs to my parents. We tried to make an emetic out of mustards and such to make him throw up, but Christopher wouldn't swallow that. So finally my father gave him a shot of apomorphine to induce vomiting. And it surely did! Poor little guy. He just kept on and on, long after his stomach had lost all its contents. Then he lay back, pale and exhausted. My mother was alarmed and thought he was dying. Did he still have a poisonous dose of medicine in his stomach? We could not be sure. So we took him to the local hospital emergency room to get his stomach washed out.

When the doctor tried to get a stomach tube down, Christopher woke up in a hurry! He bit through the first tube, but eventually he got washed out, and we saw no sign of any pills. When that was all over, he weakly said, "Can we go home now? I'll never do that again!" Poor little fellow; he thought this was all a punishment for swallowing the pills or exploring someone else's dresser drawer.

Back home, as I tucked him into bed, he looked up anxiously and asked, "Aren't we going to have 'din-dins'?" He was famished. When I asked what he wanted to eat, he listed every kind of food he knew. We had quite a celebration meal!

&

In May 1945, Paul completed his year at University College Hospital and made his second try at qualifying for the FRCS. This time he was successful. By August of that year, the war on all fronts, including the Pacific, was over. Although Paul assumed he would soon be required to perform two or three years of military duty, which had been deferred up to this point by his training, he and Margaret needed to start planning their future for when he returned. Their interest and commitment to medical missionary work was as unwavering now as it had been when they first talked about their dreams at the chemistry bench some eight years before, and they began applying for overseas assignments. Surprisingly, Margaret's parents, despite their own history of leaving England to work in a foreign land, were not happy with this decision.

We applied to the Regions Beyond Mission, which worked on the Nepal border, but at the time they could not use us. We also applied to the Sudan Interior Mission, thinking that we might work in Addis Ababa, Ethiopia, but then we found that it would be a long time before the hospital we thought to serve in would be built.

My parents didn't like our applying to go overseas. Dad knew and loved Africa, and he was less unhappy at the thought of our going there. He was even encouraging about our application to work in Ethiopia. But he never liked the idea of our going to India.

By 1946, with the war over and civilian travel resuming, the Brands had a special visitor, as Paul's mother returned to England for the first time in ten years. She arrived in March of that year and stayed in London until March of 1947. Evelyn ("Granny") Brand had never met either her son's wife or her daughter's husband. Paul's sister, Connie, had married David Wilmshurst, and they were now working in Nigeria, she as a nurse and midwife and he as a teacher. When Granny Brand returned to England, Connie and David happened to be there, Connie because of complications during her pregnancy and David because of illness. So Granny Brand was able to see both her children, and to meet her new daughter-in-law and son-in-law and her grandchildren.

Paul's mother had had some reservations about her new daughter-in-law, and hints of this surfaced now and again. But as she got to know Margaret, any concerns seemed to disappear, and ultimately the two had a wonderful relationship.

Margaret found a striking similarity between Evelyn Brand and her beloved Granny Morgan, two women living their commitment to Christ with an intensity rarely seen. Mother Brand would become another mentor for Margaret, encouraging her and Paul's similar commitment, both in their beliefs and their desire to serve God in a foreign land.

Paul was working with Dr. Berry in his practice and doing assorted surgical jobs while he waited to receive his military assignment.

And then the telegram arrived: "There is urgent need for a surgeon to teach at Vellore. Can you come on short-term contract? Cochrane."

Chapter 8

India

"Right now? Is it really safe to come?"

Margaret had no idea who this Cochrane was nor exactly where Vellore was located. Paul, however, remembered a Dr. Robert Cochrane, a world-famous physician who had lectured at Livingstone College when Paul was a young student there. He also knew that Vellore was a small city in southern India, home to the Christian Medical College Hospital, which was not far from the hills where Granny Brand lived and served and not far from Paul's own birthplace.

The city of Vellore is in the south Indian state of Tamil-Nadu, some ninety miles from the large coastal metropolis of Madras (now called Chennai). The Christian Medical College there had been founded by a truly extraordinary American woman, Dr. Ida Scudder. As a young girl with her medical missionary parents in India in the late nineteenth century, Ida Scudder had been dismayed at the lack of medical care for Indian women. They were not allowed to be seen or examined by male physicians, and there were few, if any, trained women physicians or nurses in India. With this need foremost in her mind, she went on to become one of the first female medical graduates from Cornell University in New York in 1899 and returned to India in 1900 with funds to start a small hospital for women. In 1907 she began a school for nurses, the first in India, and in 1918 opened a medical school for women.

The Vellore Christian Medical School began with fourteen graduates completing the four-year LMP degree (Licensed Medical Practitioner) in 1922. To the credit of Dr. Ida and her limited staff, all fourteen women passed their qualifying residency examination in Madras, compared to only 20 percent of the four hundred men who took the examination. Throughout the 1920s and 1930s the hospital remained a women-only facility, and all of the teaching staff of the medical school were women.

By 1940, the standard of training for physicians throughout British India had become the six-year MB, BS qualification (Bachelor of Medicine, Bachelor of Science), identical to that which Paul and Margaret had completed. For Dr. Ida's school to remain open and to achieve the status of an accredited medical college, major changes were needed, and the LMP qualification offered by CMC was to be phased out. Typical of the relentless efforts she could mount, Dr. Ida set about soliciting funds and personnel to meet this newest challenge, which threatened the very existence of her hospital and schools. Dr. Robert Cochrane, one of the foremost physicians in all of missionary medicine and considered to be a world expert on leprosy, had been director of a large leprosarium in India when he agreed to temporarily step in at Vellore and help Dr. Ida with this task.

The preliminary inspection by the accrediting body had been in 1946, and Vellore, with its changes newly in place, had passed. But the final inspection would be early in 1947. Dr. Cochrane's task was to oversee the admission of men, to build nearly a million dollars' worth of new buildings, double the number of teaching beds, introduce four new departments, and add twelve full-time teaching professors to the staff. In the fall of 1946, just six months before the final inspection, one of the two general surgeons at Vellore had to depart due to illness, and Dr. Cochrane desperately needed to find a replacement.

In 1945, Granny Brand had been in Madras at a lecture given by Dr. Cochrane, where he discussed his efforts at upgrading Vellore to meet the new accreditation requirements. She asked him if he would be interested in her son, who recently had attained his FRCS. Dr. Cochrane did not commit himself on that occasion, but the following year when he needed to find a qualified surgeon, he decided that Paul Brand would be the one to recruit.

Paul was obviously tempted, but he said it was out of the question. I asked, "Why?" And he said, "Dozens of reasons. For one thing, we're going to have another baby." So I said, "*I'm* going to have another baby, and I'll probably have it just the same whether you're in London or the Far East or India."

Paul said, "It's out of the question; it wouldn't work out."
I said, "Unless God wants it to."

Margaret had become pregnant again in 1946. She had had several miscarriages after her pregnancy with Christopher, and with a near-miscarriage at sixteen weeks during this latest pregnancy, thought that she would most likely not have any more children.

Paul was rightly concerned, and despite Margaret's support for his going to India, he wrote back to Dr. Cochrane listing the reasons he should not be considered: the Central Medical War Committee would not allow him to stay in civilian service (because he'd been deferred during his years of medical training, he would now have to fulfill his military obligation); he was too young for a faculty position; and he and Margaret were expecting a second child. Dr. Cochrane responded by letter telling Paul to meet him at a certain date and time under the clock at Victoria Station in London, and they would discuss this further.

The two men met, and by the time Dr. Cochrane was finished, Paul had agreed to take a one-year post at Vellore. Dr. Cochrane subsequently convinced the Central Medical War Committee to allow Paul to waive his obligation to the British military services, and suddenly, on very short notice, Paul was to leave for India.

Paul, Margaret, and Christopher moved into Nethania (which means "gift of God"), the home of Paul's aunts, Eunice and Hope, where he had lived during his boyhood and where Granny Brand was staying. Here he could start his packing for India while they awaited the birth of their second child. The baby was due in October, and Paul was scheduled to depart by ship the first week of November. Meanwhile, Granny took advantage of her time with Christopher, teaching him how to be a witness for Christ.

> **Granny was in England on furlough when Christopher was two.
> She would take him on the bus and give him gospel tracts to hand out.
> Christopher was very solemn as he handed them out saying, "You should
> read this. It will do you good." He was so cute people couldn't resist him.**

Jean Margaret Brand was born October 18, 1946. Her birth was uneventful, but Margaret developed some temporary complications, which made it difficult for her to physically participate in helping Paul prepare for his one-year post in India. It was a difficult time emotionally as well, as Paul would be leaving his young family for the first time. He needed to be in Vellore as soon as possible, so the plan was for him to go alone. When Margaret recovered, she and the children would follow.

> **By this time, my parents were finally, reluctantly, accepting reality. Their daughter was determined to go to India. Even so, they would often say, "There are a lot of poor people over here. Why do you have to go to India?" I tried to convince them that Paul had accepted the job for one year only to stand in for a sick colleague, and that we had no plans for the future beyond that.**

During this same time, Dr. Berry decided to retire, selling his Northwood home and medical practice and moving to the small coastal town of Seaton in Devonshire in southwest England. Shortly after Paul departed, Granny Brand also returned to India. Margaret and the children stayed on at Nethania, commuting to Northwood to help her parents with their move. Later, she too moved to Seaton to stay with her parents at their new home where she awaited word from Paul.

This period was one of the darkest times for Margaret. Her understanding of India was extremely limited, and even Paul didn't know what to expect. He hadn't been back to India since he left twenty-two years before. He had maintained constant correspondence with his parents and then with his mother through all of those years, but she moved in a world of Christian missionaries in Madras or in the remote hills of southern India. He had been given an overview by Dr. Cochrane, but this focused on details of the medical college, not the politics of India as it moved toward independence from Britain.

Contrasted against Margaret's perspective that she and Paul had been called to a God-given opportunity in an exciting new land reminiscent of her childhood in South Africa was the daily news from India in the British press. Here the image of India was all rebellion, bloodshed, and mutilation as Indians battled the British for independence and Hindus battled Muslims for control of territories and regions. For the English citizenry it was more of the same stories of war that had filled the newspapers for the previous eight years, except that this was civil war, and the British, only recently hailed as heroes in World War II, were now being portrayed by some Indians as the enemy.

The day before Paul left we had a long discussion and decided that he would go and do the job and evaluate the place to answer the question, "Is this the kind of place we would like to work permanently or at least for a long period?" I wouldn't do anything until I heard from him. Communication was slow, as letters traveled by sea mail. There were telegrams, but they were expensive. So I knew I should not expect to hear from Paul about Vellore or advice about my further travel plans for at least six weeks.

A complicating factor was that my health was not the best. I had a severe case of psoriasis, a condition that had troubled me intermittently since my adolescence. I couldn't sleep, and this affected the baby. The dear aunts were very concerned and arranged for me to see Sir John Weir, physician to the royal family, a famous homeopathic doctor. He was kind and helpful, and the prescription he gave me seemed to work, at least partly. Then my father said, "What you need is ultraviolet light," and he treated me with an almost blistering dose of UV light.

My parents kept telling me, "You see what it's going to be like? You'll never make it in India. You'll have to be shipped back as an invalid!" Paul's cousin, Dr. Vincent Harris, who had just returned from military service in India, said, "That's not my experience. A lot of the soldiers there had psoriasis, and they did better in the heat." While this gave me comfort, it didn't convince my parents.

Emotions play a big part in any chronic disease. Mine were no exception. I knew it was right to go to India, but I had all sorts of uneasy feelings. How I missed being able to talk to Paul.

Paul had arrived in India in the cool season. The climate was perfect as far as he was concerned, and he immediately fell in love with this land of his childhood, sending back letters describing the incredible beauty of the place and the friendliness of the people. Most of the friction and fighting between Hindus and Muslims, along with the strong antipathy to the British, was occurring in the north of India. The south had a rather different culture and lifestyle. In the south little was said about the troubles in the north, either in the newspapers or on the radio. Therefore, Paul had no idea what Margaret was hearing and seeing through the British media. His letters reflected only how wonderful everything was and how certain he was that God had a plan for them to be there.

Paul's letters about Vellore and India were almost lyrical. He told me about the other families there with young children. I was thrilled with his letters but realized I needed, desperately needed, more reassurance about the political situation—not just for my family's peace of mind, but for mine too. I did not want to sound alarmist, but the forecast of what was ahead for India once the British pulled out was decidedly gloomy. My vision for our work in India was fading, and Paul seemed so far, so very far away.

Early in 1947 Margaret made provisional reservations on a ship leaving mid-June for Bombay and moved forward with preparations for a three-week voyage to India with a toddler and a baby. She had to determine what clothing she and the children would require during the trip, after they arrived, and six to twelve months later when they would need different sizes and the seasons would have changed.

Although heavy-hearted at the prospect of their daughter and grandchildren leaving them, her parents bravely tried to help in the preparation. Greta made several little garments while Will made plans to crate the crib for travel. Questions arose as to what professional equipment and books would be needed, what immunizations were required, and what medicines Margaret should take with her and for what diseases. It was difficult enough in postwar England to find many items. They wondered what shortages and rationing existed in India in the aftermath of the global war that had ended less than twelve months earlier and what complications might be disrupting the very fabric of society by civil strife and rebellion.

Margaret tried to prepare, but despite her faith in Paul and her belief that God had called her and her young family to India, it was becoming difficult to ignore what seemed so obvious to everyone around her.

I had not made any close friends in Seaton, my parents' new home. I had no Christian comrades nearby, let alone missionaries who had been overseas, who could help me, pray with me, encourage me through that time. My moods swung violently. There were days of "everything will be fine" to others when I would ask myself, "Do I really have to go? Am I crazy?"

The ship reservation had to be confirmed or canceled by 10:00 a.m. on June 7, and as the deadline approached, I desperately needed to hear from Paul.

Everyone I spoke to said, "Don't go." My parents said, "Don't even think of going." There was tension and sadness in the house, and I was not getting encouragement from anyone. In that crisis of indecision I took the children and walked downtown to the post office and sent Paul a telegram. It was brief, but I knew he would read my feelings between the lines. I simply said, "Is it really safe for us to come now?"

The decision was now up to Paul, but I had the gut feeling that I would be going as planned. I returned home and got on with preparations and packing. There was no time to sit around and wonder what his answer would be. I had to be ready to act quickly.

When Paul received Margaret's telegram, he was still dazed and dazzled by India and the challenge of the work around him. He saw wondrous countryside, grateful people, and a Christian hospital community of dedicated staff living the commandments of Christ. It was absolutely clear to him that this was what his life had been leading toward, that this was truly God's calling for him. And he knew that this was where Margaret and the children should be. There was also the fact that he missed Margaret desperately and wanted her to share in the joy of this place; he also missed his children, having not seen them for six months—a critical period in the development of a toddler and a baby girl.

"When I received Margaret's telegram," Paul said, "I was puzzled. I knew she would never send a telegram unless she was quite worried, and so I checked into what she must have been reading.

"I was planning to go over to meet them on their arrival in Bombay, which I had assumed would be quite peaceful. Now I had to make certain of that. When we finally obtained some accurate news reports, they were not reassuring. In the rioting in Delhi, people were being killed by the hundreds. The British papers said that the quieter places were only peaceful until the British would pull out in August, and then the fighting would begin there as well."

There was no time for a lengthy letter discussing the options. Margaret needed immediate advice. How should he word his answer to her rather desperate telegram?

⁓

Margaret could not await Paul's reply in Seaton; she had to proceed to London to prepare for departure. Leaving her parents' home was heartbreaking. Her father, who was now sixty-eight years old, thought he might never see her or the grandchildren again. Never mind that he had done the same thing himself in 1921, taking his wife and three little daughters to South Africa, another potential hotbed of civil war.

Margaret was deeply affected by her parents' sorrow. The only consolation she had was the knowledge that she would be staying with Paul's aunts and other Harris family members in London; they would be supportive of her plans while feeling sympathy for her own parents' concerns. It was also a comfort to her that she would receive Paul's reply to her telegram soon. Surely he would tell her to come.

> On June 6 we loaded the car in Seaton and drove to Nethania in west London, about a three-and-a-half-hour drive. It was a very sad trip. After a loving welcome by the aunts, I said a tearful goodbye to my parents. My poor mother could hardly bear to let go of baby Jean.
>
> The atmosphere at Nethania was very healing for me. The aunts had read the same newspapers and knew of the situation in India and my struggle to decide, but their quiet faith made a difference and was such a help to me.
>
> The very next morning after the children and I arrived, June 7, was the deadline for the decision to cancel or confirm our booking for a passage to India. I had about three hours in which to make up my mind. Then the phone rang. It was my father with Paul's answer. He read the telegram to me: "Better you don't come now. I will return at Christmas."
>
> My parents were delighted! They had thought Paul was uninformed, plain stupid, or worse, just selfish to want us to go into such danger. Now they realized that he was none of those and that he had given me sensible advice. But somehow I still had no real peace. That awful burden of indecision remained, and time was slipping by.

As it turned out, Margaret's decision would determine the rest of her life, not just the next year. And rather than relying on human counsel, she placed her dilemma in the hands of the Lord, and He took over, bringing light to her life at that moment as He brought the dawn's light into Nethania.

> I was full of doubt and fear. Everyone, even Paul, was saying, "Better you don't go." Then I looked at the aunts, whose eyes were filled with

tears. They loved him so, as did I, and they knew what it would mean to him if we didn't come. Eunice said, "Let's pray, right now."

We knelt by the telephone, and Auntie Hope began to plead, "Oh, God, you've just got to show Margaret unmistakably what she has to do!" While she was still praying, God was answering in a totally unexpected way.

I saw a figure, a shining figure. I opened my eyes. It was still before me, silent, but with one hand upraised and pointing to the east, where the sun was coming up. I remember thinking, "God, if you want me to go east, to India, I'm absolutely willing to go. But you've got to take away this fear and give me assurance about what you want me to do." Then the figure began to fade. Still no voice, but I began to feel an incredible sense of peace. It was as though I had walked in from the bitter cold to a welcoming house and someone had wrapped me in a warm blanket. I now knew what "the peace that passes understanding" meant.

The aunts hadn't seen the figure. Its message was for me. "I know what I'm supposed to do," I said. "I'm going to go!"

I got up from my knees and went downstairs. The local newspaper, *The Daily Telegraph*, had just been delivered. I looked at its front page. The headlines and the news were just as before, of how awful things were in India. Then I looked down to the bottom of the right-hand column, to the Scripture verse for that day. (Years earlier, someone had chosen a verse for each day and paid for its insertion on the front page of that newspaper.) On June 7 the verse was from Deuteronomy 31:6, the encouragement given to Joshua by Moses, who was soon to die, leaving Joshua to carry on a difficult leadership. The verse reads: "Be strong and of good courage. Do not fear nor be afraid of them for the Lord your God, He is the One who goes with you. He will not leave you nor forsake you."

What a confirmation! I phoned my parents and told them I couldn't explain it right then but I knew I had to go. Dad replied, "I'm not going to try to say anything else to you. Bon voyage." The tone of my voice had changed. And so had his.

Invigorated by the light that had flooded in and by the power she felt, Margaret set about, over the next three days, to complete her packing. Aunt Hope was an expert and was a great help. Another encouragement was that

Paul's cousin, Monica Harris, also had a reservation on the same ship. She was traveling back to her mission station in south India and would be a great help to Margaret on the trip. Monica would travel almost all the way with them, leaving them at the junction near Vellore, where she would take a different train further west to the Salem district, about three hours from Vellore.

Margaret's burden and heaviness had been lifted. Not only had she made a decision, but she felt it was the right decision, even though it seemed to be against all sensible human reasoning.

> I called the shipping company to say, "We're on." Had I not been given such a clear message that I was to go and to trust God with the consequences, I might certainly have canceled. And who knows if or when I would have had another opportunity to go. Passages were not easy to get. Waiting lists were long. I had, by default, nearly made a bad mistake. In God's mercy He intervened with just two-and-a-half hours to go!
>
> Eight hours after I had called the shipping company, Lord Louis Mountbatten, the British Viceroy of India, gave the nation dramatic news. The Muslim leader Jinna and the Hindu leader Ghandi had agreed on the partition of the Indian subcontinent into the two new countries of Pakistan and India. The changeover would take place on August 15. Already the rioting was calming down.
>
> This wonderful news reassured my family. I was glad, however, that I had had to make my decision before Mountbatten's announcement, while the news still looked bleak.
>
> Dr. Ruth Harris, Granny Brand's niece who had worked for some years with her in India, was in England on sick leave at this time. When I shared with her about the vision, she said, "Remember this, because there will be times when Satan will say to you 'What do you think you're doing here?' And you'll be able to say 'God brought me here.'"

Unlike her goodbyes with her parents, Margaret's leave-taking from Nethania was joyous, with the encouragement of Paul's aunties, who were happy to see Margaret and the children on their way to join their nephew in his work abroad. Along with Monica, Margaret would also be traveling with other missionaries who were returning to India from furlough. They would help prepare her for a new country and a new culture.

At the port of Tilbury, south of London, at the mouth of the Thames, Margaret and her children boarded the ship. She was departing England after sixteen years by the same gateway she had entered it.

Our ship had been a troop carrier during the war and was not quite fitted for civilian passengers. Monica, myself, and the children were in a cabin with five other single women, but it was a happy atmosphere with plenty of fellowship. We had our own bathroom, which was certainly convenient, and seawater, hot or cold, was readily available. Fresh water required the help of a cabin steward.

Being confined on the ship provided time for Monica to tutor me about India. We talked about the cultural and political differences between north and south, about food, about domestic help and babysitters. In the dining saloon, my cabin mates tried to introduce me to hot spicy curries. I was a slow learner, not caring much for them at the start. (The addiction developed later!)

The English summer that the travelers left had offered the best of British weather. The sea air in the Atlantic was refreshing; and, though warmer, the Mediterranean air was delightful. But moving further south through the Suez Canal and into the Red Sea, they entered the heat of the tropics, and June in the tropics was not so pleasant.

We were in the Red Sea and had a "following wind"—not a good combination. When a ship is moving into the wind, the ventilators pick up that refreshing air and duct it below decks. Not so with a following wind. The tiny fan in our cabin was not much comfort to the eight of us. We all got heat rash to some extent.

Also, the seawater became a problem when we sailed into a hotter climate. In my ignorance I had been bathing Christopher several times daily with cool seawater. Not having fresh water readily available to rinse off the salt, his skin remained too moist and he developed infected heat rash. He slept poorly, and by the time we reached Bombay he was quite sick. Jean had developed diarrhea and diaper rash and was not getting much sleep either.

Margaret was on her way, children and baggage in tow. But Paul didn't know that. His final message to her, after days of agonizing, had been "Better you don't come now." As far as he knew, he would not be seeing his family for another six months, when he hoped to return to England at Christmas, the end of his one-year commitment.

When the ship reached Port Said, Egypt, at the Suez Canal, the northern starting point of the Red Sea, Margaret telegraphed Paul that she and the children were on their way. He was joyously stunned by the news and hurriedly made arrangements. He secured living quarters for them at the college and reserved a train compartment for the family to travel to Vellore. Then he set off to meet them in Bombay.

Chapter 9

Becoming Part of the Vellore Team

"Vellore will pull you through."

Margaret and the children arrived in India at the beginning of the hot season, the most miserable time of the year for westerners. Sweltering heat and high humidity muted some of the joy of the family reunion, but Paul was exuberant when he met them at the dock.

> Paul was so cheerful, and we were anything but when we arrived. We still had a long train trip ahead of us, and none of us were in the best of health. (The trip from Bombay to Vellore took two nights and one day on the first train, followed by a three-hour wait, one-and-a-half hours on a second train, and then a short road trip.) Added to that, it had been seven months since Christopher had seen his daddy, and even before leaving for India, Paul's many hours at the hospital meant that he was not living much of the time with us. Paul so wanted to bond with his boy, but Christopher was a little uneasy with him for the first two or three days. Jean was just a newborn when Paul left England. Now she was a six-month-old who didn't know him and wouldn't go to him at all.
>
> People often ask me about my first impression of India. My first impression was the poverty and the beggars. (The African situation I grew up in was rather paternalistic, but the people were not hungry, and begging was uncommon.) The beggars were so obtrusive; they would pull on your sleeves and make themselves very apparent. I wondered how one ever learned to deal with this situation.

I arrived in Bombay burdened by lack of sleep and a strong sense of guilt. Why had I not trusted Paul? Why did I allow myself to get so depressed? What had happened to my faith?

After transferring their trunks and luggage from the docks to the railway station, Paul and Margaret and the children, along with Monica, boarded the train for south India. Traveling on the train was not much more comfortable than being on the poorly ventilated ship, but at least Margaret and Paul were together. Once they arrived at Arkonam Junction they had to change trains for Katpadi Station near Vellore.

As we sat on the platform at Arkonam in the blistering heat, surrounded by our luggage, awaiting our next train, we must have been quite a spectacle for the Indian onlookers. Paul entertained Christopher by taking him up to see the locomotive. It was a great idea and Christopher loved it, but back with our stuff I was not enjoying my experience. Jean was in her pram (buggy), her sweaty little body attracting flies, and she started screaming. I was feeling nauseated from the lack of rest and the heat, and was trying, unsuccessfully, to keep the flies off her.

To make matters worse, several Indian ladies from among the onlookers moved in closer to see this rather strange little white baby who had no hair (Indian babies have beautiful thick hair within a few months) and to do what they naturally do so well in soothing their children—they reached forward to give her cheeks a gentle pinch. No one had told me of this custom, and Jean reacted quite negatively to it. I was on the edge of a panic attack when an angel, in the form of Monica, who was also waiting for her train to Salem, appeared. With her excellent Tamil she knew how to communicate, and after expressing proper appreciation for the loving intentions of the ladies, she suggested they should move back a bit and leave the baby to her mother.

After another hour-and-a-half train ride, they completed the final leg of their journey and arrived in Vellore around noon on June 29, 1947. It had taken Margaret and her children about three weeks to reach this destination from England.

Vellore Christian Medical College Hospital (CMC) consisted of the hospital and clinics (both the main campus and the small older campus associated with Schell Eye Hospital) in the heart of Vellore, as well as the college campus, with dormitories and classrooms for medical students, about four miles outside of Vellore. CMC owned houses in the neighborhood of the hospital where clinical staff could be lodged. The other surgeon on the staff was Dr. Jack Carman, an American, and he and his wife, Naomi, typically shared their house with new families. It was here that the Brand family was to stay for the immediate future.

Our first home was in an area called Viruthampet between Katpadi, where we arrived at the train station, and the hospital. A wide riverbed runs past Vellore. Once in a while it has water in it, but most of the time it's just a sandy bed about a mile wide. Our new residence was on the opposite side of the riverbed from the hospital, so we had to cross a bridge to get to the hospital. We were staying with Jack and Naomi Carman, whose home had been part of a mission complex. Whenever new people came, particularly those with young families, they were put in with the Carmans, who were wonderful people to introduce us novices to the country, as well as being most generous in sharing their home. Their own children were away in boarding school at this time of year.

Jack and Naomi welcomed us warmly and, upon our arrival, served us a nice Indian meal. Christopher was sitting next to Naomi, and when he'd finished he turned to her and said, "Can we go home now?" Home for him was still somewhere in England.

The first colonial settlements in India were those of the Portuguese in Bombay and Goa on the western coast in the 1500s. Subsequently the British had occupied and governed the country—the "jewel in the crown" of the British Empire—for over two hundred years. For centuries, the dependents of these westerners had practiced a seasonal migration pattern, as western women and children escaped the heat of the plains during the hot season and emigrated to the cooler hills and mountains. Many of these "hill" villages were located up to five thousand feet above sea level, and some looked almost European. Most of the permanent British residents of these areas were either owners or employees of tea plantations, shopkeepers and other business people, or retired expatriates whose careers had been based in India. There were also boarding schools located throughout the cooler regions: some British and modeled after the British educational system, some European, and some American.

Paul was sensitive to my needs after the recent difficult months and weeks, and he didn't press me for an explanation of my poor attitude when we arrived in India. Instead, he thoughtfully arranged for us to have a vacation up in the mountains of Kotagiri after we had unpacked. We needed to get away, to get cool, to let the children sleep and recover— especially Christopher with his infected heat rash—and most of all for Paul and I to talk and pray together as we had done so many times in the past.

Paul, Margaret, and the children took an overnight train journey across the steaming plains to the foothills in the west of southern India. From there they boarded a bus that ascended, via innumerable hairpin bends, to a charming little town called Kotagiri in the cool and welcoming Nilgiri Hills.

Kotagiri was home to the Kotagiri Medical Fellowship (KMF), a mission station which included a small hospital, dispensary, and area clinics that served mountain tribes as well as summer visitors, retired missionaries, and tea estate personnel. In exchange for Margaret working as a physician volunteer for the Fellowship, she and her family could stay at one of the bungalows for free.

Paul was able to remain with them for two weeks, and by the time he had to return to his work in Vellore, Margaret had met the staff of the Fellowship, Granny Brand had arrived to provide companionship as well as to assist Margaret in learning Indian culture, and they had hired a local nanny—or "ayah"—to help mind the children while Margaret worked. The children were healthy and enjoying their newest home, and this looked to be just the mission community Margaret had hoped to find in India, although for the next two months she would once again be separated from Paul, who would be working some two days' journey away.

The children and I stayed in Kotagiri for about two months. It was an enjoyable time, during which my health quickly improved and my depression lifted. And even though Paul was working in a different town, at least we were in the same country and letters didn't take weeks to pass between us. Mother Brand, also called Granny, came up and stayed with me after Paul had gone back to Vellore, so I did not feel alone. Also, we attended a nondenominational church where there was plenty of fellowship.

It was fun learning so many new things, from the Tamil language to a new system of shopping for household groceries. In walking to the hospital from our bungalow, we would pass a little store owned by a group of Badaga merchants. (The Badaga were one of the mountain tribes.) There we could buy our staples such as flour and rice. Then there were all sorts of itinerant merchants hawking their wares around the neighborhood in large baskets carried on their heads. Mostly they sold fresh fruit. I soon learned the art of bargaining and to look not only at the fruit on top, but also at what was down beneath, the less than fresh stuff. I probably got to be too good because Mother Brand would say, "Now don't be too hard on them. They need to make a living too!"

Employing servants was a novel experience for me. It sounded so opulent, but in a society where there was such high unemployment, it was one's duty to employ as many people as possible and give them a chance to earn a living with dignity. So we hired a cook and an ayah. The cook came daily with his wife, who helped in the kitchen or went shopping for us. I was always so glad that I didn't have to wrestle with the strange open fires commonly used for cooking in smoke-filled kitchens.

The ayah we hired was a sweet lady, very much a hill woman and not used to European culture. She knew little English, so conversing with her was done by action rather than word. But she obviously loved children, and I needed someone who would faithfully mind ours while I was over at the hospital.

My early days with the Kotagiri Medical Fellowship were a real learning experience for me. My courses in London had not prepared me for what I would need there, and I doubt I was much help to them at that stage. My mentors were Dr. Pauline Jeffries, an American doctor who had started KMF and who treated mostly eyes and ear, nose, and throat problems, and a Danish doctor, Lydia Herlufsen, who did all the rest. I suppose there were reference books around somewhere, but I learned by doing and observing these women. I even had to relearn pediatrics. I thought I was fairly well up on that field of medicine, but India was different. I had to adjust to a new range of tropical diseases and to new standards of normal height and weight.

As each child came to the clinic, we recorded the usual data: name and address, age, history of previous and present illness, height and weight. The next step was always a stool test, for almost every child in that rural area would have one or more kinds of intestinal parasites. The most damaging one was "hookworm." These nasty little pests would get into the child's body through the skin of the bare foot. By the bloodstream they could reach the intestine and there settle happily, feeding on the child's blood and causing profound anemia. Normal hemoglobin readings in a healthy child would run around 12 to 14 grams, but with severe hookworm infestation we would see poor little kids ever so weak and pale, with hemoglobins of less than 1 gram. The medication available at that time to clear out the hookworm was also toxic to the host. To use it would have been a death sentence for a small child already so weak. We would have needed to give a blood transfusion first, but we had no blood bank. Using what means we had, some of the children got well, but we lost others.

Margaret soon insisted on her own children wearing shoes out of doors. She had developed a healthy respect for hookworm. But there were other problems, like the potential for serious accidents with little boys who have a great sense of curiosity and not enough sense of danger.

We did not have running water in the house, but we got beautiful water from our next-door neighbor's well. It was a deep well, with the water surface about fifteen feet below ground level and the water depth another fifteen feet. A protective wall surrounded it and a wooden platform partially covered it, with a pulley to help lower and raise the bucket.

We employed someone to come morning and evening to draw water for us. Three-year-old Christopher was quite fascinated by the process, and whenever the boy went to draw the water, Christopher went along to watch him.

One afternoon I was napping, with Christopher supposedly doing the same, when I was wakened by an unusual sound, a mixture of clanging and scraping, outside the bedroom. *That's odd,* I thought. *The water boy is delivering early this evening.* I was about to snooze again but somehow felt compelled to get up and check on the noise. And there was Christopher, wearing the shoulder yoke, which was about ten sizes too big for him, half dragging, half carrying the large buckets and making his way "like a big man" to go and draw our water supply.

It was another occasion when the Lord graciously intervened. If I had gone back to sleep, Christopher would have reached the well. He was a good climber, and getting up onto the platform would have been no difficulty for him. He might have had trouble attaching the bucket to the rope, but he knew just how the water boy tossed the bucket over into the water (he loved the resounding splash he'd heard many times). But could he have done that without tossing himself over too? I still get chills thinking about it!

While Margaret remained in Kotagiri to work, Paul continued his duties in Vellore. For a young surgeon newly trained, Paul's responsibilities were impressive. He was performing a wide variety of elective surgeries and taking calls for emergency cases. He saw patients in the clinics and helped with the administration of the medical school. He was responsible for teaching basic medical science courses as well as basic surgical courses to medical students. Paul had been inspired by Dr. Cochrane to make Vellore one of the best medical schools in the British Commonwealth and was excited to be part of this vision.

Despite Margaret's own qualifications, she did not have any sort of appointment or stipend as such, as was true with the wives of other staff members. She had come to Vellore as Paul's spouse. The salary paid to him by Vellore included only living allowances for his wife and children. She wanted to practice medicine in some fashion and would offer her expertise where it might be needed, but she had the freedom to devote as much time as she wished to her family responsibilities.

⁓

By the end of September the hot season on the plains was ending as the monsoon rains swept through the country. Paul returned to Kotagiri and brought his family back to Vellore.

The city of Vellore was reasonably large, with a population of approximately 300,000 in 1947. The surrounding area was agricultural, and much of its economy was based upon marketing produce. There were also scores of small businesses. The average daily wage of a nonskilled worker was around one rupee.[1] A family of four could survive on that, but it left little for unexpected expenses such as medical care. The options for health care consisted of private practitioners, a government hospital, or the Christian Medical College Hospital. The majority of the local populace could not afford to see the private practice physicians or stay in the small hospitals owned by the doctors. The government hospital was free, but the quality of care provided was variable and not without cost.

> There was a government hospital in Vellore, and from time to time they had really good doctors working there. But patients preferred not to go to that hospital because, although it was supposed to be free, in those days there was much corruption and bribery, and they couldn't get care unless they paid. (For example, patients weren't able to get a bedpan unless they bribed somebody.)
>
> CMC Hospital charged only patients who could afford to pay, and for the most part the patients were willing to accept that, knowing that bribes were strictly forbidden at our hospital and also knowing that they would get good care. We had about eight hundred hospital beds, and much of our care was given without any cost to the patients. Indeed, the hospital's reputation brought patients from all over India and much of Asia as well. People had great faith that "Vellore will pull you through."

With the ability to apply basic hygiene theory to common problems, to rehydrate patients dehydrated by diarrheal illnesses, to clean wounds, sparingly administer penicillin, set fractures, and perform basic operations, CMC Hospital was not far behind the care being offered in the most advanced of London hospitals at that time.

> When I started work at the hospital, pediatrics seemed the best area for me, since one of their pediatricians, Dr. M. D. Graham, was on leave in England for special training. Dr. Graham was the only doctor with a graduate degree in pediatrics on staff at that time, and I knew I could

---

1. Probably today's salary would be about four or five rupees minimal wage. By today's exchange, one U.S. dollar is equivalent to forty-four rupees. At the eye hospital, in the 1940s and 1950s, patients who could afford it were asked to pay one rupee for a cataract operation and eyeglasses.

not possibly take her place, but I could be a bit of help. So that was my assignment. I had two doctors to help me. They were Indian and were pleasant, earnest Christians. Both had a lot of experience, but neither had a university degree. They had what was called a "Licensed Medical Practitioner" diploma (LMP). Without them I could not have gotten through that first year. Partly because I was trained in the West they expected more of me, but I needed to learn as much from them as they from me.

Many of the medical conditions were quite unique from my perspective. My London training, for instance, had not prepared me for "swami hair." Our students and other sophisticated Indians would shampoo and then oil their hair daily. But in the villages where availability of water, let alone shampoo, might be a problem, this was not done. Head lice were common, and the combination of lice and unwashed, often uncombed hair could result in the hair becoming matted. When this happened, the senior family members would be consulted about it. "Is this now swami hair?" was the question. Which meant, "Has the (Hindu) god that favors this sort of hair put his mark on the child?" If so, the hair would be left uncut, unwashed, and uncombed until the appropriate annual festival came around; then with a fancy ritual the child would be taken to the temple where the hair was shaved off, mixed with coconut and other offerings, and dedicated to the god. Some of the children who had to go most of the year in that pitiful state would come to our outpatient clinic with horrible abscesses on the scalp and be really ill. Generally the parents would agree to the hair being cut and the skin taken care of, but others might insist that the decision was in the god's hands, and the child taken home to live, or perhaps die.

Another new treatment to me was the therapeutic use of cow dung by village midwives as a dressing on a newborn baby's umbilical cord. Some of those babies developed tetanus. Why they didn't all get it remains a mystery to me.

I also had to learn that death was regarded as inevitable for a proportion of the children in any village family. But the death was expected to happen in the heart of the family, at home, not far away in some unfamiliar hospital. It was not always easy to make a judgment on that, and we didn't want to let a child go if there was even a slim chance of recovery. There were times, however, when the outcome seemed inevitable and we needed a bed for a child we really could help. Then we would let the family take home the one we judged terminal.

❧

When Margaret first returned to the Carman household from Kotagiri, she made arrangements that would allow her to work in the mornings at the hospital while spending her afternoons at home with the children. Naomi Carman recommended that Margaret hire the Carmans' previous ayah, Martha, to look after Christopher and Jean when Margaret began working.

In England, Christopher had always been tended to by a family member, Aunt Anna or Grandma Berry, while his mother worked. In India he now was under the care of someone from outside the family when Mother was away in the mornings. He did not always find this to his liking. After one particular difference of opinion with his ayah, he determined to take matters into his own hands.

One day Martha and Christopher were very much at odds. She felt her authority was slipping, so she threatened that if he didn't obey her, she would lock him up in a dark room. There was no such dark room, but Christopher didn't know that and had no intention of staying around to find out. He decided to walk to the hospital and find me.

Christopher wasn't yet four years old, and the hospital was two miles away across a narrow, busy bridge thronged with buses, cars, ox carts, bicycles, animals, and pedestrians. He took along an old purse of mine to impress any bus driver who might stop for him. He stood at the bus stop and waited, holding up his handbag. A bus came, but the driver ignored him and went right on by. So Christopher started walking because he knew which way to go.

Meanwhile, Martha discovered he was missing. She and the other servants checked the wells, fearful that he might even have committed suicide. Then, finally, they decided that the garden man, Manikam, should take his bicycle and look for Christopher on the roadway. Manikam found him, already halfway across the bridge.

Manikam tried to persuade Christopher to get on the bike, but he refused. So Manikam walked between little Christopher and the traffic all the way to the hospital.

I was doing my rounds in the children's ward when the senior nurse came and said, "There's a little boy here who says he must see you. I don't recognize him." I wasn't surprised. I hardly recognized my little boy. He was smothered in dust.

The moment he saw me, the tears started. He ran to me saying, "Mummy, don't send me home. I've got such a lot of work to do here!" I cut short my ward rounds, washed his face, hugged him tight, and then we went to have a bite of food before going home.

After that, we decided to employ a different ayah who happened also to have the name Martha.

Besides enjoying the assistance of an ayah, Margaret was freed from a good deal of household responsibility by the presence of a cook in the Carman household who would go to the marketplace daily to buy items for the day's meals. Shopping for groceries required navigating through the main bazaar and among the countless little stalls where vendors sold fruits, vegetables, spices, oats, rice, and grains—all at negotiable prices. Despite whatever interest Margaret might have had in learning to cook, given the difference in equipment and techniques, she preferred to stay out of the kitchen in India.

We ate all our meals with the Carmans, and I had great respect for their cook and the work he managed to do so well. I could not have coped. He cooked over firewood, even producing very nice cakes. (Many villagers could not afford such expensive fuel and used dried cow dung as their main source of fuel.).

Since Vellore had a sizable Muslim population, we had butcher shops. The cow is sacred to the Hindu, but the Muslim butchers were allowed to slaughter and sell beef once the cow or ox had had a long life of hard work. Unfortunately by that time the meat was quite tough and stringy and only chewable after grinding and pressure-cooking it. Occasionally we could buy chickens, which both the Muslims and Hindus were allowed to eat. Also pretty tough!

With the wonderful variety of vegetables that were available, however, I looked forward to the midday meal, which was a vegetarian curry and rice. At first I did not enjoy the hot spices but soon became quite addicted to them and still find Indian food my favorite. If it was too spicy, a banana (always available) and some curd (yogurt) would cool it down.

In India, as it had been for Margaret in South Africa and England, the mainstay of breakfast was some kind of porridge. Her father had been able to obtain his favorite Scottish oat porridge in Bloemfontein, but such authentic porridge was rarely available in Vellore.

> For breakfast each day we had a "kunjee" of some sort, a type of porridge. We often had a kind of cracked wheat, which the children liked. Sometimes we had ragi, a variety of millet; this was highly nutritious but not a favorite of the children, who compared it to eating sand! Oats were not grown in India. Some were imported, but often by the time they got to our market they had been invaded by weevils and had a distinctly "weevilly" taste. We could also have eggs, although they were not always fresh.
>
> Vitamin A deficiency was a common problem with many Indian children. We were frequently prescribing shark liver oil to prevent this. I was advised to give it to our children too. This was not a popular move! It had a strong fishy, oily taste. In all fairness to them, and since I was the one who thought it important, I had to take some myself. Their dad, however, didn't think we both needed to set an example!
>
> The only way we could get the dreadful stuff down was to float a teaspoonful of the oil on a tablespoonful of jargari (similar to molasses), then swallow it as quickly as we could. When Christopher was about five years old, he thought he had a solution to this unpleasant routine. He decided that if he mixed the jargari and oil with his kunjee he wouldn't taste it at all. I could not persuade him that he would spoil his whole breakfast. He was so sure he was right. I then threatened him that even if he didn't like it he would have to eat it. He saw no problem at all with that.
>
> An hour later Christopher and I were still at the breakfast table. He had truly struggled to eat it all, but finally I gave way and let him go. A lesson learned!

As Paul's commitment at the hospital came to an end in December of 1947 it became increasingly apparent to him and to Margaret that they would stay longer than one year. The challenges in such diverse areas as patient care, teaching, research, evangelism, and even hospital construction were utilizing every facet of knowledge Paul had acquired since he first left high school in England. It would be hard to find such a stimulating post anywhere in Britain. And Margaret had established a regimen that gave her a satisfying balance between her roles as mother and doctor, with time as well to teach evening Bible classes to medical students. She found herself in a loving Christian community with associates as sincere in their dedication to serving the Lord as she and Paul were. There was no longer any doubt in her mind as to how accurately Paul's letters had captured the spirit of this place. And as her letters home reflected her own joy, her parents began to accept her original decision to join him in Vellore.

Paul had also been correct in describing the turmoil of political struggle as being a North Indian issue. But the move toward independence continued throughout the country, and on August 15, 1947, the Brands witnessed the official lowering of the Union Jack and the raising of the Indian flag. Besides separation from British rule, the terms of independence included the partition of the country into the separate countries of India (predominately Hindu), and East Pakistan and West Pakistan (predominately Muslim). The bloodbath of civil war in the north only intensified as the partition proceeded. But in the south the Brands never experienced such events firsthand.

Margaret was now pregnant again, with the baby due in October, and as the summer of 1948 approached, plans were again made for her and the children to escape the heat and move up to the cool Nilgiri Hills. This time, however, their trip to Kotagiri would include a visit to Paul's childhood home in the Kolli Hills. Mother Brand had given Paul money for the purchase of a very used car—a great luxury for them—so the family no longer needed to rely on the crowded trains and buses. (Unfortunately the car developed serious "health" problems, and they sold it after about seven or eight months.)

The presence of Paul and Margaret and their children in India was a great blessing to Mother Brand, who had been separated for so many years from her family. At the time she was working mainly with her mission group in Madras, but periodically she was able to visit her son and his family in Vellore, and on this occasion they were able to visit with her while she was vacationing with her niece, Dr. Ruth Harris, in the Kolli Hills.

The journey required an all-day drive to the village of Sendamangalam in the foothills of the Kollis, followed by a climb by foot up a steep, ancient goat path to Valavandhi, the small community that had developed around the work of Paul's parents and which was the original home of Paul and his sister Connie. The work started there by Jesse and Evelyn (Granny) Brand was now being carried forward by a missionary couple, the Morlings, as well as Dr. Ruth Harris, one of Paul's cousins. Ruth was as courageous and devoted as her Aunt Evelyn, being the only physician for hundreds of hill people in a remote region still plagued by malaria.

The visit to Valavandhi was a wonderful opportunity for Paul to relive his childhood memories and to show Margaret the landscape of his birthplace and early childhood. For Margaret it was a precious time that gave her new insight into her husband and allowed her to share his memories. She hoped that one day he might be able to see Bloemfontein where she, too, could share her earliest memories.

From the Kolli Hills the family drove to the Nilgiri Hills and to Kotagiri, where once again Margaret and the children would reside at "The Gows" and she would resume her work with the Kotagiri Medical Fellowship. Paul was able to stay with them for a few weeks, and, having their own car, they could explore other areas of the region, though the reliability of the transportation was a constant concern. Both of them were enjoying their young family.

One evening there was a particularly beautiful sunset, and Christopher was outside enjoying it. Suddenly he rushed in excitedly, seized my hand, and tried to drag me outside as he almost shouted, "Come and see the sky. It's unnecessarily beautiful!" I don't know how he'd learned that long word, but he pronounced it so correctly and his words have stayed with me ever since. Yes, God didn't have to make the world so beautiful, but I guess He just couldn't stop doing so!

When Paul returned to Vellore, Margaret was left alone with the children and the puppy Winston. Winston was good at barking at outside noises, but if a door actually opened, he would hide behind Margaret. Knowing that they were living close to a forest and thus to wild animals that might not always be friendly, Paul had acquired a shotgun, and before he left gave Margaret some instruction on using the gun if need arose. The only time she took it out of the closet was to try and scare away some crows. While Paul was there, the birds, who were smart and bold enough to enter the house if a door was left open, had come to have a healthy respect for that gun. But in Margaret's hands the gun seemed harmless, and they sensed they really had nothing to fear. It was fortunate for her and the children that their lives did not depend upon Margaret's firearm ability.

> **The crows were so smart they knew I couldn't shoot them. I would point the gun at them and they would just look at me. Those cheeky things! I never did fire the gun. It was a two-barrel shotgun, and at least I knew which end to use. So there I was in that little house alone with the children and Winston and a gun that even the crows didn't take seriously.**

Back in Vellore, Paul was enjoying the excitement and anticipation of new living quarters that would be available for his family when they returned from Kotagiri in September. The medical college campus was four miles outside of the city of Vellore in an area called College Hill (Bagayam). It had been built in 1932 on a two-hundred-acre site, with a dormitory for the women medical students, a chapel, an assembly hall, classrooms and laboratories, and a large bungalow and small bungalow for housing the female faculty staff and guests. At that time, the construction of the campus fulfilled Dr. Ida's dream of moving the school away from the crowded hospital site in the city center where it had started. With the next expansion in progress to admit men students and increase faculty, construction had been ongoing at College Hill to build a men's dormitory and add new duplex houses for staff. The Brand family was assigned one of these new houses, and the Carmans would be their next-door neighbors. Gradually this collection of houses and bungalows at College Hill would become a village-like community of CMC staff, families, and visitors.

Despite Paul's experience in the building trades, one problem that arose at the site of the new house was something he had not encountered in London.

> **Initially the house lacked a septic tank for the sewage system. One was dug and appropriately lined. Septic tanks are not supposed to have any odor, but this one soon did. It turned out that an experienced staff member had suggested leaving a dead animal in the tank "to get the bacteria going."** *What a good idea,* **thought one of the anatomy department's lab assistants, who was not highly educated and whose responsibilities included digging holes for the disposal of dogs used for dissection.**
> **After a few weeks, the smell from our septic tank had taken over the**

entire neighborhood, and the odor, in Paul's words, "changed from a mild pink to a rich purple." Time to open the tank and take a look. There he discovered not just one dog, but six, in various stages of decomposition. Not such a good idea after all.

The unhappy lab assistant then had the unpleasant task of removing the remains and burying them underground. But after all was done, the smell cleared and the tank worked beautifully.

By September Margaret was more than ready to return to Vellore, anxious to move into their new home and to prepare for the new baby. As soon as possible after their return, Paul drove the family out to their new home at College Hill.

With great excitement the children explored everything. Christopher was attracted to the upstairs balcony with its protective parapet, and while Paul and I were busy unpacking the car, decided to see whether he could walk along the top edge of it. He could indeed.

He confided in me later what he had done, but added, "I was very scared looking down on the ground far below, and I had to keep asking God not to let me fall!" We then had a serious discussion about "not tempting the Lord our God." Needless to say, it was not the last time that topic came up for discussion in our family!

Upon her return, Margaret found that she was not needed in the Pediatrics Department, as Dr. Graham was back from study leave and had resumed her position on the faculty. With the baby due in a few weeks, Margaret was content to put off any decisions about where she might apply herself next. She looked forward to being a full-time mum and concentrating on the demands of a newborn, a two-year-old, and a four-year-old. She anticipated being able to enjoy that role for several months.

The Brand's third child, Constance Mary (who would go by the name of Mary), was born on October 22, 1948. She was a healthy addition to the growing family, and after a few days in hospital, mother and daughter went home to College Hill.

Margaret settled in happily, taking care of the baby and managing her active toddler and growing boy. Clinical medicine was not on her mind.

Chapter 10

Eyes and Leprosy

"You'll learn."

It was a Friday, early in November 1948, and baby Mary was just two weeks old. The weather in Vellore at that time of year was delightful, and I was enjoying being a mother at home without any additional responsibilities. That afternoon, a messenger came to the door and handed me a chit (a note). We had no phones on the campus, so to communicate around the college we would send a messenger by bike, who would then return with the reply. The chit was from the acting director of the hospital, Dr. Carol Jameson.

> Dear Margaret,
>   We don't wish to hurry you, but we must have more help in the Eye Department as soon as possible.
>   Carol

The Eye Department! I thought. *She has to be joking!* Earlier when they had asked me, "Where do you want to work when you return?" I had said, "I don't mind where you put me, just as long as it isn't in the eye department." I felt so helpless when I saw children come into the Pediatric Outpatient Department with eye diseases. I would think, *What on earth is wrong with those eyes? How on earth are they going to take care of this?* And I was so glad I didn't have to deal with it.

I turned the piece of paper over and wrote:

Dear Carol,

I don't mind being hurried, but I know nothing about eyes. You'll have to look for someone else. Sorry.

Margaret

I assumed that was the end of it. But one hour later the messenger returned with another chit. It simply said:

You'll learn. Please start on Monday.

Carol

So six words on a little slip of paper changed my life!

In future years I would come to see this request as a "God event," but not at the time. I felt woefully inadequate when it came to eye diseases, having had almost no training in the subject in medical school as I couldn't physically get to my opthalmology rotation due to lack of transportation. Just as I had learned very little about tropical diseases during medical college, so I had learned very little ophthalmology.

Despite her reluctance, Margaret's self-discipline, coupled with her desire to contribute to the effort at CMC gave her the will to tackle this new task. Three days later she appeared dutifully at the eye clinic, carrying her two-week-old infant with her.

Dr. Victor Rambo had been running the ophthalmology service at CMC, but he was presently on leave so that he could work at a large mission hospital in northern India that had unexpectedly been left without any doctor whatsoever. Until they could get a replacement, Dr. Rambo had to take charge, doing everything from eye care to obstetrics, doctors having to be flexible in what they might have to do in those days. No one had any idea how long he might be away from Vellore.

I was told that it was not my expertise they needed (certainly I could not replace Dr. Rambo!) as much as my Christian presence in the hospital. There was a trained eye doctor there, Dr. Rao; but he was a non-Christian, and they were concerned that he might not treat the patients in the way the hospital wanted them treated. Actually, Dr. Rao was as courteous and gentle as any Christian might be, and he certainly was a great help to me. Also, a few eye specialists from the city of Vellore came in two or three times a week. It was a bit of a patchwork, however, and lacked continuity. Since I did not hold a salaried position, I was known as the "honorary ophthalmologist."

Already feeling helpless when it came to dealing with the diagnoses and treatments of eye diseases, I couldn't have started on a worse day. It was the height of an epidemic of keratoconjunctivitis, an infectious inflammation of the eye, and that first morning we had nearly four hundred patients to see. We were just mobbed. After a while I recognized what I was looking at, but not at first. Talk about being "thrown in at the deep end"!

The Schell Eye Hospital, consisting of an eye clinic and approximately eighty in-patient beds, had been the original small general hospital built by Dr. Ida Scudder in 1902. It was known as the Mary Taber Schell Memorial Hospital and was built with a generous gift from the Schell family. It was located about one mile from the main Christian Medical College hospital, which itself had been built in 1928 as the Vellore Missionary Medical School Hospital. Schell provided important services to thousands of people in the region.

At this site Dr. Ida had begun her own journey from a rudimentary knowledge of medical care to creating what became one of the most sophisticated hospitals in Asia. Now Margaret was about to begin a similar journey, from novice to a position of leadership in ocular leprosy, but she didn't know that yet. As far as she was concerned, when Dr. Rambo returned she would be finished learning about diseases of the eye and would be offering her services to some other CMC department.

Dr. Rambo was gone for about two months, and when he returned to assume his duties at Schell, I went to say goodbye to him. "You are not leaving," he said. "I am going to train you" and made a lot of complimentary comments about my hands being the perfect hands for an ophthalmologist. (Actually I do partially agree with him on that. Women do have good hands for the delicate instruments used in ophthalmic surgery.) After that I settled down and spent a lot of time following him around. Talk about shadowing a doctor! I learned because I had to, but at the same time the subject intrigued me.

The work of the ophthalmology department was divided into three categories: provision of eyeglasses, medical treatment of eye conditions, and surgical treatment of eye diseases. CMC employed an optometrist in the eye department to do refractions (analyzing the vision of patients) in order to prescribe corrective lenses. Lenses were relatively inexpensive and could be made by a commercial optician located near the hospital. Frames for eyeglasses were more of a problem, however, because of their expense.

Whenever possible we re-used frames that had been donated and shipped over from Britain or America or elsewhere—collected by churches, the Lions Club, and others. Sometimes we could even find an appropriate prescription among all the glasses that had been sent, since some organizations would analyze each pair and put stickers on stating the lens correction. If the patient needed to have a new prescription, the optician ground the lenses after we gave the patient the frames. If we didn't have frames, the patient had to pay for both frames and lenses. Still, eyeglasses there cost only about ten percent of the price we would have paid in England and elsewhere.

Eye problems treated at the hospital primarily consisted of acute diseases related to a variety of infections. Penicillin, which had only been introduced into clinical use some seven years earlier, was the mainstay of treatment. It could be administered as eye drops, by injection, or both.

Glaucoma was a disease that in most cases was considered a nonsurgical problem. Glaucoma is a condition where excessively high pressures develop either within the eyeball or in the chamber between the iris (the colored disk) and the overlying cornea. Eventually the optic nerve is damaged and vision is lost. Eye drops were the primary treatment, but such medications were expensive for most Vellore patients, and it was difficult to assure that patients would use medications appropriately. Therefore one of the first surgical procedures Margaret had to learn involved making a small opening through the edge of the iris to drain fluid from the front of the eye into the back.

Another eye problem correctable by surgery was an infected tear duct system that would not drain into the inside of the nose; the blockage had to be corrected or replaced with a new opening.

But the most common eye problem was cataracts. Behind the iris of the eye is the lens, a crystal-clear structure through which light enters the eye.

For a variety of reasons the lens may become cloudy, and when this cloudiness progresses far enough, sight is lost. A clouded lens is called a "cataract." Surgical removal of this diseased lens can restore vision, although the person then needs corrective lenses to replace the focusing function that the natural lens of the eye normally provides. Why this condition is so prevalent in India is not known, but cataracts were the most frequent surgical eye problem the ophthalmology department encountered.

My first experience doing eye surgery was learning to deal with infected tear sacs. This was a common problem and contributed to more serious complications. Then I needed to learn cataract surgery. I started "operating" on the eyes of dead animals, which we obtained from the butcher. I also observed Dr. Rambo, hearing what he said and watching him operate. When he didn't have time to teach me, he would send me off to his library to look up some assigned topic. It was like a one-on-one residency.

Finally the day came when I attempted my first cataract operation on a real person. I was understandably nervous. Dr. Rambo was very tall, and he leaned over my shoulder and steadied my hands as I made my first incision. Soon I became confident enough to do it without that help.

Looking back at my mentor, Victor Rambo, I realize that as important as all the technical and scientific aspects of my training under him were, none were to stay fixed in my memory like that of his consistent example of compassion. I recall many instances when a family came with a young child who had a poor prognosis (either for sight or even for life) and Dr. Rambo, having given them the bad news, would kneel right by the child and pray simply and briefly for him or her, pray for the family, and ask God to make His love in Jesus known to them. Sometimes he wept with them. He could not speak much Tamil, the common language in that part of India, but they knew his heart.

One of Dr. Rambo's most cherished ministries was the "eye camps," where he would take a team to outlying areas, within a distance of one hundred miles from the hospital, and provide education, eye care, and even surgery. The CMC eye department could thereby help people who had no means of traveling to the city. The team consisted of doctors, nurses, medical students, skilled and nonskilled assistants, translators, evangelists or "Bible women," and cooks. There were even musicians, as patients who had to lie quietly day after day after eye surgery needed something pleasant to entertain them. Some of the team stayed for only a day or two, while others stayed for several days to care for the patients who were recovering.

Margaret did not become involved with the camps at first since the expedition involved at least one overnight stay for all the camp team and she was still nursing baby Mary. Later those camp trips became a great joy to her and an important part of her improvised ophthalmology training.

We would run an eye camp about every seventeen days. Our camp coordinator was one of the key people, arranging for camps to happen and alerting the villagers about them. Traveling on his bicycle (later he was upgraded to a motorbike), he would scout out a good site for the camp, which included an improvised operating room and a place to let the patients rest quietly after surgery. Occasionally he located a village with a small government health clinic that would be glad to lend us space. More commonly, he negotiated with a school to let us use their facilities, to the great delight of the students who got a bonus holiday! On one occasion we were able to use an abandoned rice mill. It had been commandeered by a variety of small birds that had nested under the roof. We couldn't clear them out, so we hung sheets over the operating tables to keep the bird droppings off the patients—an arrangement that was acceptable to all parties!

Next, the camp coordinator notified the villagers about the upcoming camp. He told them where and when to bring anyone who was blind or losing vision, and, if they could, to bring some food as well, since the patients needed to be prepared to stay in the camp for several days after surgery. We always got a good response. Some villagers walked ten or more miles to get to the eye camps, led by a family member.

Once a site was chosen and a date picked, we decided who would be on the team. Typically the departure time was at the end of a regular workday at the hospital. We loaded an ambulance and a trailer with medical instruments and supplies, musical instruments, food, operating tables (simple stretcher type), and everything we might need. We carried drinking water and distilled water for boiling the surgical instruments, and since we did not expect to have electricity, we took along several good flashlights and batteries. Often, we had medical students with us. They loved camp experience, were eager to help in any way, and appreciated learning how to make do with minimal resources.

By the time the hospital team arrived, the patients were already there and had had their visual acuity assessed. This was a simple test. The coordinator, who had been formally trained at Vellore to do refractions, stood three meters in front of a patient and held up his hand, extending one or more fingers for the patient to count, one eye at a time. If the person couldn't see enough to count fingers, could they see a hand movement? If not even that, could they see light and dark? (We reckoned that an eye able to count fingers at three meters still had useful vision and would not have high priority for camp surgery.) The result of the vision test, along with the patient's name and age, were recorded on a piece of paper and securely pinned to their clothing.

Usually when we arrived at the camp, we found three to four hundred people waiting to be seen before we went to bed that first night. As soon as it was dark, we lined the patients up and screened each one with a good flashlight. The night sky was a wonderful "darkroom" for this. We examined the eyes for any abnormality in addition to cataracts and especially looked for any evidence of infection. We also did a rough estimate of the pressure in the eyeballs just by finger palpation. Most of the blind people had cataracts. Providing they had no complications, we were able to operate, give them glasses, and send them home to a reasonable expectancy of useful sight. Any patients with complications we took back to Vellore.

In addition to the many cataract cases, we saw scores of children who were in danger of blindness because of vitamin A deficiency. This condition, called keratomalacia, was most common in toddlers who had been off of breast-feeding for a few months. Due to the lack of vitamin A, the marvelous clear shield over the center of the eye became dry and soft, then became infected. We could treat the infection with antibiotics, but we also had to restore the cornea to health. We brought large stocks of injectable vitamin A to stave off a crisis; later the condition could be treated and managed with proper diet and supplementary shark liver oil, which is rich in that vitamin.

Efforts were later made to find an inexpensive way to provide vitamin A and other nutrients to prevent keratomalacia. Research done in the Indian city of Conoor showed that a sort of milk could be made from the residue left after extracting oil from peanuts. This source of vitamin A became known as "peanut milk." Our public health and pediatric departments at CMC found another excellent source of vitamin A in the leaf of a plant, kiri, common to villages in our area. Soon toddlers throughout the region were being given a combination of peanut milk and kiri, and the incidence of keratomalacia progressively declined.

Some patients had eye problems that could be relieved by medication, and we gave them what help we could. But there were always those who had no sight at all and for whom, sadly, we could not do anything physically. For them, as for all the others, we did have the good news of the gospel. Many had never heard the gospel; they knew only that they had to please some god in their village. To hear of God's unconditional love and His gift of Jesus to the world was indeed news. They heard it in song, in Bible reading, and in the testimonies of those who themselves had come to trust Jesus.

⸙

When we had finally finished screening all the patients and had chosen who would have surgery the next day, we found a place to sleep. If we were in a school, we slept on wooden benches. Or one might be lucky and find a metal bench (these didn't harbor bed bugs!). We always carried mosquito repellent with us and tried to cover ourselves as much as possible. The village people who were staying over for surgery would just lie down anywhere they could.

The next morning after breakfast and a time of devotions, we scrubbed up and started work. We might have a hundred or more cataract surgeries to do in a day.

Water was often one of our main problems. During one period of time, when the monsoon rains had failed for five consecutive years, the surface wells were dry and the villagers starving. We took as many tanks of water as we could, as well as plenty of rice and other food items to be able to feed both our own camp staff and the patients. People said to us, "Just let me stay and have something to eat and drink. I don't care what you do with my eyes." It seemed almost criminal to use precious water on washing when people were dying of thirst. So we were very frugal about our surgical washing.

Since we didn't have surgical gloves, we soaked our hands in alcohol between cases. Instruments and suture and needles were boiled and sterile, but not our hands or the patient's skin. If we touched skin, we were considered "dirty" and had to scrub again. We were taught never to touch the skin, but to manipulate the skin with a sterile applicator and only touch the handles of the instruments, never the instrument tips or the suture or needle. This policy and practice paid off, and the Lord was good to us. We rarely encountered surgical infections, in spite of our limitations. Many of the patients rarely washed their faces, but on this occasion they did, and typically had their eyelashes trimmed and oftentimes the eyebrows shaved off. They then went to another table where they received a nerve block and eye drops in preparation for the operation.

In those early days we stitched the eyeball closed after cataract removal, using J & P 100 grade sewing thread, which could be sterilized by simple boiling. The stitches were removed once healing was complete, which usually took about ten days. This meant that patients had to stay at the site for that length of time. After staying quiet in camp for ten days with their eyes bandaged, the patients had their sutures out, were given the thick glasses they would need to compensate for the absent lens, and after a service of thanksgiving to God would be on their way home.

During their stay in the eye camp, patients were cared for and fed either by their families or by our staff. Men were placed on one side and women on the other side of whatever large room, such as a classroom, was available. The surgeons had to leave after the first few days to return to their work in Vellore, which might mean up to one hundred in-patients waiting to see them upon their return. Other members of the eye camp team stayed to care for the patients—to change their dressings, to keep them as still as possible, and to provide any other care needed until they were ready to return home. The surgeons visited the camp patients on alternate days.

Each patient was asked to pay one rupee to cover the surgery, ten days' stay at the camp, and a pair of glasses. This was not enough money to be of much benefit to us, but it was absolutely necessary for the dignity of the patients and their families, and to show them respect. Those who didn't have money might bring a chicken or part of a chicken. Many Indians just can't accept anything for free. And, sadly, it's those who really have a hard time becoming Christians. God's grace is free. None of us can ever deserve or work for it.

Restoration of sight to the blind and prevention of blindness in those with failing eyesight seemed to be almost miraculous to the afflicted. But the eye camp teams couldn't "cure" every problem.

> Most of the people were illiterate. I have one particular memory of a man who, after his surgery was successful and he was given the standard type of glasses, a +10 diopter strength, complained that he couldn't read with those glasses. So I took him over to our optometrist to get him fitted for a reading correction. Still no use! He was obviously disappointed. He'd expected more from the surgery. The optometrist then asked him, "Did you ever learn to read?" He answered, "No," as if to say, "What has that got to do with it?"

Through the lessons she learned from the lives of these wonderful people, Margaret was humbled to find that at times she herself suffered from a form of blindness.

> One girl, a teenager, came into the outpatient clinic one day carrying a toddler and a six-month-old baby. The baby looked fine, but the toddler was suffering from extreme vitamin A deficiency.
> As long as a mother was breast-feeding, her baby would get sufficient vitamin A. But when the next baby came along, the older child would be upgraded to toddler diet, which was nothing but rice and rice water, maybe a little sugar, practically no protein, and almost no vitamins.
> The absence of vitamin A was disastrous. The child's hair would become brittle and lose color, the skin and mucus membranes would become very dry. The conjunctiva and the cornea of the eye would dry and have no resistance against even a mild infection. Ulceration would follow, and within a day or two the whole cornea would "melt." We saw this all too frequently. If the child came to us in the "dry" stage, before the cornea ulcerated, we gave him or her a shot of vitamin A and then a good diet with supplementary vitamin A. In most instances we could pull them out of this condition, which threatened not only their sight but even their life.
> So in comes this tired young mother, the toddler draped across her shoulder. Too weak to cry, he simply moaned. His eyes were swollen tight shut. We laid him down, and I carefully opened his eyes. The mother

stood close by watching him and also my face. First one and then the other eye. I just shook my head; it was too late to do anything for him.

"You say he has been seven days like this, his eyes closed?" I asked. She nodded "yes."

Somewhat angrily I asked her, "Why did you wait so long? If you had come sooner we could have done something for him." I was seeing her as an uncaring, stupid mother who wasn't concerned about her child. I added, "And now you've got a blind child on your hands."

Then I noticed there were tears running down her cheeks. She looked at me and quietly said, "I've been seven days walking to get here."

She had been carrying those children for seven days, trying to get them to our clinic. She was exhausted. Her milk supply was exhausted. And she had arrived too late for the help she needed. How insensitive, how blind I had been!

Margaret was not only learning about the science of treating eye diseases; she also was learning lessons that profoundly affected her thinking—many of which she has carried throughout the rest of her life.

We were short of help at one particular camp. For some reason the medical students were not able to come, so we drafted local village children and they were delighted! They were not only getting holiday from lessons, but they were allowed to help in the eye camp. I was assigned a young boy who said he was twelve years old, but was very short for his age. His job was to hold the flashlight and shine the beam right on the eye as I operated. He understood all the instructions and took his place, standing on a box to give him height, right beside me. How important for him, now capped, masked, and gowned, to feel part of our team. He became so enthusiastic I had to remind him to hold his other hand behind his back. I was afraid he would feel he had to help in the surgery.

He was getting along fine until we got to the fifth patient, when he suddenly went to pieces and seemed unable to look where the light was supposed to shine. I thought maybe he was feeling a bit squeamish and asked him how he was doing. He said he was all right but didn't want to watch that operation. Then, pointing to the patient, he added, "She's my mother." We found a substitute for him, and I finished the job.

The woman was only in her mid-forties but already had advanced cataracts and had gone blind before her son was born. She had never seen him.

By the tenth day, my young helper was bouncing up and down with excitement, saying, "Amma, can you see me now?" It took her several minutes after the new glasses were put on her to realize that she could see again. She gazed at her son for a long time, and then, breaking into a smile, said, "My son, all these years I thought I knew you, but today I see you."

Her words impacted me emotionally at the time, but their lesson has also stayed with me throughout the ensuing years. So many times I think I know a person. I make up my mind about them, and my opinion is not always favorable. Then God has to stop me and say, "Now just a minute. Let me show you how I see that person." In those moments I have to admit my own blindness and let God open my eyes. How patient He is with me!

Dr. Rambo embodied the spirit of so many of the faculty at the Christian Medical College. One of Dr. Ida's greatest gifts was her "audacious confidence in human potential." Many of the staff that she attracted to her project in Vellore came to believe the same about having confidence in what other people could accomplish if one assigned them a task and helped them get started. This was a principle at the heart of the training of medical students at Vellore, but it also was part of the way in which senior staff approached junior staff. Dr. Carol Jameson had seen Margaret's potential, as had Dr. Rambo; and thanks to their own "audacious confidence" in Margaret, she herself began to feel that she could master this difficult area of ophthalmology.

By the nature of the organ involved—the eye—ophthalmology called for a delicate touch, something most doctors going into surgery at that time did not possess. Margaret had been blessed with special abilities and did indeed possess the delicate, fine motor skills required for eye surgery.

Working through His servants, Dr. Jameson and Dr. Rambo, the Lord had brought Margaret to where He wanted her to be.

Chapter 11

Lessons from the Family

"I can never out-give God."

By the fall of 1949, Margaret was pregnant with their fourth child, due in early 1950. This didn't interfere with her daily routine, which included home schooling Christopher, caring for Jean and Mary, and continuing her medical work at the clinic.

Dr. Reeve Betts, a thoracic surgeon from America, had joined the staff of Vellore, and he and his family moved into a house near the Brands. Before long, Margaret and Reeve's wife, Martha, joined together to start a home-school program based upon an American system (the Calvert system) with which Martha had been working. In the mornings Margaret traveled into town to work at Schell Eye Hospital, and in the afternoons she and Martha homeschooled the older children. The Betts and the Brand children shared some things in common, but their approaches were not always the same.

One summer afternoon when the monsoon clouds were getting heavier and a few drops came, the Betts and Brand children shrieked with joy, and each family dashed indoors to get ready to play in the rain. Peter and Anne Betts came out dressed as they would in the States: waterproof coats, hats, and boots. The Brands came out in their underwear.

Jean was more cautious than her brother, but she had her share of accidents. One time it was a scalp laceration, stitched up by Dr. Betts on the

kitchen table with the assorted Brand and Betts children providing an audience, and another time when her father closed another scalp laceration with
metal clips. Both procedures were done without any local anesthetic. The
first time Jean kept a stiff upper lip during the repair, perhaps due to the
audience present. The second time she toughed it out thanks to her father's
bribe.

> We were enjoying the loan of the Carmans' piano while they were on
> furlough. While Jean and Christopher were having a lively game, she fell
> against the stool, resulting in a two-inch gash in her forehead. Paul was
> home then, but all he had were some skin clips (small metal clips pressed
> into the edges of the wound to close the skin), so he told Jean that for
> every clip he put in without her fussing she would get one anna. One
> anna (no longer used) was 1/16th of a rupee, a rupee being a day's wage
> for a manual laborer. So an anna wasn't a lot of money, but to Jean this
> seemed like vast wealth. She earned at least twelve annas that evening!

Margaret benefited from her children's thought-provoking statements and
enjoyed being the recipient of these lessons.

> Living so close to the Betts family, we were in each other's homes a
> great deal. Jean loved to visit them, as she was allowed to play with their
> toys, and also she regarded Martha as a special friend and confidante.
> One morning after I had left for work, Jean went to visit Martha, who
> was just finishing dressing when Jean arrived. She watched with great
> interest as Martha carefully applied her lipstick. I didn't use cosmetics,
> so this was something Jean never saw her mother do, and she was most
> intrigued.
> "Why are you doing that?" she asked.
> "To make my lips pretty," was Martha's reply.
> "My mummy doesn't do that." Pause. "But then, she never gets her lips
> unpretty."
> Three-year-old Jean didn't mean that in a spiritual sense at all, but
> when Martha told me what she had said, I was reminded that I needed to
> take it that way and that I needed repeatedly to pray the way David did in
> Psalm 141:3: "Set a guard over my mouth, O Lord; keep watch over the
> door of my lips."

Another lesson came from Christopher. He often had nosebleeds. One afternoon he and the Betts twins were playing behind our house. I was in the living room close by and overheard their conversation. Anne had climbed up on the play-gym with a sizable rock in her hand. She inadvertently dropped it on Christopher's head, and his nose began to bleed. The twins were alarmed, as they had heard of nose bleeding being a sign of fractured skulls and they knew people died of fractured skulls. Clearly, they thought Christopher would die very soon.

I heard Peter say, "You're going to die, and I think it is mean of God to let you go so young!" Christopher immediately responded, "Don't blame God. He didn't drop the rock. Anne did!"

In 1949, Margaret's parents moved from England to Cape Town, South Africa, the area that had so appealed to Dr. Berry some thirty-five years earlier when he stopped there during World War I. Their oldest daughter Anna and her husband, Anthony, were working in Kenya, while daughter Frieda and her husband, Jim, were working in Rhodesia. Although there was still considerable distance between them, Will and Greta would be much closer to two of their daughters if they moved to Africa, and even Margaret and Paul were nearer to South Africa than to England. The Berrys had not seen Margaret since the sad farewell in Devon three years before, when Christopher was a tyke of three and Jean an infant of eight months, and they had never seen Mary.

Margaret's parents made their first visit to Vellore in November of 1949. They loved seeing their grandchildren and were happy to be reunited with Margaret and Paul. Will appreciated the happiness his daughter was enjoying, but he still could not bring himself to give his blessing to her choice of locale and declined any offers to show him the hospital or clinics. It was odd that he should not be more interested, being a physician himself who had worked in a similar setting. Whatever his motive, Margaret felt some sense of disapproval from him.

The Berrys had timed their visit so that they would be present for the birth of their next grandchild. As it happened, however, they departed before the baby appeared. They arrived in November, planning to spend Christmas and then be on hand at Margaret's due date in January. But babies have their own timetable, and Grandpa and Grandma Berry were halfway back to their home in South Africa when Estelle Frances was born on February 25, 1950. She would be nearly two years old before they would finally meet her.

⤳

With the birth of her fourth child, Margaret became a full-time mum. She still led some Bible classes for medical students but found her days very full with the two older children to homeschool, her newborn, and an active toddler who seemed to have more curiosity than the average child.

Paul would come home in the evening and be met by a catalog of Mary's adventures. She loved the sound and sensation of ripping paper, so we had to keep our books well out of her reach. She was also very fond of butter, which we sometimes bought for special occasions. One day she opened the refrigerator and took out our whole stock (about four ounces), took it off to a quiet spot, and consumed the lot. I was sure she would have a bad stomach upset, but she digested it uneventfully. A pity! That would have been an excellent teaching moment.

Mary also loved to experiment. For some strange reason she was fascinated by the pictures in my ophthalmology book, which was often lying around the house. Perhaps it was that fascination that encouraged her to try one of her more frightening experiments.

She had a teddy bear and soon discovered that she could extract its eyes, which were on stiff wires about two and a half inches long. One day I heard Estelle, who was normally a very quiet baby, screaming as if in pain. I rushed to see what was going on. Mary had her on my bed, head firmly held between her knees, and was trying very hard to insert an extra "eye" (borrowed from Teddy) into Estelle's upper eyelid. (Fortunately she was above the eyeball, sparing the eye itself!) She was saying reassuringly to her baby sister, "Don't worry, darling, I'll soon be done."

Paul, who was away in the quieter atmosphere of the hospital and so missed most of the excitement (and frustration), took it very philosophically. "I don't think there are enough good things for Mary to do in one day!" he said. On another occasion when Mary and I had had a particularly difficult day, he said quietly, "Remember, dear, even the most incorrigible child is *encourage-able*."

That quote has stuck in the family's phrase book! And it has a great deal of wisdom in it.

The summer of 1950 saw Margaret and the children once again making their exodus to Kotagiri as the hot season approached. The journey became increasingly complicated as the family grew, but every holiday in the mountains afforded wonderful experiences and lessons.

That year we rented a dear little cottage, Lindeth, in the heart of the community. It was perfect for us. The little kindergarten school run by Miss Woods, one of Christopher's favorite people, was almost next door, a little lower on the side of the hill. Jean was not quite old enough to start, but she eagerly awaited her brother coming home each day and would learn each song, each word that he gave her.

On June 19 we planned a little celebration for my thirty-first birthday. Paul had returned to the hospital in Vellore, but Granny Brand was with us, and we invited another family to join us at 4:00 p.m. for tea, cake, and whatever else we could offer. The older children, Christopher and Jean, helped plan the party.

Four o'clock came and went with no sign of any guests, and Christopher began to feel uneasy. He was afraid we might not celebrate at all, and he couldn't let that happen. So he slipped away from the house, rushed down the path to his school, beat on the door to get Miss Woods's attention, and then breathlessly told her of the crisis: Would she please come and be the guest so that the party could get started?

Poor dear Miss Woods. She had been taking a nap and was quite confused about the situation. But realizing how important it was to Christopher, she promised she'd get ready and come right up to the house. He thanked her and dashed away, feeling he had saved the day.

He was barely back at the house when we saw the invited guests coming up the road. Off he went again to try and head off Miss Woods. He met her on the path, all dressed for the party, and told her that since the other guests had come there was no need for her to bother.

I met her the following day, and she told me the whole story. I would have felt most embarrassed had she not been enjoying the joke so much, her rosy cheeks jiggling with laughter as she gave me all the details. We had a lot of leftovers, so I invited her to tea that day and she helped us finish them.

～

I was always learning lessons, but one in particular stands out—a lesson in God's faithfulness.

The early summer months up in the hills were delightful. As the monsoon season drew near, however, the rain and cold made the heat of Vellore seem not such a hardship after all. But since we had already paid the minimum required rent (three months), to leave early would surely be wasted money, and thus bad stewardship. We could sublet and recoup some of the money, but who would want to rent a wee cottage with no heating in it for a cold wet month? So it looked as though we should either put up with the cold or go back to Vellore and forget about the money we'd "wasted." Torn between the two choices, I prayed about it, and the answer came in an unexpected way.

It was a cool blustery day but not actually raining, so I took the family out to play in the little yard. Then she arrived—a poorly dressed woman and two thin little children walking wearily toward us. She spoke good English, was probably of mixed Anglo-Indian descent (a group of people who did not feel they belonged to either race and were somewhat ostracized because of that). She was widowed, had a poorly paying job, and was hard-pressed to find enough food for the children. She asked outright for any financial help I could give. I asked her to wait while I went indoors to see what money I had and what I might spare.

I found exactly enough for two weeks' housekeeping in my money bank. An inner voice told me to share what I had with her, one week's worth of food money. A different voice told me not to be so foolish. How would I feed my own children if I did that?

Oswald Chambers has defined faith as "Obeying God and trusting Him with the consequences." Listening to that first voice and the reminder that we are to take care of the widow and orphan, I took half my money and a few clothes that our children could easily spare and went back outside. The woman accepted the cash and the clothing and wept as she tried to express thanks.

I did not know how I was going to manage our finances for the next few weeks, but somehow that seemed unimportant. And I was very conscious of a peace and joy that had nothing to do with the woman's gratitude.

Something else I did not know was that, even then, a couple was on their way to see us—strangers to us, as this woman was. They didn't need money. They needed a house. Would we be willing to sublet our cottage for a month? Would we indeed? Our financial problems were more than solved!

Many times since that day I have needed to be reminded that I can never out-give God and that He is utterly faithful.

Chapter 12

Expanding Responsibilities

"Be glad you aren't married to a sailor!"

Dr. Paul Brand was broadly trained in all of the surgical fields, and although he had special interest and experience in orthopedic surgery, he was capable of teaching and performing procedures in other surgical specialties. At CMC Paul's assignments were primarily in general surgery and orthopedics, but until other qualified staff joined, he had to cover anesthesia and dentistry too. He lectured in anatomy and other basic medical subjects as well as the clinical ones.

Though unrelated to his primary duties, Paul became more and more intrigued by the deformed hands and feet of leprosy patients. He wondered at the cause and effect and whether some kind of reconstructive surgery might be offered to these patients. Dr. Robert Cochrane, the director of the Christian Medical College who had brought Paul to Vellore, was himself an expert on the disease and ran a major leprosarium east of Vellore. Paul's interest in studying leprosy found a sympathetic ear. But leprosy patients were not admitted into the hospital at Vellore nor at any general hospitals in India. So great was the public's fear of this disease that if it became known that leprosy patients were in the wards and outpatient clinics, most other patients would leave.

The bacterial organism that causes leprosy was discovered in 1873 by Dr. Armauer Hansen, a physician working in a leprosy hospital in Bergen, Norway. Hence, leprosy is called "Hansen's disease." The leprosy bacterium is similar to the tuberculosis bacterium. In fact, Hansen's discovery led the

German Dr. Robert Koch to look for and find the organism responsible for tuberculosis. But while the spread of TB through respiratory secretions was clear, the transmission of leprosy was not (nor is it yet understood). Leprosy seemed to strike randomly, affecting one family member yet not others. It was usually associated with the poor in tropical climates, but members of all classes of society and in a variety of environments could contract the disease. Father Damien in Hawaii and other westerners working abroad had gotten leprosy. And at one point the state of Minnesota in the U.S. had a high incidence of leprosy due to its Scandinavian immigrants.

The Bible has been blamed for the stigma associated with leprosy throughout the world, but the leprosy of the Bible is not Hansen's disease. Scholars now believe that the Hebrew word *Tsara'ath* originally translated as "leprosy" in fact refers to a collection of skin diseases that caused the individuals so afflicted to appear "unclean" or "defiled." Such uncleanliness became associated with sin and with the need for Hebrew priests to isolate such individuals and perform ceremonial cleansing. In the mid-twentieth century efforts were made to universally replace the word "leprosy" with the term "Hansen's disease" because of this stigma. But as one patient told Margaret, "It isn't the name. It's what the disease does to you that leaves its stigma."

For decades many mission societies had provided simple leprosy facilities at sites located far from population centers. Dr. Cochrane had worked for many years at one of these facilities sponsored by the Church of Scotland. He was a highly qualified dermatologist, but his research facilities were minimal and he had no specialists in other fields of medicine or surgery to help address the many mysteries of the disease that he knew must be solved. With millions of cases in the world, leprosy missions shared his hope for better treatments. It had been his dream that one day he might persuade such societies to build a leprosy research center close enough to a medical college so that interested faculty members could provide assistance and expertise at such a leprosarium. Part of Dr. Cochrane's motivation to serve as Principal at CMC was his hope that just such a facility could be built near Vellore. He succeeded, and under his leadership two years of consultation with the British Mission to Lepers and the American Leprosy Mission had led to plans to build a facility in the area of Karigiri, four miles outside of Vellore.

Paul understood that a world-class center near Vellore was in the planning stages, but he became somewhat impatient. And at the time he was focused on a specific aspect of the disease: the damaged limbs and what might be

done for them. For a brief time he was allowed to begin experimental reconstructive surgery on such patients at CMC hospital; but the administration
decided that even the two beds allotted him were needed for more standard
cases. Yet Paul's first results at this pioneering hand surgery were encouraging enough to warrant pursuing this effort.

Eventually Paul's exhaustive and unique research, a revelation to the experts at the time, would demonstrate that the pathology of the disease involved the organism having a preference for the cooler portions of the body.
The bacterium never invaded the body organs deeper than the skin and superficial tissues, and it especially settled into the coolest nerves of the arms,
legs, and face. Paul determined, therefore, that the destruction of the hands
and feet was not due to digits "falling off," but to the loss of sensation in
hands and feet. Because they felt no pain, patients, without realizing what
was happening, literally walked holes in their feet or destroyed their hands
by grasping hot utensil handles and sharp tools or didn't recognize infected
wounds. The lost nerves also resulted in certain muscle groups becoming
paralyzed. The antibiotic sulphone could slow down the disease, and for individuals who still had some active immunity, this might be enough to cure
them. But it could not reverse damage done before treatment started.

Paul also discovered that deeper nerves to the hands and feet were unaf-
fected, so that certain muscle groups and their tendons in the forearm or
lower leg were perfectly functional. This led to the possibility of transferring
working tendons to the other side of digits where the tendons did not work
so that the clawed hand could be made to move and grip and work again.
Sensitivity would not be restored, but function would be.

With his college faculty duties taking priority, Paul's research into reconstructive surgery for the hand was something he could pursue only in his free
time. As a result, he had to bring his work home with him in a most unusual
fashion.

> In the early days of Paul's investigations into which tendons could be
> used for various muscle deficiencies in the hands, he had to have a hand
> he could study. So he chose to keep a cadaver hand in our small freezer
> in the kitchen! The temperature wasn't as frigid as freezers are now, but
> it was cold enough to keep it from going bad. When he had time, Paul
> would take out the hand, let it thaw (which didn't take long in the India
> heat), and play with it. He would pull different tendons, see what moved,

and imagine what would happen if he moved this tendon over to that area and so on.

Our cook, Aruldoss, came to me a couple of times and said, "Madam, is that bacon in the freezer?" (He was longing to make something with bacon.) I would say nothing other than to leave it alone, that it was something the doctor wanted to keep cold. Mary remembers her dad demonstrating the marvels of this human hand to her, though this is a part of our homeschooling that I don't recall.

Paul's research soon gave him reason to hope that many of the deformities of leprosy might be corrected surgically. The next step was to find some way to admit leprosy patients into a facility close to the Vellore hospital where he could work with them. In his free time Paul continued to investigate the pathology of the disease and to pursue the creation of a small leprosy research and rehabilitation center. In 1950, through the intervention of an angel in the form of a retired American missionary, he was able to begin his project.

"Mother" Eaton was a retired missionary, living in India, who had come to Vellore seeking treatment for severe arthritis. She heard Paul speak about his desire to create a small village-like center where leprosy patients could have reconstructive surgery, undergo the complex post-operative physical therapy, and be taught a useable trade to take home with them. Paul's vision meant that a life of begging could be replaced with a life of productive employment, that those who had relied upon alms could support their families. Mother Eaton gave Paul and Vellore five hundred pounds of her savings, saying that she didn't want to meet the Lord and have to explain why she had left this money sitting idle.

"Nava Jeeva Nilayam," the New Life Center, was built near the Brand house on the medical college campus. Paul planned the simplest of mud-walled and thatched huts, designed to be like Indian village housing. The center, which could house twenty boys, included simple living quarters for the patients, sheds for instruction in trades such as carpentry and simple tailoring, a chapel built by medical student volunteers, and a small hut for surgical operations, using a pressure cooker for sterilizing instruments.

For the first few years, the New Life Center was surrounded by a firm barbed wire fence because of the very real fear of infection should the patients start to wander out into the campus. Gradually, with a better understanding of the disease, there was recognition of the low risk of transmission.

Only about 5 percent of any population had the defect in their immune system that allowed them to contract the disease, and the boys at the center all
had "inactive" disease. Soon the medical students started coming to assist
Paul, many of them participating in the spiritual education of the boys, and
the fence was ignored. Eventually, the barbed wire was removed.

At first Paul would spend just his evenings at the center after his work at
the hospital was done; but as the hospital surgery staff expanded, he was able
to put in daytime hours as well. Margaret fully understood Paul's passion for
his work but was not altogether satisfied that the children were getting their
share of their father's time. He would be away in the morning before they
were up and seldom home before they had gone to bed. She complained now
and then.

> One day my complaints drew an unexpected response from Paul. "Be
> glad you aren't married to a sailor!" he said.
>
> I realized that I had married a very special man, and that the children
> and I must learn to share him with the world. I also knew that he loved
> his children passionately.
>
> Paul always kept Sunday mornings (when he had every right to sleep
> in a bit later) for the children. Just for them. When it was barely light,
> he got up quietly, trying not to disturb me, roused Christopher, Jean,
> and Mary (at that time Estelle was still too little for such adventure), put
> some bananas or other snacks in a bag, then set off with the children up
> the rocky hill near our house to a cave near the top, which was home to
> a large colony of bats. Paul and the children would go into the cave, sit
> quietly, and watch the bats returning home from their night's foraging,
> folding their wings and hanging themselves up to sleep. Then came the
> snacks and a story.
>
> Paul was a fantastic storyteller. He generally made it a serial story, so
> on Saturday evenings the children would excitedly remind themselves
> of where Daddy was in the story and wonder what the next chapter
> would be. Or he would tell a story from the Bible in a way they would
> not forget. And finally there would be a short prayer of thanks to God
> for bats and all the other beautiful things He'd made. Those Sunday
> mornings made up for a lot of missed moments with Daddy!
>
> Vacations were also times for Paul to exercise his storytelling gift. He
> had the imagination to make up exciting stories involving children who

"just happened to have" the same names as our children. In addition, he would quietly add in little character insights. For example, if one of our children was rather quiet and bashful, he would create an opportunity in the story for the child of that name to be the heroine. It was delightful to see how the children glowed when this happened.

As the children got older, the stories became more exciting and even scarier, including wild adventures. Then, when the children were on the edge of their chairs, Paul would say, "Good night. We'll have to see what happens tomorrow."

Paul was not only busy day and night, but increasingly his interest in leprosy took him away from home. He traveled throughout India, either trying to find funds for his project from various mission organizations or meeting with other physicians who were involved in research on leprosy. On one such occasion when Paul was away, Margaret had an unexpected encounter related to Paul's new interest, which proved to be a crucial experience in the life of the family.

By 1951, Paul was getting to be quite well known around India. The word was, "There's a doctor down in Vellore who is willing to operate on your hands so that you might be able to work with them." People were coming from many parts of the country to get help for their hands and their feet as well.

One weekend when Paul was away in Madras giving some lectures and I was at home with the children, a man who had heard that there was hope for people like him showed up.

It was a Saturday afternoon, and I had walked to the college campus to place a phone call. (There was only one phone on campus, and it was about a quarter of a mile from our house.) As I started home, a cycle rickshaw drew up beside me and the passenger stepped out. I could tell immediately that he was a leprosy patient. His feet were roughly bandaged so that his shoes hardly fit over the dressings, and his fingers were clawed. His eyes were odd, but at that time I did not understand enough about eye complications with the disease to say more than "odd."

"Excuse me, madam," he started politely, "but could you tell me where Dr. Paul Brand lives? I want to see him." He was soft-spoken, with excellent English, and I could tell he was an educated man.

"Yes" I answered. "He lives in that house over there, but he is not home right now and won't be back until Tuesday. I am his wife and perhaps I can help you."

The man's face fell. His name was Mr. Sadogopan, he said, and he had heard that there was hope for people like him at Vellore. He went on to tell me all the wonderful things he'd heard about Paul's genius with leprosy patients. I had to break in and repeat that Paul was not there and wouldn't be back until Tuesday. Could Mr. Sadagopan stay somewhere in Vellore and come back on Tuesday?

He looked doubtful for a moment. His home was in Madras. He had traveled by train to Katpadi, where he boarded a bus for the rest of his journey. But the bus conductor, recognizing his disease, had angrily pushed him off.

He had found a rickshaw cyclist who was willing to take him to the college, a seven-mile trip, but it had cost all his money. He knew he was not wanted anywhere, and he had no more money. Mr. Sadagopan wasn't a beggar; he was a proud man from a high caste Brahman family, and it wasn't in his nature to sleep on the street.

That very morning I had been reading a commentary by Oswald Chambers on the Sermon on the Mount, which over and over again had come down to the point: "Are you ready to obey this? Are you really willing to do this?" I had also been reading the story about the sheep and the goats in Matthew 25, where Jesus talks about the last days when all the nations will be judged. They will be divided like sheep and goats, the sheep on His right, the goats on the left. The sheep would be those who had taken care of the hungry, the needy, the sick, the stranger. The goats were those who had neglected them. In verse 35 I read, "I was a stranger and you took me in." The phrase had stuck in my mind.

As I stood talking to Sadagopan, suddenly it was as if somebody were speaking out loud to me: "Isn't he your stranger, and are you really willing to take him in?"

Leprosy was still little understood and greatly feared by many people, and statistics indicated that children were more susceptible than adults.[1] Was I crazy even to consider taking Sadagopan home with me? Yet to say no to the question "Was I willing?" seemed like saying no to the

---

1. We now know that those statistics and assumptions were not correct.

Lord, as if He didn't understand the situation. So I gave the matter over to Him.

To Sadagopan I said, "Come over to our house. We don't have a spare room, but you may sleep on our verandah, use the nearby bathroom, and we can find food for you. All right?" With a beaming smile, he made an eloquent speech of gratitude.

The children were delighted to have a guest. I gave them instructions on how to behave, and they were quite good about keeping a respectful distance yet getting close enough to talk to Sadagopan and hear his story. We fixed up bedding for him on the verandah, which was close to the bathroom. (I could not help but notice the footprints left by the soggy bandages around his ulcerated feet.) Our cook fixed his food and took it to him. Being from the Brahman caste, Sadagopan was a strict vegetarian and normally would not eat food prepared by a non-Brahman. But his was not a normal situation. He was glad to get a simple vegetarian meal three times a day.

On Tuesday evening Paul returned from Madras and wondered who this stranger was on the verandah. He looked quite alarmed when I told him. "But Margaret," he said, "what about the children?" I told him that they had been pretty good and kept their distance, but they had been so thrilled to have this houseguest. "Besides, he had nowhere to go." Paul understood, went and greeted Sadagopan, and assured him that he would be admitted to the New Life Center the next morning.

Sadagopan became known to the other patients and to us as Sadan (pronounced Suh-duhn), and his friendly nature endeared him to us all.

Years later when author Philip Yancey asked Sadagopan what was the best thing that ever happened in his life, he said that it was being taken in by a family and treated with love and respect when he had just had the miserable experience of being humiliated and thrown off a bus.

Although our treatment of him made such an impact on him, he did not become a Christian—at least he never declared himself one. Paul and I often talked about this, and Paul felt that in his heart Sadan did believe. He certainly acted as if he was filled with God's love.

In the caste system the Brahman is at the top, just a step away from heaven, and to the members of that caste it seems they have worked to get there. They cannot accept something given to them; they must earn it. So they find it hard to accept the free gift of God's grace. It seems a special miracle when they do!

That same year another incident deeply affected the Brand family. For five years they had lived unharmed by the variety of dangers that a country like India could pose—not only the risks of exposure to a variety of illnesses in the civilized areas of India but also the ancient dangers that roamed the wild regions.

Estelle was fourteen months and Mary two-and-a-half years old when the family, including Winston, our beloved little dachshund, went up to Kotagiri for the hot months. Winston had been part of our family since the summer of 1949, when the purebred dachshund had been given to us as a puppy. He was much loved and a great little fellow.

One day we climbed to the top of Queen's Hill, just behind the house where we were renting rooms, and settled ourselves for a pleasant morning in the warm sunlight. Paul was getting an oil painting lesson from Granny Brand. I was knitting. The children and Winston were playing around the rocks.

Suddenly Winston started barking fiercely, and Paul went to see what was happening. Right where the children had been playing, at the base of a big rock, was a large Russell's Viper, a highly venomous snake. It was rare to find venomous snakes at that elevation. They did not like the cool temperatures. But with several days of warm sunny weather, things could change, and this one must have been enjoying the sun too until Winston noticed and raised the alarm.

It might easily have been one of the children who disturbed the creature, now raised up in a fighting pose. They were all standing by in horror, not knowing what to do. We called them off immediately, but Winston's battle instincts were aroused. Had he been a mongoose, he would have known how to attack a snake—to get it by the back of the neck and then hang on until the snake was overpowered. Winston was a courageous fighter but hadn't been bred for snake fighting. Paul tried to pull him away, even as he used a stout stick to kill the snake.

Winston had wounded the snake before Paul killed it, but the snake had also wounded Winston—right on his nose, which soon started to swell. We took him to a vet as soon as we could, where he was given an injection of anti-venom. We thought he was going to survive, and he did last a week. But then our little hero died. This was a tremendous sorrow to us all, especially to the children.

Paul got permission to bury Winston and plant a young jacaranda tree, which has a stunning blue blossom, over his grave in the garden there at Queen's Hill missionary guesthouse. Mary's prayers were nearly always about animals, usually sad-looking, mangy stray dogs. That night, after a solemn burial service, she prayed, "Jesus, please help Winston to be happy growing into a jacaranda tree."

Margaret and Paul had now been in Vellore for five years, their original "one-to-two" year commitment having been extended each year. Missionary families typically were given a one-year furlough (home leave) every five years, so as 1952 approached, they planned what they would do on their furlough and what they wanted to accomplish.

When they first went to India, the Brands had been a family of four; they would be returning to England as a family of six. Before leaving India they had to obtain passports for the newest family members, which was not a simple feat to accomplish in one of the most foreboding "jungles" of India—the governmental bureaucracy.

Christopher and Jean were already on my passport from when we came from England, but now I needed to add Mary's and Estelle's names. In order to do this I had to submit birth certificates to the British High Commissioner in Madras. Their births had each been registered promptly and legally with the local Indian offices in Vellore at the time of the events, and I had written several times to the registrar of births and deaths asking for extracts from the registers so that I could get official British birth certificates and also get their names on my passport. My letters drew no response. As time went on I became quite anxious and decided that I should go in person to see the registrar in Vellore.

I thought my request was fairly straightforward, but I was obviously wrong. I was referred from one desk to the next, from one office to another about a mile away. No one could understand why I should want to get an extract of the register. Finally someone seemed to know about it. However, he took a lot of time explaining why I should have done it by mail and not be interrupting other office duties. My explanation did little to satisfy him. He then told me to go back home and write out exactly what I needed, attach a "one anna corfee stamp" to it and mail it. That "one anna corfee stamp" was evidently the critical thing I had missed in earlier attempts. I rehearsed the words over and over, lest I forget them, and walked back the mile to the original office to find the stamp vendor.

The stamp vendor had gone home for the day, and no one knew just when he might be there next day. But I dared not take any chances, so I returned early the next day to find him. He had gone to have coffee. Frustrated, I went to the eye hospital to see whether I could use the time there. Sure enough, there were plenty of people who needed attention, so the morning was not entirely wasted. Then I delegated our cook for the job of buying the crucial stamp. He would communicate better than I could—and he did! He came home triumphantly with several "one anna corfee stamps." I looked at them and read "One Anna Court Fee."

I mailed my requests, giving all the details they might possibly need and carefully attaching the "magic" stamps. Then I waited. Several more weeks passed, and I began to wonder if I would be able to get the passports done at all. Finally two elegant certificates arrived. Parchment paper, meticulous calligraphy. What more could I want? The girls were identified by their annual numbers and monthly numbers in the register. But no sign of a name. And we, the parents, were listed as "Paul Wilson Brand" and "Margaret Elizabeth Berry" with no indication that we were married!

I returned to the office of the man who had given me the instructions about the "corfee stamp," but he was in a hurry and tried to dismiss me. I stuck to him, explaining all the time that the certificates would not do, that I had to have proper ones with the children's names. He finally realized that he had to deal with the problem, that I wasn't going to go away! He was exasperated, and I was stubborn. But the outcome was that we understood each other's cultures a bit better.

I learned that, according to the local customs, it was considered bad luck to give a child a definitive name before he or she was six months old. Often the temporary name would be somewhat disparaging, like "trash can." The Evil Eye would leave a child with that type of name alone. Or the child might be referred to as "Little Baby" (a name that could stick through life). My friend in the office learned that we westerners firmly decided on our child's names before registering him or her. It would be most unusual to change our minds after that. All this meant that the names we had registered for the girls had been ignored, that it was now too late for them to be officially named without special permission from the local authority, and that after permission was granted (which might take several weeks) we would then have to start afresh and apply for necessary documents.

The man in the office was getting quite impatient with me and told me to return later that day and he would show me the book of rules. I was quite impatient too. It all seemed too foolish for words, and our departure date was getting closer. I decided that I would return to that office but seek the help of a more senior official. I went home, rested, prayed, and returned to the office. A line had formed outside the commissioner's office. He was comparable to the local magistrate and could adjudicate on minor grievances. I reckoned I qualified and joined the line.

The aggrieved person ahead of me was politely heard and advised of his rights. He rose, stretched his hand across the table, and asked the commissioner for his name, adding, "You are the first official I have talked to that has bothered to hear my grievance." The commissioner respectfully shook his hand and answered, "My name is C. R. Richards, Indian Christian." It was a small thing maybe, but it gave me great joy. Joy just to hear his quiet witness and joy to realize that I could talk to someone who would understand!

Mr. Richards was indeed most helpful. He called his clerk and dictated a letter requesting immediate attention to our need to have the names inserted appropriately in the register and to then issue new certificates. I then ventured to ask that the word *formerly* be inserted before the name Berry, to indicate that I was legally married to Paul. He nodded to acknowledge my request and dictated, "After the names Margaret Elizabeth Berry write, 'spinster'." He was puzzled as to why I did not think that would work!

Several minutes later our discussion ended in a friendly way, and within a week I received the new certificates. Both the children had their proper names, not merely institutional numbers, and I was unquestionably Paul's legal wife.

Preparations for the Brands' furlough year were daunting and almost endless: arranging for the storage of their household goods that would be left behind for a year, packing four seasons of clothing for two adults and four children, making complex round-trip travel plans, securing a residence in which to stay in England and schools for the children, and planning what Margaret and Paul would hope to accomplish while on leave. Besides passports, proofs of inoculations had to be rounded up. Tickets had to be booked both for the train travel from Vellore to Bombay as well as ship passage from Bombay to England. A reservation for rooms in Bombay to use prior to sailing needed to be secured. Each child had favorite toys or books to pack. Precious photos and simple gifts for family in England must not be forgotten.

Margaret's parents and sisters were no longer in England, but Paul's aunts were more than happy to offer their home to the young family, just as they had done years before when their sister Evelyn had brought Paul and Connie home from India. The aunts had lived through having young children in the house once before, although their furniture, banisters, china, and crystal hadn't been endangered in recent years.

As if Margaret did not have enough to do before leaving on furlough, one other task arose. She had to arrange the marriage of one of the household servants, their ayah Martha.

Early in 1952, when we were getting ready to go on our first furlough, I received a letter from Martha's father. He indicated that since Martha had been in our employ for three years, we should now regard her as our daughter and take responsibility for her future. He didn't mean establishing a pension fund. He meant finding a husband for her and arranging the marriage!

Neither Paul nor I had any idea of how to set about this, so Paul wisely suggested we get his mother's help. Granny Brand understood the nuances of Indian culture. Also, she had raised a number of orphan girls and had to find husbands for them, so she had had plenty of experience behind her when she advised me.

Granny Brand drafted letters for me to send to various missionaries and organizations that might know of suitable young men. Replies began to come back and interviews were arranged.

Martha made it clear that she did not want to be part of the process. The arrangements would be between Paul and me (more likely just me) and the man and an interpreter. I was touched that she should so trust me to make a good match. I did the best I could, after praying frantically about it, and a choice was eventually made. (Martha did coyly view her future husband's back as he walked away from the house. She would next see him at her wedding!)

The wedding took place in Namakaal, about four hours' journey from Vellore. Granny Brand, the four children, and I were there as Martha's family. None of her biological family was able to get there. When Estelle, who was nearly two years old and loved Martha dearly, saw her ayah across the church, seated solemnly by some strange man, she wailed in protest at being firmly held back from going to her. The noise interrupted the ceremony. Martha got upset, stood up, and beckoned to Estelle, who immediately dashed to her, climbed on her knee, and all was quiet again. The rest of the wedding proceeded with our little girl sitting confidently on the bride's lap.

The match seemed to be a good one, and Martha visited us a few years later with her own two happy and healthy little girls.

The plans for the Brands' twelve-month furlough were ambitious to say the least. Margaret had two goals, along with caring for the children, visiting family and friends, and taking some vacation time: to take training in optometry so that she would be able to refract eyes and prescribe glasses, and to gather information and materials on a British-based homeschooling program. She had begun homeschooling Christopher and Jean, working with the American program that Martha Betts was using. But if the children were eventually going to enter the British school system, it would be better for them to be in a program consistent with the curriculum of standard British primary schools. The program she hoped to explore was that of the Parents' National Education Union (PNEU), a system developed by Charlotte Mason in the nineteenth century and ahead of its time in its philosophy of educational techniques.

Paul's plans included several months to be spent in America. To his delight he had been granted a Rockefeller Foundation Fellowship, which would pay his expenses to study anywhere he wished for an almost unlimited time. Paul's work in discovering and clarifying the pathology of nerve damage in leprosy and creating new operations to reconstruct hands and feet had caught the attention of a regional Rockefeller representative touring India. His scholarly research and analysis of his experiments and outcomes were meticulous, and he had published excellent articles detailing his work to date. He was just the sort of medical pioneer the Foundation sought.

The other significant task Paul needed to accomplish was to obtain financial support so that he and Margaret could continue working in India. For the past five years his salary had been paid by the college, but that would not be increased, despite his growing family. He needed to find a mission sponsor in England that would guarantee continued support, including the expenses of his family.

> The college made it clear that they would like us to return after furlough, but it was also clear that they could not increase our allowance. The current allowance would not support boarding school fees or the travel entailed by having the children in boarding school, should we be unable to continue homeschooling. We felt confident that we would find a missionary organization that would sponsor our further service in Vellore. So we left for our furlough expecting to be back. The house would be used by another family while we were gone, so we took what we needed and left the rest in storage.

In April, the Brand family, along with their trunks and luggage, boarded the train in Vellore and left for Bombay. Christopher and Jean, who were now eight and five, could help with some of the baggage, but three-year-old Mary and two-year-old Estelle needed assistance and close attention. After a two-day journey on a coal-powered train with open windows, they arrived in Bombay travel-stained and weary.

> We stayed at the Christian Missionary Society Guesthouse, a quiet, pleasant home, which was just what we needed at that point. After getting cleaned up and having a good night's sleep, we felt ready for what we had to do during our day-and-a-half in Bombay. We had to clear our luggage through customs at the docks, Paul had an appointment to meet with other research workers in his field, and the children were looking forward to exploring the city.
>
> Paul asked me to take our luggage to be checked through customs prior to shipping while he went off for his appointment and the children remained at the house. I then would return by taxi, collect the children, and take another taxi to a home where we had been invited for supper.

Clearing customs took much longer than I had anticipated, and by the time I was through it was rush hour—and Bombay rush hour is a unique experience! Every taxi was taken, but finally one stopped for me. I climbed in and sat back, relieved that I had accomplished what I had to do.

The driver had a friend in the front seat with him, and they were chatting. Then, after he dropped off his friend, the driver tried to engage me in conversation. His comments were casual enough until he asked if I had been up the mountain to a famous viewpoint. When I said no, he told me we would go up there right then. At that point I became uneasy. What was in his mind? Trying to keep my voice nonchalant, I said, "I don't have time to do any sightseeing. My husband and children are waiting for me. Please just take me to my destination." He half looked over his shoulder at me and said, "What's a husband and what's the hurry? You and I can have a lot of fun tonight." By then I was shaking and getting nauseous. Just a few months earlier two women missionaries had disappeared. Was I to be the next statistic? No one knew where I was.

I tried to say in my sternest voice (but since I was shaking so badly my voice was too), "If you don't let me out right now, I shall report you to the authorities."

Perhaps he looked in his rearview mirror and saw my pale face and didn't want to have to clean up his cab if I did vomit. Whatever his reason, he drew up to the curb and let me out.

What a relief to see his cab disappear into the traffic. I just stood there shaking for some seconds; then my stomach settled down. I caught another taxi and was soon back at the guesthouse.

Later when I told Paul about my unpleasant experience, he simply asked me why I didn't get the cab number. All I had been thinking of as I saw the cab drive away was that I was alive and safe! If I had not already realized it, this was one more illustration of how different men and women are!

I had difficulty sleeping that night. Some of my restlessness was caused by reliving the fear, and perhaps a bit of it was self-pity that no one else seemed too concerned about my ordeal. All told, I was glad to leave Bombay the next day and ever after was uneasy whenever I went to that city.

The Brands' journey to England took them across the northern part of the Indian Ocean and into the Arabian Sea, then up the Gulf of Aden to the Red Sea. At the northern end their ship passed through the Suez Canal and into the Mediterranean. Heading west they passed the Straits of Gibraltar and on to the Atlantic Ocean and, finally, England. This was one of the most historic and spectacular ocean routes in the annals of seafaring. But while Margaret enjoyed some moments of pleasure on the voyage, for her the trip was chiefly memorable for two things: laundry and losing Mary.

The *Mooltan* was a nice little ship but with very limited air conditioning. The weather was hot. Our cabins were hot. The only way we could get the children to sleep was to put them down on top of the covered hatches under the cool night sky. Then later we carried them to our cabin and their berths.

As a result of the heat I spent a good deal of time in the laundry room, which was like taking a daily Turkish bath! No automatic washers in those days. But we mothers surely got to know each other well, and that was fun.

We should have been used to Mary getting lost by that time. She had ventured off on her own many times, but in places where we had no concern. We knew that she would be well treated and would show up again. Then came Aden.

We anchored at Aden, a major trading port for the Yemeni people, where the traders could come on deck and we passengers could buy souvenirs or we could go ashore and explore the ancient city. Estelle wasn't well, so I stayed on board with her while Paul took the three older children ashore. Then when he returned with the children, I went ashore for a little visit on my own.

When I returned from my visit ashore, the Arab traders were gathering their things to get off the ship. Paul assured me that the little ones were both asleep, and I peeked into the cabin to check on them. Estelle was sound asleep, but there was no sign of Mary. Had she gone to the bathroom? I went to check, calling her name at all the various bathrooms on our level. No answer. Had she gone back up on deck to see the traders again? I could not rule out that possibility. She was such a friendly little girl.

By now I was getting more than a little concerned, as I knew the ship would leave soon, and bad stories I'd heard in my childhood about the "white slave trade" kept surging up in my mind.

I found Paul and shared my concerns. He was completely confident that she was somewhere on the ship and we'd find her. But he agreed to go to the purser's office and report that she was missing. By then the loudspeakers were announcing, "All visitors ashore, and all passengers should now be on board."

After we'd given a description of little Mary to the purser, Paul said, "Well, we've done all we can. Let's go and have lunch." As we were sitting in the dining saloon (I, distraught, had lost my appetite, but Paul, at peace, was having a good lunch), we heard the sound of the anchor coming up. And I didn't know where my little girl was, on board or ashore.

It turned out that Mary had gone to the toilet but, being sleepy and somewhat disoriented, had not returned to our cabin. Instead she had gone down to a lower deck, found a nice cabin, and gone fast asleep on someone else's berth. Our own little Goldilocks! The lady who brought her back to us, about a half-hour after lunch, looked very like an angel to me!

As the *Mooltan* docked in Liverpool, Margaret was thankful that her family had survived the voyage intact and felt excited about setting foot in England. When they had left five years earlier, the physical destruction of war was still present everywhere in the landscape, and the economic and emotional damage was even greater. Would rationing still be in effect? How would England look and feel? Margaret couldn't wait to find out.

Chapter 13

First Furlough

"I had nothing else good enough to give."

Spring was the perfect time of year to arrive in England, with colorful buds starting to open and lush greenery everywhere. The Brands' return began with a joyous family reunion with Paul's aunts in St. John's Wood in northwest London. Jean had been eight months old when Aunt Eunice and Aunt Hope had last seen her, Christopher had gone from tyke to young boy, and they were meeting Mary and Estelle for the first time.

Besides family activities, Paul and Margaret were busy with the tasks they had planned to accomplish while on furlough. Paul visited medical and surgical colleagues, gave addresses to publicize the Christian mission of CMC, and began soliciting support for his own continued work in India. After considering several organizations and offering much prayer for guidance, Paul and Margaret chose to join the British Mission to Lepers (subsequently renamed the Leprosy Mission International), which had offered to support the Brands as missionaries. Meanwhile, Margaret investigated the homeschooling system she wanted to start upon her return to Vellore.

I learned that all the books I would need, the curriculum I should follow, and the examinations I would give would be mailed to me in India. I would then mail the answer papers to London for grading and advice. This became the basis for the primary education of Christopher, Jean, Mary, and Estelle.

She also found courses in optometry that perfectly met her professional needs.

I had come a long way from the state of terror I had been in back in 1948 when Dr. Jameson said, "You'll learn. Please start on Monday." But I was very aware of significant gaps in my knowledge of ophthalmology, particularly the whole science of optics and optometry. I had originally been fearful of dealing with eye problems because I simply knew nothing about diseases of the eye. With Dr. Rambo's teaching and my time spent at the eye hospital and in the eye camps, my knowledge and competence had grown, and the more I learned, the more I wanted to know.

During our furlough I was able to spend time at one of the Polytechnic colleges, which offered a good education in optics and optometry. Through my church in England, a teacher in optics at one of the colleges heard that I was looking for just that sort of training, and he volunteered to teach me. He was a fine Christian and generously gave me his time and expertise. I didn't take any exam or receive a diploma, but I became proficient in doing refractions.

Paul, who had been working alone in India on reconstructive surgery in leprosy for the past five years, was now able to consult with some of the finest minds in the fields of neurology, pathology, and surgery. One such meeting resulted in an astonishing invitation—an honor he never expected and one bestowed upon only one member of the Royal College of Surgeons each year.

Paul was able to meet with the renowned plastic surgeon, Sir Archibald McIndoe, at his hospital in East Grinstead, Surrey. Sir Archibald was famous for the stunning results he had achieved in reconstructive techniques for British RAF airmen who had suffered severe burns during the war, especially to their hands.

As a result of their meeting, during which Sir Archibald asked Paul about his work in India, Paul ended up presenting his research to larger and larger audiences, organized by Sir Archibald. After the third presentation, Sir Archibald asked if he might recommend Paul as a candidate to give the Hunterian Lecture that year to the assembled Royal College of Surgeons of England, in London. Of course Paul agreed and then frantically began refining his presentation. The committee read it, considered its value and uniqueness, and then gave their official approval to Sir Archibald. It was indeed a unique presentation. No surgeon had ever tried to work on the hands of leprosy patients as Paul was doing.

> At the end of October, Paul was duly robed and in solemn ceremony led into the lecture hall of the Royal College of Surgeons of England, where he delivered a lecture entitled simply, "The Reconstruction of the Hand in Leprosy." At the conclusion of the lecture, the macebearer led him off the platform and escorted him from the hall. Paul had now acquired a new title, Hunterian Professor of Surgery, 1952.
>
> At a small reception following the lecture, Paul was warmly thanked and significant interest was expressed in our work.

With Margaret getting her new training in optics and her orientation to the homeschooling curriculum and with Paul successfully presenting his revolutionary approach to the extremity deformities of leprosy, both felt that their immediate future in India was secure, particularly with the new sponsorship of British Mission to Lepers.

> The Leprosy Mission didn't give us a greater monthly salary, but they did give more generous "allowances" than the medical college in Vellore had been able to afford. They created a budget based upon the size of our family, the cost of boarding school, the cost of transportation for school and for furloughs, and other things applicable to a family. Looking ahead, the Leprosy Mission also made contributions on our behalf into the Government Pension and National Health Service of England.
>
> Rather than having a separate salary, I received what was called a "wife's allowance" as part of the family budget. That worked well for me, as it meant that I was free to take any necessary days of leave if one of the children was sick.

Money itself was never a major issue for Margaret and Paul. For them, wealth was measured in the richness of the love within their family and the pleasure of each other's company, and they enjoyed the simple lifestyle that missionary medicine provided. They preferred making their own music rather than buying records. Hand-me-down or homemade clothing was always appreciated and very acceptable. They ate simply, wore jumpers (sweaters) and socks knitted by Margaret, and reused gift-wrapping paper over and over again. They did not consider this a sacrificial lifestyle but rather one that freed them to concentrate on much more important treasures.

The one luxury they did allow and save for was family holidays, and the short holiday jaunts they were able to take during their time in England provided fond memories.

We had the use of a car and traveled west to the Severn Estuary, where we stayed in a delightful little cottage overlooking the water. We also spent a memorable holiday at West Runton on the east coast of England—an area particularly loved by Paul, as many of his childhood holidays had been spent there. And we visited the scenic Lake District in northwest England, where we stayed in the lovely home of Dr. T. Howard Somervelle and his wife, Peggy. Dr. Somervelle was a famous surgeon, a famous Everest climber, and a musician (and in his later years he became known for his paintings). Since the Somervelles were out in Vellore filling in for us, they had urged us to use their house, which overlooked Lake Windermere, and we spent several marvelous weeks there.

Paul had long wanted to teach the children the art and joy of sailing, so one day we rented a little sailboat and packed a picnic lunch. We had visions of a brisk wind and the fun of tacking and all the other stuff one does when sailing. The wind was strong and steady enough to get us away from the dock and out to the middle of the lake. Then it stopped. And so did we. The boat had no motor. Oars? Yes, but we sat and waited for the wind to revive. It didn't—and then the rain poured down. We had a small tarp, which covered about six square feet of the front of the boat. Not a lot of shelter, but under it I tried my best to prepare our lunch without getting everything soaked.

Christopher, with his father's spirit, thought it was fun. Jean was less sure. Mary asked why we had come out there to get so wet. Finally we had to resort to the oars and rowed our way back to the dock.

That experience on the lake was not wasted, however, as it prompted us to begin reading, as a family, a truly wonderful series of books by Arthur Ransom for children and families who loved camping, sailing, and outdoor fun. The first one we read aloud as a family was *Swallows and Amazons*. Two other titles I recall were *We Didn't Mean to Go to Sea* and *Pigeon Post*. We read those books many times and were always delighted.

In the midst of furlough responsibilities, medical training, and holidays, Margaret and Paul also began the homeschooling program with the two oldest children. Jean was an earnest student, her brother, Christopher, less so. But even if Christopher didn't appear at times to learn much from his mother, she was learning lessons from him.

When decorations and seasonal preparations heralded the coming of Christmas, the church at which we worshiped, Mt. Zion Baptist Church, St. John's Wood, which had been Paul's home church in his youth, gave notice of "Toy Sunday." The children were to select one of their toys that was in good condition, wrap it, and bring it to the service on that particular Sunday. These gifts would then be distributed to children in a poor area of London.

We didn't have many toys with us—mostly hand-me-downs from neighbors and friends who had outgrown them and generously shared with the children. But the children looked over what they had, seriously and thoughtfully, trying to decide what they might give away.

A cousin had given Christopher an early Christmas present of a small model dump truck. It was a little bit of heaven to him. He parked it by his pillow at night and carried it in his hand all day. I never saw him without it.

When Toy Sunday came, all the children went forward with their gifts, some awkwardly wrapped. I hadn't asked our children what they were giving, but when Christopher returned to his seat he looked rather pleased, so I asked him what he had given. He whispered, "My dump truck."

I am ashamed to say that my immediate thought was that the cousin who had given it to him might think the gift wasn't appreciated. Christopher must have read my mind, and what he said was unforgettable: "Mummy, I had nothing else good enough to give!"

So often we give only what we can easily spare. Christopher taught me that God sometimes wants me to give what I treasure most.

⌒

As the end of 1952 approached, the Brands prepared for the next phase of their furlough. Paul sailed to the United States in early December, where his Rockefeller scholarship would cover his visits to three or more major research and surgical centers. He selected a neurologist in Boston and two hand surgeons, one in the Midwest and one in San Francisco, anxious to glean whatever he could about nerve damage in leprosy and the latest techniques of hand surgery. His time would be taken up observing, sharing, discussing his own findings and experience, and at times assisting in surgery as well as lecturing on what he was doing. He had received a generous allowance from the Rockefeller Foundation, and he planned to spend as little as possible for his travel so that he might use the excess for other family necessities. He traveled by train, stayed in less luxurious accommodations, and by the end of his tour had saved enough to purchase a car. The new Vanguard sedan, made by the Standard Motor Company, would be shipped from England to Madras and from there driven to Vellore. Named "the Bungi," this vehicle played a major role in family affairs over the next ten years.

While Paul sailed for the U.S. on the *Queen Elizabeth II*, Margaret and the children departed England on *The Cape Town Castle*, sailing to South Africa on December 18. After several frightening incidents with wandering children—particularly Mary, who was prone to "adventures"—Margaret had devised a "buddy" system to use when she had to handle all of the children by herself.

> The children had small cards with their name, cabin number, and ship pinned to their clothing. In addition they wore dog leashes around their waists. Christopher's was linked to Mary's, Jean's to Estelle's. Thus I had peace of mind as I maneuvered children and luggage through cities and onto trains, through customs and onto ships. Christopher was quite embarrassed by all this and was relieved when the ship pulled away from the dock and the labels and leashes came off.

At Cape Town they were met by Margaret's parents and her sister Frieda and family, including husband Jim and their children Malcolm, Graham, and Bunty, who were visiting from their home in Buluwayo, Rhodesia. Anna and her family would come later from their home in Nairobi, Kenya. It had been five years since the sisters had been together, and some of the cousins had never met. They celebrated this marvelous family reunion as well as a second Christmas with lavish gifts from grandparents—lovely homemade clothing and wonderful toys. This atmosphere of generosity and good cheer was almost overwhelming for Margaret.

Will and Greta Berry had rented an apartment for all of them at Fish Hoek, a beautiful beach resort south of Cape Town. The family crowded in and had a few wonderful days together. It was high summer in South Africa, and the sea was a perfect swimming temperature and safe for both children and adults. Most mornings were spent at the beach, with the afternoons occupied by homeschooling activities. When Aunt Frieda and her family had to leave, the farewells were hardest for Christopher, who had quickly bonded with his cousin Malcolm, no doubt appreciative of having another boy in the family with whom to play.

Margaret and the children spent three months with Grandpa and Grandma Berry. Paul joined them in late March, and a great deal of time was spent catching up on his experiences in the States while he learned about the extended Berry family's recent activities. Anna and her daughters Ruth and Janet had arrived from Kenya, and there were birthdays to celebrate— Christopher's ninth and Estelle's third.

On the last leg of the family odyssey, the Brands traveled by train to the city of Durban on the east coast of South Africa, where they boarded a ship to Bombay. The train from Cape Town to Durban passed through the city of Bloemfontein. Margaret considered stopping over to see her childhood home but decided that she preferred to leave her memories of the veld unspoiled by the changes that had occurred.

Margaret and Paul's remarkably productive twelve-month furlough had enriched their professional careers, enabled them to visit loved ones in England and Africa, given them time to enjoy each other's company and family holiday time, and established a solid sponsorship that would allow them another five years of working at Vellore. They felt truly blessed.

Chapter 14

Return to India

"My mummy's going to have another baby!"

Upon their return to Vellore in early May of 1953, the Brands were assigned to new quarters on the second floor of what was known as the
Small Bungalow, which Dr. Ida had built in 1932 to house female staff on
the medical college campus. These quarters provided them with four rooms,
plus a screened room on the roof above for the children's sleeping quarters.
This would be the Brands' home for the next eleven years.

The children wasted no time in returning to the fun of being free to roam,
explore, and climb. Paul had always said, mostly jokingly, that it was better to have a few strong survivors among the children than a large group
of weaklings. He did, however, instruct them on what he considered to be
proper, versus foolish, risk-taking. But sometimes it seemed the children forgot the difference.

> About two hundred yards from our new home was the anatomy
> department, and near it, the animal lab. To the children, this was like
> their own small private zoo, a favorite place to visit. Most of the animals
> were of the ape family and were caged, but one, a gibbon, was allowed
> some freedom in the mango trees above his cage. Gibbons are quite large
> apes, and this one had an uncertain temper.
>
> One hot afternoon, soon after we returned from furlough, five-year-old
> Mary and three-year-old Estelle wanted to go and see the animals. They
> particularly wanted to see the gibbon, to watch him swing gracefully in

the trees above his cage. That day he was nowhere in sight. Mary then had a bright idea. She would climb up on top of his cage to get a better view.

Whatever Mary did, Estelle was sure to follow. (Mary made up Estelle's mind for her many, many times!) So up they both went.

Suddenly Mary sounded an alarm. "The gibbon's coming!" The animal had seen the girls and was swinging across from one tree to the next to investigate.

Mary got down quickly, but little Estelle couldn't decide which foot to put down first. While I tried to reach up and guide her feet, the gibbon reached down with his long arm and grabbed her hair. Poor little girl. She was suspended between the two of us, with me pulling down on her ankles while the ape pulled up on her hair. After several seconds of pain and terror for her, the gibbon let go and went off to his trees again.

In spite of all Mary's encouragement, Estelle was reluctant to revisit the animal lab.

Mary was an inventive child who needed fairly close supervision. Not long after the gibbon incident this became even more evident when I engaged some home help so that I could go back to the eye hospital, at least temporarily. Unfortunately, the woman we employed did not speak much English, nor was I proficient in Tamil. And she certainly didn't understand our Mary.

There were several beautiful tamarind trees near our new home, which offered all kinds of potential delights for the children—climbing, making tree houses, and, in the harvesting season, eating the deliciously sour fruit. The children loved to stand in front of me and suck on the sour beans, knowing that it would make me pucker up my face in painful sympathy. The college sold contracts on the fruit to local merchants who organized the harvesting, but staff could take a few pods now and then. The harvest began when the pods turned brown and were easily pulled or knocked off the branches. Until then they were green and fairly tough, a condition that saved Estelle from a possibly serious accident.

Mary had spotted some pods on the tamarind tree near the house. They were a bit out of reach for her tree-climbing skills, but she organized a way to get them. She and Estelle would get up onto the kitchen roof, then climb up further onto the chimney. Difficult but not impossible. Then, while she held Estelle's dress firmly "so that she wouldn't fall," Estelle could reach over to the nearest branch and grab a pod.

Paul and I returned home from the hospital just in time to see Estelle, like a little bridge, hanging between the flat kitchen chimney and a branch of the nearby tamarind tree. Mary was holding onto Estelle's dress while Estelle clung to a tamarind pod. Beneath her, twenty to thirty feet down, was hard-packed earth.

Paul leapt out of the car and, trying to keep his voice steady, told the children to hang on tight and stay just as they were. He then took the stairs three at a time, got out on the roof and up on the chimney beside Mary. Meanwhile, I positioned myself under Estelle, hoping that if the tamarind gave way and she fell I might be able to prevent a fatal injury.

Thankfully, the tamarind pod was not ripe enough to give way, Paul was given wings to make it up those stairs, and the Lord lovingly heard our panic-stricken prayer!

In early June of 1953, Christopher started boarding school, which marked the beginning of significant changes in the Brand household. After careful thought and prayer, Paul and Margaret had chosen to enroll Christopher in Breeks Memorial School in Ootacamund (known as "Ooty"), a hilltop town in the Nilgiri Hills. Breeks was run by a devoted Christian staff and had a good reputation for preparing children to pursue further study in Britain. About half the student body was comprised of day scholars from the local Indian community. The others, about a hundred, were children of missionaries working in remote parts of the country or in other parts of Asia. They attended classes with the day scholars but were boarded in a residential facility called Lushington Hall, under the care of Christian house parents, about a mile from the school.

Since Christopher started classes in early June, he was able to attend as a day student while the family remained in the hill area during the hot summer months. But once they returned to Vellore, he moved into Lushington Hall. The initial separation was not easy.

Christopher began his day-scholar studies quite happily, but reality hit him a week before we were due to return to Vellore. We were in church, when he suddenly realized that this would be the last time he would be in church with us for a long while. He clutched hold of me and burst into tears, sobbing his heart out. Other parents who had been through this agonizing ordeal looked on with sympathy.

After a short burst of heavy sobbing, Christopher seemed to feel better, but I felt terrible. And when we said our final good-byes in his dormitory, he kept the bed between us. He didn't want to be hugged or kissed in front of the other boys.

Christopher made friends easily and soon settled in at school, at least socially. Scholastically, it was more of a challenge for him. He was joining a class that had started back in January. Also, even though his reading ability was advanced, he was relatively weak in his other subjects. The principal advised that he repeat that year. With hindsight, probably he was right. But Christopher pleaded to be allowed to continue with the new friends he had already made, and we agreed.

Meanwhile, at home in Vellore, Margaret began homeschooling Jean and Mary, using the British-based system she had acquired. The motto of the Parents' National Education Union (PNEU), was part of the logo on the front cover of every notebook: "I Am, I Can, I Ought, I Will." This perfectly reflected Margaret's philosophy as well: "I am able. I can do it. I ought to do it. I will do it," and was exactly the attitude toward life that the Brands wanted to instill in their children.

Estelle was enrolled in a small nursery school that had been started for children whose parents lived or worked on campus. The nursery school was under the direction of a competent energetic woman named Jessie, and the children loved her.

Margaret resumed some of her duties at Schell Eye Hospital, although at the time her skills in optometry were not being used much since there was a full-time optometrist on the staff. But being mother of three active little girls was enough to occupy most of her time. Adding to those demands, she was pregnant (with a due date in June 1954) and did not have a great deal of surplus energy to expend. The children were excited about another baby coming into the family.

Estelle rushed to her nursery school and breathlessly announced to teacher Jessie, "My mummy's going to have another baby, and she says I can have a turn too!" I had shared the news with them that we were to have another baby and that I'd need their help in taking care of him or her. They would all "take turns" in helping bathe or change their new baby brother or sister.

One of the most significant accomplishments during the Brands' furlough in England had been the recruitment of John and Alison Webb. John was a pediatrician, trained at Oxford. Alison, like Margaret, had completed medical college but had not done a specialty fellowship. When the Brands first met them, John and Alison were living and working in Newcastle-upon-Tyne in northern England. Both were interested in entering medical missionary work and had applied to the Church Missionary Society for a post abroad. When they heard Paul speak about Vellore and his work at a CMS recruitment meeting, they became very excited.

> The Webbs were excited about the work in Vellore, and we had a meal together so that the four of us could meet and discuss India in general and Vellore in particular. We soon realized that we had more than a common desire to serve the Lord; we shared a common interest in promoting health in an underserved part of the world. Along with that, from the very beginning we bonded in a personal way. John and Paul were soon talking fishing, painting, and even bird watching, while Alison and I discussed how best to prepare for parenting in India.
>
> The Webbs, along with their three-year-old son, Michael, and one-year-old son, Andrew, arrived in India in 1953, shortly after we left Christopher at boarding school. They quickly threw themselves into the work, and John became an excellent head of the pediatrics department. Alison gave her attention to her two lovely boys and also worked part-time at the hospital in pediatrics. She eventually specialized in child psychiatry.

The Brands and the Webbs were destined to become lifelong friends, as were the Brand and Webb children. Eventually there would be one Brand son and five Brand daughters, and one Webb daughter and four Webb sons. Over the next several years, as the families grew ever closer and spent holidays together, they became four parents and eleven children calling themselves "The Wends."

The Brand's fifth child, Patricia Nancy (soon nicknamed "Trish"), was born June 28, 1954, at the Kotagiri Medical Fellowship in the Nilgiri Hills. She was named for Paul's two beloved cousins: Patricia Harris, who had endeared herself to the children when they were staying in Westmorland in 1952, and Dr. Nancy Robbins, who worked for many years with Amy Carmichael in Dohnavur, India.

Paul and John Webb had already returned to Vellore when Patricia put in her appearance. Since the two families had rented a house together in Kotagiri for the summer hill season, Alison was on hand to care for the Brand children and keep a watchful eye on Margaret.

Trish was delivered by Margaret's old friend Dr. Lydia Herlufson, of the Kotagiri Medical Fellowship. Margaret had thought her maternity leave of only two weeks after Mary's birth was short. In Kotagiri she would have less than two days.

Looking back to Christopher's and Jean's births in the Royal Northern Hospital, London, I realize how pampered I'd been. For two weeks I had had no responsibilities and could lie pleasantly in bed or walk around if I chose. But times and needs had changed. In India I soon found I had other responsibilities, despite having just gone through a delivery myself.

When Trish was less than two days old, the hospital needed help. Both Dr. Lydia, who was the general practitioner, and Dr. Pauline Jeffries, who specialized in eyes, ear, nose, and throat, became ill. A doctor was needed at Kotagiri, and I was it!

A poor Badaga (tribal) man came to the hospital with a deeply infected and intensely painful eye. The old man was moaning as he squatted, rocking back and forth, outside the hospital ward. Only immediate, rather radical, surgery could help relieve the pain. The eye was too far gone and had lost sight, so it had to be removed.

The senior nurse recognized what was needed and asked for my help. So I got dressed and went to take care of him. While I was out of my room, another nurse came to do a routine check and procedures for me. Not finding me, she became a bit concerned until she was told I was in the operating room. (She rightly assumed that I was not the patient.)

Dr. Lydia Herlufsen was very ill with malaria, so I took over her clinic for several days. While I worked, newborn Trish slept in her bassinet in the little X-ray room next to the clinic.

After Dr. Herlufsen was back on the job, I became full-time Mum again. Alison and the Webb children returned to Vellore, and Paul's mom, Granny, came to share the family with me.

When Trish was six weeks old, Paul was able to return to Kotagiri to meet his new daughter and to help with the family's travel back to Vellore. But the excitement of that meeting was dampened by his having an attack of dengue fever ("break-bone fever"), a viral illness caused by the bite of mosquitoes. Ill with high fever and severe muscle and back pains, he spent the first days after his arrival in bed. After a week or two he felt well enough to face the drive back to Vellore.

With young children and the climate in which they lived, health issues were often on their minds, but most could be handled with traditional medications. Then a serious problem arose. Paul and Margaret thought they were going to lose their beautiful baby Trish. Her survival was due more to ancient Indian ways than the modern medicine of Vellore.

Trish was about five months old and beginning to wean onto foods other than breast milk. Her four older siblings had had their share of problems with this transition, but nothing compared to hers. She developed severe diarrhea, then an infant's bowel obstruction, which happily resolved without surgery. But then she went into a long phase of irritable bowel syndrome and was unable to absorb fats or carbohydrates.

She had been such a robust little infant, but quickly that changed. She lost weight, muscle power, and interest in life—except for raging hunger.

Dr. John Webb, our dear friend and pediatrician, tried everything he could think of to help her. Still, she seemed to be slipping away from us. We were preparing ourselves for the worst while we hoped and prayed for the best.

Then one Sunday evening, after chapel service, a close friend, Dr. Ruth Myers, asked us, "Did you ever hear what Bishop Packenham Walsh would do for those children whose mothers couldn't breast feed them or who had been orphaned?" (This famous bishop of an earlier generation in India had taken care of many orphaned children in famine times.) No, we had not heard.

Dr. Ruth then explained how the village people would put an unpeeled banana into the embers of the fire until the pulp turned golden. Then they would mash the pulp with water (presumably boiled) and spoon it into the infant's mouth. Scores of babies had survived on nothing more than bananas and water.

The idea sounded incredible, but we were desperate. Instead of baking the banana, we boiled the fruit in its peel. We also found that it helped to scrape the soft lining of the peel into the pulp/water mix.

Apparently baked banana is easily absorbed, because within twenty-four hours of starting this strange diet we noticed a difference in Trish. There were days when she consumed seventeen bananas, and her health rapidly improved. Then, very cautiously, we added other foods. A grain grown in South India called ragi was well tolerated, but wheat much less so. We tried out one item or another and were always ready to go back to simple bananas.

After about five or six months, we were thankful to have our baby Trish fully recovered and healthy again.

Besides Trish, there was another major addition to the Brand family in 1954. Aruldoss, a young single man, was engaged to be their cook. He had been employed at a missionary guesthouse in Kotagiri where he had learned to prepare Western dishes. Over the next fifty years, Aruldoss and his family would become as much a part of the Brand family as their own children and grandchildren. One of Margaret's most important contributions to the creation of Aruldoss's family was finding him a wife.

We hired Aruldoss as our cook, and after about a year he asked if I would find him a wife. Once again Paul and I found ourselves acting more as parents than employers. This time, however, I knew a little more about how to accomplish the task.

Even though other people were looking for a wife for him, I had to give final approval or it wouldn't do. He finally asked me to see a girl named Manomani. She was a lovely girl, quite a bit younger, but that was all right. She couldn't speak English but had had a bit of English education and could read and write a little English. The marriage was successfully arranged, and the wedding was held in a little Tamil church in Vellore.

Manomani became our ayah after the marriage, and the couple remained with us all the rest of our time in India and became part of our family. When they asked us to name their first child, we suggested a combination of their two names, Arulmani. Little Arulmani became a real companion for our daughter Pauline.

Without the help of dear Aruldoss and Manomani, Paul and I surely couldn't have accomplished all that we were able to in India. They were vital to the management of our household and the care of our children. Every morning after Paul had gone off to work the three of us would get together and talk about the coming day. We would then pray together, they in Tamil and I in English. It was a good relationship.

Along with five healthy children, faithful household staff, and good friends, the Brands were blessed by the nearby presence of Granny Brand. She was the only member of their families they could see on a frequent basis. For Granny, who had been separated for decades from her own family, this was a blessing as well. Margaret respected and appreciated Granny, even though being her daughter-in-law could sometimes prove a challenge.

Granny, in her seventies, came down to Vellore fairly frequently from her little mountain cabin when her work allowed, but she refused to live with us permanently. She valued her independence, and she also valued our independence. Perhaps she recognized that she could not live with us without wanting to manage us.

Sometimes we knew she was coming, and sometimes we didn't. She would often come by jutka, a small horse-drawn cart, and as she came up the road to the house she would call "Paul," almost as if singing, the first part of the world, "Pau" nearly an octave lower than the last "l." As she usually arrived in the wee hours of the morning, we would be wakened by her clear voice announcing her arrival. We would go downstairs to greet her and help her upstairs to our apartment.

Her journey would have begun at least twenty-four hours earlier. First of all she had to come down about four thousand feet to the foothills. There were then no roads, only a goat track. A horse could manage it, and as long as she could, Granny rode on horseback. In her later years, she allowed herself to be carried in a "dholi," a canvas hammock slung on bamboo poles carried on the shoulders of four men.

The remote tracks that served as roads could not be traversed by regular cars, so once she got to the foothills, she would hire a jeep to drive her to the bus route. Once on the bus she had to travel several hours to the nearest train station, followed by an overnight train ride to Katpadi, our closest station. And then ten miles or so from the train station in a "jutka"—a small horse-drawn wagon—to our home.

Sometimes Granny brought a patient or two with her for Paul to treat. One such person was Karunainesan (Kuh-roo-ny-nay-sun), who had been a beggar, moving from village to village in the hills. He had leprosy, and although his face had not been too badly affected, his hands and feet were badly deformed. Granny felt sure Paul could help him. Karunainesan (K) had never been off the hills and had never seen trains and buses, but he trusted Granny completely, so when she said she would take him to her son who would fix him up, he had no doubt that she would.

K began the journey riding Granny's little pony. That too was a first for him. When they finally reached the train station, she bought third-class tickets for them both, and they boarded the train. Things were fine until the conductor came around checking fares. He didn't question Granny but immediately turned angrily on poor K and told him he had to get off the train at the next station. At that point, Granny rose up like an angry mother cat and scolded the conductor for his attitude and behavior. He crept away ashamedly.

When Paul saw K, he told Granny that there was absolutely no room in the ward for him. Unfazed, she said simply but firmly, "Then he can stay here until there is room for him," referring to our verandah. End of discussion.

K was our guest for a few days until a bed became available in the leprosy ward. He needed a long hospitalization, but during that time he was taught to read. He learned to read simple parts of the Bible, and as he read, he learned that he needed Jesus. While Paul was able to restore function to his hands and help heal his feet, the Lord gave him new life. When K eventually returned to the hills and shared his new knowledge, he was no longer regarded as a beggar. He was accepted as a teacher, indeed, almost a pastor!

Granny was an artist, and throughout her life she painted scenes of the natural world around her. She always carried her watercolor paints with her, and whenever she had moments of free time, or if something remarkable caught her attention, she would find whatever scraps of paper were available and captured what she saw. Margaret shared with her an awe of God's creation, especially as manifested in the exquisite beauty of flowers. Together they imparted to the children the wonder of the landscape the Lord provided.

Granny gave the children a love of the mountains, and especially of the flowers they found there. They always looked forward to art lessons from her and to her enthusiastic singing, to her wonderful storytelling, and to evening prayers with her. They enjoyed her and she them, especially their singing and their attempts at memorizing Scripture.

At the same time, Granny also demonstrated her conservative Strict Baptist beliefs in both her life and her opinions.[1]

If Granny disapproved of something, she forthrightly said so. She disapproved of any kind of card game, no matter how innocent it might seem to most people. So we put away all cards during her visits.

Granny also strongly disapproved of smoking and made no secret of it. Some of the Vellore staff were smokers, and they would get a bit irritated with her constant criticism of their habit. But they were able to balance this against the respect they had for her outstanding qualities, such as her passionate championing of the poor and downtrodden.

If someone bragged about bargaining something down, she would interrupt them with "What about the poor person? That might have been the only thing he had to sell. Why didn't you just accept it at his price and pay him what he asked?" She was particularly adamant about not bargaining with rickshaw owners. They were indeed very poorly paid and often had to pull or cycle big loads. She got very upset if I ever tried to bargain down the fare.

When Granny disagreed with us, she voiced her disapproval; but having done so, she recognized that the final decision should be ours. And being Granny's daughter-in-law was sometimes a challenge. There were a few things she disapproved of in Paul, but she didn't tell him about it. She felt I should be the one to correct him!

---

1. Strict Baptist was the name of the denomination she belonged to. That group is now called Grace Baptist.

On the whole, however, her visits were fun. She had a great sense of humor, and although we had some differences of opinion, they were minor. We received so much blessing from her presence that those moments really didn't count. And, for the children, she was a vivid example of what being a witness for Christ meant.

Chapter 15

Leprosy of the Eye

"Is it red eye, doctor?"

It was during this busy year of 1954 that Margaret's interest in ocular leprosy began to develop. Paul, in addition to his responsibility in the surgical department, was devoting more time to the subject of leprosy; but Margaret had hardly been aware that the disease affected the eyes. In fact most tropical medicine experts focused on the disease's effects on the skin, the facial deformities, or the limbs. Yet of the two million people with leprosy in India, almost forty percent would sooner or later suffer eye involvement, many becoming blind, and almost no one in the field had studied this facet of the disease in any detail.

If one of the seminal events in Margaret's life was being told to report to the eye clinic to start what would be a career in ophthalmology, another such event occurred in an eye camp and would eventually lead her to becoming one of the world's experts in ocular leprosy.

When Trish was about three months old, I again began assisting at the Schell eye clinic as well as participating in some of the eye camps. At the end of one particular camp, at which we had operated on over one hundred cataract cases, I noticed a group of seven or eight men standing together, clutching one another, as though uncertain of whether they would be welcome. They did not seem to be part of the village community. But who were they? Hopeful eye patients who had arrived late?

I asked one of our non-professional camp staff members (called *attendants*) if he knew who they were. He looked up briefly. "Oh, they are just lepers," he said and went on working.

According to much Hindu philosophy, those with leprosy are outcasts. The Hindu belief in karma suggests that perhaps in some previous incarnation such persons have displeased the gods and now are paying for it. Those with the disease become almost non-persons. Even though the camp staff attendant may not have been a Hindu himself (he was probably a nominal Christian), he was somewhat tainted by the philosophy. But he agreed to come with me and talk to this group.

I had never seen eyes like theirs and could not imagine how they became that way. They did not appear to be in pain but obviously were blind. Only one of them could see a little, and the others clung to him.

I needed to study this problem further, and to do that I needed to take one of these men back to the hospital where we had better equipment, but I was not sure how we could accommodate a patient with leprosy at the eye clinic. We had no isolation ward at Schell, and I was aware of the taboo against admitting such a patient into our little eye hospital. (In those days we all thought leprosy patients needed to be isolated.) But my other colleagues at the camp supported the idea of taking one patient back in the ambulance and finding some way to accommodate him there.

The doctor who was in charge at Schell also was very helpful. He had done more documenting of eye complications with this disease than most ophthalmologists, but since most leprosy patients would not come to a general hospital, his experience was limited. He shared with me what he knew.

Some six years before, when Paul first had been intrigued by the effects leprosy had on hands and feet, he had asked the same questions Margaret was now asking about the eye diseases of these patients. Unsatisfied with the answers he received from almost every expert he approached, he launched his own effort to understand the pathology of the disease and the damage it caused. Now Margaret found herself in an identical situation. There was little written about ocular leprosy, and few of the faculty at Vellore could offer information. Eyes ravaged by the disease, especially among the beggar population, were everywhere around them, but no one had studied this prevalent problem in any detail.

For those without sight, the most important sense is touch. Usually by the time a person went blind because of leprosy, however, he had lost sensation in his fingers and often his sense of smell as well. This affected the performance of even the simplest tasks. There are not many jobs you can do if you are disabled to that degree, so it was little wonder that those afflicted ended up on the streets as beggars.

In many cases, the family used those with advanced leprosy for begging, and this became a significant source of income for some families. In fact Paul found that some of his patients whose hand deformities were corrected by surgery returned depressed over having lost their livelihood as beggars. This was one of the reasons that a major emphasis of his work at the New Life Center was to create job-skill training for the boys, since they could no longer work as beggars when they returned to their villages.

Some leprosy patients were cared for by their families, some were not. If the wife was the sick one, the husband would often abandon her and find another wife. If it was the husband who had the disease, the wife was much more likely to stay. Those with loyal family members who helped them would probably survive longer, but for how long?

The person in India with advanced leprosy had a quality of life that is incomprehensible. Suicides were common.

Paul had to build the New Life Center to pursue his study of the disease. Fortunately for Margaret there now existed the Schieffelin Leprosy Research and Training Centre in Karigiri. Here she could begin her investigations, learning more about leprosy itself, and ocular leprosy in particular, as she worked in the outpatient clinics.

Margaret continued to juggle her work with her family life. She cherished her time homeschooling Jean and Mary, which occupied the majority of her week. When she did have to work, she could rely on one of the other mothers on campus or on Manomani to look after the children.

◈

At the time Schieffelin Leprosy Research and Training Centre officially opened in June 1955, it consisted of a hospital with space for seventeen in-patients, out-patient clinics, a research laboratory, staff houses, and cottages for some of the patients. The first director, Dr. Herbert Gass, a dermatologist on the staff at the medical college, set a strong and optimistic tone during the five years he was at Karigiri. A key early member of the Schieffelin staff was surgeon Dr. Ernest Fritschi, a colleague of Paul's, who eventually became director from 1974 to 1987.

Ernest Fritschi, the son of Swiss parents, had been born and raised in India and had attended university and medical school in Madras. He had married a lovely Indian Christian woman, Mano. Ernest's father, a missionary, was also a horticulturist, and Ernest shared his father's fascination with the subject and was knowledgeable in all aspects of land management. The site chosen for Schieffelin, eight miles from Vellore near the village of Karigiri, was a desolate and arid plot of several acres, useless to area landowners and therefore owned by the government, which the government could fittingly allocate for a "leper colony." Before his years of service were over, Ernest, using water and land conservation techniques that were ahead of their time, had turned this scrub plot into a lush green oasis teeming with trees, shrubs, flowers, and birds. He even made certain that snakes were part of the population to keep the rat population in balance. It was also Ernest who named the bullocks pulling the watering wagon for his landscaping projects "Herb" and "Paul" and insisted that it was a coincidence that Dr. Gass and Dr. Brand had the same first names.

Ernest nurtured the staff at Karigiri as much as his beloved land, seeing to it that everyone who worked there, in whatever capacity, would be as fruitful as possible. He practiced the same audacious confidence in people's potential that Dr. Ida had exemplified. It was he who encouraged Margaret to use the facility at Karigiri to start an eye clinic devoted solely to the problem of ocular leprosy. He helped to turn one room into an examination room, painting the walls black and covering the windows with drapes so that she could examine eyes in a dark environment. It was the first step that would lead to more than thirty-five years of ongoing research and education for "Dr. Margaret."

○◌

Most people cannot contract leprosy (Hansen's disease). It is estimated that only approximately 8 percent of the world's population are susceptible, and within that small group there is a range of low risk to high.

The most susceptible person gets the form of the disease known as "multi-bacillary" (i.e., many organisms). A person who is host to billions of mycobacteria may develop multiple skin lesions, loss of eyebrows, nerve palsies, and loss of sensation in the hands and feet. Individuals with better resistance get the form of the disease known as "paucibacillary" (i.e., few organisms). Though the volume of infection is less and skin involvement usually limited to a single insensitive patch, certain nerves may be affected and result in severe consequences. The variety of immune responses leads to diverse reactions in Hansen's disease and to different problems within the same organ such as the eye.

Margaret found the peculiar varieties of ocular leprosy to be fascinating.

The leprosy bacillus has this peculiar affinity for cooler parts of the body, so it doesn't invade deeply into organs such as the lungs. Within the back of the eyeball is the retina, which receives light and transmits messages to the brain—the very function of "seeing." The retina in the back of the eye is about six degrees Celsius warmer than the cornea on the front surface of the eye. The bacteria don't trouble the retina, whereas the cornea—the clear, shining window in the front—is very cool and, thus, very much at risk.

I never cease to marvel at the creative wonder of the corneal structure. What design! To enable us to see clearly, it must be transparent. It cannot have blood vessels in it, yet it is living tissue and needs oxygen and other things the blood would supply. Instead, the cornea depends upon the tears on its surface and the fluid in the chamber behind it for those needs.

The cornea has to be maintained at the right shape to focus the light rays, yet it has no rigid skeleton. It depends on fluid pressure in the chamber behind it. It has no bony protection, no skin or muscles covering it. Only when the eyelids close is it protected. Otherwise it is out there, naked, facing all kinds of danger.

So, what does protect the cornea? A simple answer would be "its nerve supply." It has the richest network of sensory nerves in the body. Lubricating tears and the eyelid muscles enabling us to blink regularly play a valuable back-up part, but it is that exquisite sensitivity that is essential.

Since the eyelids are so important to the defense of the cornea, and therefore to our sight, they too deserve our appreciation. And so does their Designer! Normally the eyelids close in sleep, protecting the cornea. They close in defense of the eye if there is some threat of injury from outside—the defensive blink. But their busiest time is during our waking hours when they are in the "automatic spontaneous blink" mode. A normal individual needs to blink about four or five times a minute to maintain a clean, wet, healthy cornea. Not only must the blink be frequent enough, it also must be complete, with the lids touching each other, and it must be efficient.

For a blink to be efficient in keeping the cornea clean and wet, the lids need to be shaped just right, the margins must keep in touch with the cornea (like efficient windshield wipers), and there must be a steady supply of normal quality tears. (Tears are quite complex in their chemical makeup. They are much more than simply water.)

Coordinating all this, at a conscious or subconscious level, are the brain and the nerves to the eyelid muscles as well as the sensory nerves in the cornea itself. A defect somewhere in this complex system may allow the cornea to become dry, and a dry cornea, like a dirty window, is not good for seeing through; a dry cornea is easily damaged by quite minor injuries. And once the cornea is irrecoverably damaged, the sight in that eye is gone.

It was becoming apparent to Margaret and a few others that the loss of sensation and other nerve functions caused by leprosy was not only responsible for the deformities of hands and feet but also for many of the eye problems of these same patients. This was new territory, as little was known about what caused the blindness and how it might be prevented. Margaret's growing interest and investigation would lead her to acquire revolutionary insights into ocular leprosy.

It took Margaret years of study to learn the subtleties of the different forms and phases of ocular leprosy and to know which treatments were appropriate and at which times. Fortunately, at the Schieffelin Centre she had not only the encouragement of Paul and Ernest but also the assistance of Dr. Vimala (Chowdery) Seshumurty, one of their former students in the medical college.

Ernest had plans for me. He urged me to apply to the Indian Council of Medical Research for a grant to study the eyes of five hundred newly diagnosed and untreated leprosy patients. The British Leprosy Mission provided a grant through which we were able to retain an assistant for me, a dear Indian colleague, Dr. Vimala Seshumurty. Eventually the mission provided a corneal microscope to Karigiri , and the Ciba-Geigy Corporation also contributed equipment. Being able to evaluate the corneas of these cases with a microscope was crucial to our study. Doctors at Schell, such as Dr. Roy Ebenezer and Dr. Anna Thomas, were helpful to my study as well, acting as consultants whenever I needed them.

Many of the patients came to Schieffelin for hand problems or foot ulceration, and while they were there I would see them and do a brief eye exam. By doing this, I could determine whether they had some active disease in the eye and needed to be seen once a week or every two weeks or more at my regular follow-up clinic. In doing this, I also was trying to find untreated cases of leprosy to document the spectrum of ocular leprosy as a baseline study. Vimala assisted with these examinations and then did the final analysis with the help of a statistician.

At the beginning, we had many questions. At what stage in the disease of leprosy did eye problems become manifest? What were the first signs? What was the progression of the disease in the eyes? What were the factors? Did the eye problems respond if you treated the underlying leprosy?

When Karigiri began admitting patients in 1955, it was exclusively for leprosy. We had about twenty in-patient beds and a small pathology lab, about 10 feet by 15 feet and divided into two parts, with one-half given to me for an eye clinic. That was convenient, as patients would come to the lab for various routine tests and then come right on to the eye clinic to let me examine them. In that way I "lost" fewer patients. Although the hospital was built on a simple plan, it was considered complicated by the average villager, who could get quite confused by directions like "turn left at the end of the corridor" and would be tempted to instead turn toward home at that point. We also had one operating room at Karigiri where I did some minor surgery. Major procedures were done at the Schell Eye Hospital.

As I began my study of ocular leprosy, I learned that, in general, two categories of eye problems led to damaged corneas. The first type had no corneal sensation but could still blink; the second type had corneal sensation but could not blink. Multibacillary patients with direct infection in the cornea from leprosy organisms suffered damage to the fine sensory nerve endings, which led to loss of corneal sensation. Paucibacillary patients were more at risk of infection of the nerves to the eyelids themselves. These patients might retain corneal sensation, but their eyelid muscles were paralyzed and could not react to protect the eye. In either situation the precious cornea was at risk.

Another unusual reaction could occur, for unclear reasons and more commonly in the paucibacillary patients. After several weeks or months of treatment, the patient's immune system suddenly triggered an aggressive attack on any sites where the infection was still present. The severity of this immune response was actually harmful. The nerves became swollen and there was severe pain, loss of muscle power, and numbness in the area, which affected nerve supplies. If the nerve to the eyelid muscle was involved, then the eye did not close properly.

Many leprosy patients showed up with bad corneal ulcers. When we asked them what had happened, they hadn't a clue. "It just came," they said. But as we spent more and more time observing them, we began to understand the problem. If we get a little irritation in the eye, we close the eye and give it a gentle rub. We've all done this. But these patients didn't close their eyelids, either because they had some paralysis of the eyelid muscle or because they lacked corneal sensation. They would put their finger directly onto the surface of the eye and give it a good hard rub. I had one patient who had a huge callous over the base of his palm and he used that callous to rub his itchy eye. He then wondered why he went blind. He assumed it was the medicine he was taking, so he stopped taking his anti-leprosy medication. The eye was absolutely dead by the time we saw him.

The manifestations of ocular leprosy were numerous, but one of the most dangerous was what the patients themselves called "red eye," an inflammation that developed in the deep anterior structures due to an antigen-antibody reaction. This threatened the eye far more seriously than the Western concept of "pink eye," which refers to "conjunctivitis," an inflammation of the covering of the eye. Traditionally this was often the first step toward loss of sight.

Many a patient would come to the clinic with obvious redness of the eye. As I examined it, the patient might ask, "Is it red eye, doctor?" It wasn't just the words; it was the expression on the face, the ominous tone of voice, that told me how much they dreaded the condition. Such patients were not in danger of immediate blindness, but they knew from the experience of others that once inflammation started, it would recur again and again and, eventually, take their sight.

Proper treatment for this and other eye problems caused by leprosy could help delay or even avoid altogether that inevitable outcome.

After Margaret began to define the various manifestations of ocular leprosy, the next step was to find appropriate treatments for the problems. Some therapies were the same as those used in general ophthalmology, such as antibiotics to treat injuries and bacterial infections, cortisone drops to suppress inflammation (as in the leprosy reactions), or surgery on blocked tear duct systems. Other problems required new approaches. One of the most important issues she first grappled with was a way to protect the eye when the normal protective mechanisms were lost.

If the eye is not closed in sleep, it will get dry. Oily drops (such as castor oil) in the eye before going to sleep help to protect the eye when a person's eyelids don't close completely in sleep. Other helps are the frequent use of artificial tear drops during the day, goggles to protect from direct injury from dust and sunlight, and a hat or other cover for the head and face when out in bright sunlight. Unfortunately it was not practical for our Schieffelin patients to use artificial tears; they could not afford to buy the drops and they could not use their hands for putting in the drops. And patients already stigmatized by leprosy had little desire to stand out in a crowd by wearing goggles or an unusual headpiece.

Exercise was another treatment. Although paralysis of the eyelid muscles is common in leprosy patients, it is seldom complete. Some of the muscle fibers survive. We discovered an exercise that could strengthen those surviving fibers and thus maintain, and in some cases improve, function of the eyelids. We instructed patients to try to close the lids as much as possible, hold that position while counting to ten, and then relax. This exercise was to be repeated twenty times, three times a day. We also encouraged our patients to develop the habit of conscious blinking—what we called "think-blink." This might sound simple, but it is frustratingly difficult for an individual to do without the benefit of the precious subconscious reminder of pain from an eye that is becoming dry.

If a person does not feel pain, how can they know that their eye is in trouble and that they should go to the doctor? The simple answer: by paying attention daily to how well they see and by noticing unusual redness in the eye. It doesn't require sophisticated apparatus for a person to evaluate his own vision enough to know if it has recently diminished. Thus, another important part of educating our patients meant teaching them how to monitor their own eye problems so that they might seek help before too much damage occurred. This meant cultivating two habits: checking their sight and checking for redness of the eye on a regular basis.

We taught patients to choose an object that could be seen from their home—perhaps a road sign, a gate, or fence. Standing at the same distance from it, about the same time each day, with one eye covered so that each eye was tested separately, he or she could tell whether they saw it as well on one day as they did the previous day.

Learning to look for redness also was fairly simple. It was developing the habit of doing it that required a constant reminder and help from the family or other patients.

Patients were not the only ones who needed reminding. Even experienced health care workers (sad to say, including doctors) had to learn to change their mindset. It is so easy, and so dangerous, to assume that a red eye that does not hurt is not a serious matter. It took me some months to develop proper respect for redness in my leprosy patients. I had to learn that if a patient denied pain in an eye that was red or obviously sick in some way, I should regard that as a warning. I should immediately check his sensation, and if that seemed impaired, the record must be marked "High Risk" so that he would get more of our time and attention, not less.

Margaret had no established treatment guidelines available for some of the problems she was encountering. In time she would be one of the experts writing such guidelines, but at this point she was learning by trial and error.

The most challenging patients were those who had overlapping problems that might require contradictory treatments. Dr. Margaret learned how to prioritize the problems and choose the proper treatments for each.

One of my patients was always rubbing his eyes. He complained of itching and nothing seemed to help. I could not change his habit; I just had to watch him closely. One day he showed up with inflammation ("red eye"), and I had no option but to use our routine treatment, which included steroid drops. I warned and pleaded with him not to rub. I expect he tried to heed the warning, but one week into our treatment program he came in with a corneal injury. Now he had two problems with mutually exclusive needs. His inflammation needed the steroid drops, but his corneal injury would do worse with those. Which should get priority?

Determining that saving the cornea was the more critical of the two problems, we stopped the steroids and started an intensive regimen of antibiotic drops. I did something else too: I put a stitch between the upper and lower lids to keep his eye closed over the injured cornea. I tied the ends of the stitch in a bow, not a knot, so that I easily could loosen it, open the lids, check the progress of healing, do whatever was needed, close the lids, and re-tie the bow, thus protecting the area of concern until it finally healed and it was safe to use steroids again. This patient came to us before too much damage was done, and he did well.

When teaching doctors or other health care workers, I would tell this story and show the pictures of this case. Then I would flash on the screen a little message: "CORNEAL CARE COMES FIRST."

Over the next few years, new procedures in the field of ophthalmology proved useful in Margaret's work at Schieffelin. One such technique was "corneal transplantation," which meant replacing a damaged cornea with a healthy cornea harvested from a cadaver. When corneal grafting became the standardized technique for treating corneal scars, and it was being done at Schell Eye Hospital, Margaret seriously considered it for her leprosy patients. However, the loss of corneal sensation, which had caused the injury and scarring in the first place, could seriously jeopardize the outcome of a graft. A second discouragement was the difficulty of obtaining donor corneas, most of which come from cadavers and must be obtained as soon as possible after death.

In Hindu culture, however, the dead were cremated. And even though a body was going to be burned on a funeral pyre and the eyes destroyed, they believed it was important to have the eyes with the body or the person might be reincarnated without any eyes. Very few relatives, therefore, would donate a body. The only opportunity to obtain cadavers was when a body went unclaimed—most often a criminal who had been executed. Usually families would not claim such individuals.

The Anatomy Department was always in need of cadavers, and someone at Schell had asked that the eye department be notified if a recent cadaver might be available. One dark, wet night, as I was getting ready for bed, there was a banging on the back door. Paul was away, and the children were fast asleep. When I opened the door, I encountered a messenger. He carried a smoky hurricane lantern, and he was covered with a piece of cloth to protect him from the rain. He looked quite ghoulish. He thrust a note into my hand, and by the lamplight I read the words, "Judicial hanging at dawn tomorrow. Be there to get the eyes."

The jail was less than a mile from our house, but I hadn't any instruments to get the eyes. And the thought of getting up at dawn, waiting for the body to drop, and then moving in to get the eyes before the body was even cold was a horrible, totally repugnant thought to me. I couldn't imagine myself being able to do this.

I sent a note to someone in the Anatomy Department asking that they send for the body once the hanging was done. I knew their department would have the instruments I needed, and I could go there in the morning and get the eyes. To me that seemed much more civilized than working in the hanging room.

⌒

Dr. Margaret's unique discoveries in ocular leprosy were groundbreaking, but because she was not a board-certified ophthalmologist, the credibility of her data had to be validated by members of the eye faculty.

There were times when I wished I had completed a formal fellowship or residency in ophthalmology. In my work in India, I had more opportunities to become a skilled cataract surgeon than most of my peers in formal ophthalmology residences in the West, but I was well aware that there were many areas in which I did not have experience. Paul had had a formal residency in surgery, but I had learned it as I went along. It had been a matter of "you'll learn," just as Dr Jamieson had written years before on that historic afternoon in 1948.

Then, somewhere in the early 1950s, I had an invitation from the principal of the Christian Medical College to go back to England and get my FRCS in Ophthalmology and return to Vellore to head up the eye department at the Schell Hospital. At that point the children were all very young and needed their mother, even as she needed them. Yet this was a great opportunity. What should I do?

Paul courageously said, "You do what you feel is right. If you go, we'll cope somehow." But could he? Could they? Could I? We were not talking about my being gone just a month or two, but perhaps a year or more. We prayed, and the Lord clearly gave me the answer. I knew for certain that there was no way I could leave my beloved family to go off and improve my professional status. From that moment on, I had great peace.

I cannot say I have never revisited that decision or been tempted to think I should have taken that chance. But then I recall the sense of peace I experienced when I chose to put my husband and children first.

Actually, it was a matter of putting God first. And He always takes care of the consequences!

Chapter 16

Marmalade and Boarding School

"You have to help me help you."

In early 1956, nine-year-old Jean joined eleven-year-old Christopher at Breeks boarding school in the Nilgiris. The two were very close, so he was pleased to have her joining him at school. But the school year got off to a frightening start.

We were preparing to pack the school trunks and get ready for the journey to Ooty when Christopher began complaining that he wasn't feeling well. Remembering myself at that age, I assumed he was dreading the impending separation, so I was not too concerned. But by dinner that night I could see that he really was not himself. Time to get out the thermometer. His fever was 100 degrees and still climbing. The next day, he was worse and could scarcely speak.

John Webb, our friend and pediatrician, came and examined Christopher. At that time, children were coming into hospital with viral encephalitis (Japanese B), so he suspected this virus infection and took a blood sample. If it was encephalitis, there was no telling what the outcome might be. Christopher might make a full recovery or he might be left permanently brain damaged or he might die. All we could do was watch, keep the fever down with tepid sponging, and pray. How we prayed!

Christopher was very sick for about four days, halfway conscious and halfway delirious. Those were tough days, yet life had to go on. I had to get Jean ready for boarding school, although Christopher's situation had drained away her excitement about starting school. Her heart was with him, and she didn't want to leave. But she was learning that there are many times when you do what you have to do.

We were able to link up with another party of children heading to Breeks, and one of the mothers promised to take Jean under her wing for the journey, freeing me to stay with Christopher. He did make a full recovery, and a few weeks later he too was back in school. Another event for which we praised the Lord!

It turned out that the virus isolated from Christopher's blood was a new one. It was transmitted by a mosquito bite and was not contagious from person to person. The microbiologists at Vellore became very interested in this virus and repeatedly came to him for more blood samples. Since he hated needles, Christopher did not exactly enjoy this. But he became resigned to it and ultimately earned a small prize—a football (soccer ball). And for a year or two he had the honor of having a virus named after him: the "Christopher Brand virus."

Once Christopher had recovered and returned to school, Margaret resumed her professional duties, helping out in the general eye clinic some mornings and working with eye patients at the leprosy hospital at Karigiri on other days. She was also homeschooling Mary and Estelle, using the PNEU curriculum. Trish was now old enough to attend nursery school along with the Webb's daughter, Clare. Teacher Jessie found them a handful—not a discipline problem, but quite inventive. Out of school the two were inseparable.

Besides her home and professional activities, Margaret served as one of the Bible class teachers for the medical students. All of the Christian students at Vellore attended a mandatory one-hour Bible lesson per week as part of their curriculum, something their families and home churches expected the college to provide. (Non-Christian students could attend voluntarily.) While each of the classes followed the same basic course, the lessons required several hours of prayer and preparation by the individual teachers.

For Margaret, now the mother of five, devoting any attention to her professional career required a feat of juggling her responsibilities of homeschooling, regular correspondence to the older children and other family, the supervision of Trish, teaching of Bible classes, the supervision of the household, and the usual social contacts of life on the college campus. But both Paul and Dr. Ernest Fritschi (now director of Schieffelin Leprosy Research and Training Centre), who realized the significance of what she was discovering, encouraged her to do so, and many provided help so that she could.

Aruldoss not only cooked and served the meals but did the shopping, a time-consuming job in India. His wife, Manomani, helped with the children as well as cleaning and tidying the sometimes chaotic house. The heavy laundry was done by a dhobie (washerman) whose donkey carried the loads to the river. Female medical students gladly came to babysit the children in the evening, which gave Paul and Margaret time to attend to other responsibilities. Finally there was the help of others in the Christian community, especially Dr. Alison Webb, who would help with crises with the children despite her own busy work schedule. All of this became even more essential as Margaret became pregnant again.

◌⁓◌

> The psalmist says that children are a heritage from the Lord and a reward from Him (Psalm 127:3–4). A heritage is a gift we haven't earned. We don't earn our children, nor do we own them. They are the Lord's. His to give for a while. His to use in His kingdom. As a parent, I was aware of the awesome responsibility of my temporary assignment in nurturing them for the Lord—getting the right balance of toughness and love, of teaching by word and by example. I am so aware of my failures, of the missed opportunities. I know for myself I shouldn't dare tell my own children how to raise theirs. (I admit I fail on that resolve!)

In the summer of 1957, Margaret was in the first trimester of pregnancy, which was not usually a topic for family conversation in those days.

> My shape was beginning to demand that I wear a maternity dress. This was not lost on Jean and Mary, who remembered other occasions, but Christopher was quite naïve about it.
> One day at lunch, when Christopher and Jean were both home on vacation from boarding school, Jean brightly asked me when the next baby was expected. I responded by asking her why the question. So the conversation started. Suddenly it dawned on Christopher what we were

talking about. He looked very concerned and said, "Don't do it, Mum, it's too big a risk. It might be another girl!"

℘

The Brand's sixth child and Christopher's fifth sister, Pauline Frieda, was born December 2, 1957, at CMC Hospital in Vellore. Besides the joy of Pauline's birth and the coming of the Christmas holidays, December of 1957 was also an exciting time for the family as they prepared for their furlough early the next year.

It had been five years since the Brands had been in England, and now there were two new children to introduce to family and friends: Trish, aged three-and-a-half, and little Pauline, six weeks old. Also, the older children had changed dramatically. Christopher was nearly fourteen, Jean eleven, Mary nine, and Estelle eight years old.

In 1952 their furlough had been for twelve months. This time the Brands would have only nine months, arriving in England in February and returning to India in October. There were several reasons for this, among them Mary and Estelle's school calendar in India and Paul's obligation to attend the quintennial meeting of the International Leprosy Association (ILA) in Tokyo in November.

Several important matters had to be attended to during these months. Paul and Margaret had decided to enroll Christopher and Jean in boarding schools in England. They had already selected Christopher's school, but arrangements had yet to be made for Jean. Margaret and Paul needed to investigate the options for her as well as the critical matter of finding guardians to care for Christopher and Jean during the school vacations and act "in loco parentis" for them.

Paul and Margaret were expected to spend part of the furlough doing promotional work to raise funds for the Leprosy Mission, and Paul's agenda included attending the annual meeting of the British Orthopaedic Association, where a technical film of one of his tendon transfer operations was to be presented. (This film was later purchased by the Swiss pharmaceutical corporation Ciba-Geigy for use in its educational division, which was involved in developing drugs for the treatment of leprosy. Subsequently Ciba was very helpful in assisting the work at Karigiri and in funding some of Margaret's work there.)

As they prepared to depart, the household was a busy one. Margaret did the packing, no small task for eight people and various climate conditions and seasons. She also had to pack away all their personal possessions, as others would occupy the house during their furlough. In the midst of this, she was finishing up the homeschooling program for Mary and Estelle as well as nursing the new baby.

Paul had much to do in arranging for his absence from Karigiri for eight months, as well as preparing lectures, data, and slides. In addition, he was responsible for making all of the family's complex travel arrangements. Yet he still found time to be concerned about one item: marmalade. For, as he often jokingly said, "My metabolism is based on marmalade."

After their experience of England in 1952, when the wartime rationing system still prevailed, the prospect of another marmalade famine was for Paul a dismal one. His solution was to make it and take it with them. There was a great deal of laughter as they calculated the amounts needed per family member and how best to transport it. "We don't need to pack it separately," Paul joked. "We can just pack alternate layers of clothes and marmalade as we fill the trunks."

One evening Paul brought home in triumph three large, strong tin boxes, which could easily hold ten pounds of marmalade apiece. I could tell that, all joking aside about a layer of clothes and a layer of marmalade, he was really serious now.

Paul set Aruldoss to work making the marmalade. The tins were carefully washed and dried, then filled, and the lids hammered down firmly. These containers seemed tight and secure, requiring a strong hand and a heavy screwdriver to pry them loose. My confidence was rising. Maybe this would work after all. We placed the tins in separate trunks, one to go in the cabin with us, one in the trunk for the accessible hold, and the third in the deep hold.

When we were halfway to England, the weather started to get cold, so we retrieved the trunk containing warmer clothing from the accessible hold. As I opened the trunk, I noticed an unusual smell. Then I realized how sticky everything felt. My heart sank. It was indeed a layer of clothes and a layer of marmalade, and not funny at all. The hold had been hot enough to start the fermentation process that had finally blown the lid right off the tin!

Paul and I spent the rest of the trip hand washing each garment *and* the trunk, in addition to the everyday washing that included Pauline's diapers. We saw a lot of the laundry room on that voyage.

That was just the first chapter of the marmalade story!

The older children found the voyage thrilling and exciting. Christopher and Jean were a wonderful older brother and sister, imaginative and innovative in creating games for the others to play. Best of all, the children had their father's complete attention, and he reveled in having the time to spend full days and evenings in their company. He would haul them up on deck during storms, teaching them that seasickness was best confronted in the spray of fresh ocean air, not lying on a bunk in a cabin. He was proud of the hardy band he was leading into the future.

Once in England, the Brands moved into a large three-story house near Kew Gardens, in west London, since Auntie Eunice and Auntie Hope had moved to a smaller house and could no longer accommodate the large Brand family. "Pilgrim Lodge," as the Kew Gardens house was called, had been purchased by the Mission to Lepers for just this purpose—a temporary home for missionaries on furlough. The added advantage for the Brands was that within walking distance was St. Luke's, a Church of England day school which Jean, Mary, and Estelle could attend until the summer holidays. Christopher was enrolled at another school that would help tutor him in certain subjects, such as French, in preparation for English boarding school.

One of the most welcoming aspects of their arrival at Kew was that Paul's sister, Connie, and her husband, David, were also in England on furlough from Nigeria and had been given permission to stay at Pilgrim Lodge for a few weeks to help the Brands settle in. Thanks to her brother's marmalade plan, Connie was soon put to work.

We arrived at Pilgrim Lodge on a blustery cold winter evening and were cordially met by Walter and Amy Fancutt, the host couple in charge of the house, and then by dear Connie and David. Were we ever glad to see them! While we brought luggage into the house and arranged it in the appropriate rooms, the children explored the garden in the remaining minutes of daylight.

It was a pleasant house with a spacious garden surrounded by a high brick wall. At the back of the garden was a small ornamental pool with a central fountain that no longer worked. The top of the pool had iced over and the bottom was layered with thick mud and leaves that had not been disturbed in a long time. Eyeing it, Christopher decided he could step from one side, to the fountain, and then over to the other side. Unfortunately he miscalculated the distance and went into that cold, wet, oozy mud. He came into the house dripping-wet, smelling bad, shivering, and asking, "Mum, where can I find some dry clothes?"

Before we left the ship, I had carefully packed one of the trunks with all of our nightclothes and other items needed for the first few days, and I was congratulating myself on being so well organized as I told Christopher where to find clean clothing. (Incidentally this also was the trunk where the second tin of marmalade was packed. I had checked the lid before we left the ship, and it had seemed sound.)

Christopher opened the trunk. Paused. Then called, "Mum, there's a smell of marmalade in here!"

The second tin, which had survived the voyage, had now exploded. It was quite astonishing the way that marmalade had spread itself throughout the whole trunk in a very short time. Everything was sticky. I nearly wept!

Connie, bless her heart, came to my rescue. She started laughing, and I laughed with her.

Downstairs in the laundry room was a washing machine with a hand-operated wringer. No tumble dryer in those days. A line in the garden did a nice drying job on a bright sunny day but not on a cold wet night. Undaunted, Connie set to work to wash at least the nightclothes. Then everyone had to take turns holding them before the gas fires located in various rooms until there was something dry for each one to wear that night.

I cringed at the thought of opening the third trunk, but I finally plucked up enough courage and did it. No smell.

After retrieving the tin, I pried open the lid, hoping to see at least ten pounds of nice marmalade. Instead, it was black, smelled strange, and tasted horrible. The acid marmalade had reacted with the metal tin.

The ending of the story is that when we went shopping, contrary to Paul's fears, we were able to buy all the marmalade we needed!

Since then, the marmalade story has become a favorite part of Brand family lore.

⌒

At the beginning of the furlough, Margaret's parents were in England as well, having come for a visit from Rhodesia where they had moved to be near daughter Frieda. After Connie and David departed, Grandpa and Grandma Berry came to Pilgrim Lodge, staying in rooms above the Brand quarters. They became acquainted with their newest granddaughters Trish and Pauline, and reacquainted with the older children. They also caught up with the news from Margaret and Paul. It pleased Dr. Berry to see how Margaret had been able to achieve specialty expertise in ophthalmology and had fulfilled the potential he had always seen in her.

During this furlough, the stress for Margaret was considerable, with Paul frequently gone on medical lectures and deputation talks, four of the children in two new schools, a four-year-old and a breast-feeding baby at home, upcoming summer holiday trips to plan, boarding schools to investigate for Jean, and guardians to secure for Christopher and Jean, who would be left in England. Margaret's parents had planned to stay for three months, which they did. To add to the strain, Margaret's mother suffered a heart attack during the visit and had to be hospitalized. She felt with her father the fear and despair as he watched his beloved Greta facing a life-threatening illness.

To further complicate matters, Margaret found that Pilgrim Lodge was not the best place for active young children. The manager of the house, Mrs. Fancutt, was herself under a great deal of pressure to maintain the missionary lodgings in the pristine state expected by the mission.

Walter Fancutt was a highly respected member of the Leprosy Mission, and his wife, Amy, had the responsibility of maintaining Pilgrim Lodge. It had been carefully decorated and furnished to please the artistic sense of the General Secretary of the Mission and was truly a beautiful house. The General Secretary and his wife were seasoned missionaries, but they had not had the experience of raising children. Nor had Walter and Amy. So they were at a disadvantage when it came to preparing to receive families with young children who had been raised in a very different culture and who were not used to the niceties of a sophisticated home in

England. And since we were some of their first guests, they were in for a rude awakening. A lot of grace was needed on the part of both parties.

The décor was beautiful, the wallpapers tastefully selected and immaculately applied. I shall never forget the horror of discovering that three-year-old Trish had done a "mural" in black crayon on the wallpaper in the living room. To my relief, Amy was quite understanding and helpful as together we tried to clean it up. (She loved Trish and that helped.)

Early on in our stay at Pilgrim Lodge we were given a sheet of house rules. These were all most reasonable in light of the purpose of the house: to provide a home for missionaries on furlough. Many of these were single missionaries who really needed a rest and didn't want to be disturbed by children or anyone else. But the rules did constitute a burden for parents who had plenty of other concerns to handle.

The rules also constituted a challenge for our daughter Mary, who sometimes behaved as if rules were there to be broken if one could get away with it.

We houseguests shared a common phone, which was located near the front door. Mrs. Fancutt had worked out a system so that whoever answered a phone call could summon the appropriate recipient from whichever floor they were on. A board with hooks carrying nametags of all the guests, with a bell button beside each name, hung near the phone. The system worked well. That was until Mary thought up a cute trick to play on everyone.

Both Paul and I were out of the house for an hour or two, and when I returned I was confronted by subdued-looking children and an understandably upset Mrs. Fancutt who said, "One of your children has changed all the names around on the bell board, and I need to know who has done it." None of them had owned up, though I suspected they knew who the chief culprit was. "All right," I said. "None of us will have tea (a light supper for the children) today until you tell me who did it."

In a little while Trish came and told me she had done it. So she and I went to confess to Mrs. Fancutt. Trish was her "golden girl," and it was a terrible shock to poor Mrs. Fancutt to be confronted with such a crime committed by such an adorable little girl. So she asked Trish to show her how she had done it. When Trish tried to demonstrate, it was immediately obvious that she could not have switched the tags. She was much too short and there was no chair to stand on. So she was acquitted of the original crime but guilty of another—lying! When faced with that charge she simply said, "But I was so hungry!" So the case against her was dropped, and she was given something to eat.

The remaining three—Jean, Mary, and Estelle—were all under suspicion (Christopher was away on a camping trip). Mrs. Fancutt and I waited. Presently Estelle crept in quietly and said, "I know who did it but I can't say" (she was always loyal to her sisters). I told her to go back and have a talk with whoever had done it. She returned with Mary and together they said, "We did it." (I suspect it was a rehearsed speech.)

I took them downstairs to tell Mrs. Fancutt (whose wrath had cooled by then), and they made their speech to her. When she asked the girls why they had not told her before, Mary said, "Because I was afraid you were going to kill me!"

Some weeks later Mrs. Fancutt told me that Mary's fear had really made an impression on her. She had not realized until then how her anger affected others.

Another incident at Kew has remained with me throughout the years—another example of the lessons I have learned from my children.

Baby Pauline and Trish were home during the day while the older girls went off to St. Luke's day school, and Trish was often bored because Pauline wasn't big enough to play with and spent a lot of time sleeping. One day she told me she was going to help me wash the nappies (diapers). This was in the days before disposable diapers and automatic washing machines. We used hand-turned wringers, and Trish decided that looked like fun. She was eager to "help" Mummy.

We found a box she could stand on, to put her at the right height, and I began to explain just what she would have to do. But she brushed me off, saying, "I know how to do it!"

I began to feed the cloth diapers through the wringer and told her it was time to turn the handle. But she couldn't do it. I loosened up the rollers a bit, but still she couldn't. No matter how much encouragement I gave her and how hard she tried, she simply could not do it.

She finally stood back, hands on her hips, and looked at me almost in defiant desperation. "Mummy," she said slowly and firmly, "you know I want to help you, but can't you see you have to help me help you?"

Then she put her little hands back on the wringer handle, I put mine over hers, and together we did it beautifully. She beamed with satisfaction.

Many times I have thought of that moment of insight and prayed, "Lord, You know I want to help You. But I need You to help me help You." He does not tell us to stand aside out of His way. He will allow us to use the strength and wit we have, but He provides the real power.

A dear friend of mine, a chairman of several nonprofit organizations, has on his desk in front of him a little framed reminder: "The Lord loves me too much to allow me to succeed in any of my endeavors without relying totally on HIM."

⟳

Greta Berry recovered from her heart attack, and she and Dr. Berry returned to Rhodesia while the Brands finished their furlough. As the summer holidays began, the family enjoyed camping and seaside trips. Friends generously loaned them the needed equipment and even housing for short stays. It was a delight for the children to have the undivided attention of their father, as they had enjoyed on the ship, and they rejoiced in this family time together. But boarding schools and guardians for Christopher and Jean still had to be determined after the family holidays were over.

The British boarding school system was, and remains, a controversial subject, largely due to the separation of the child from the parent for long periods of time. While boarding school was the only option for families living in many foreign locales or when there were no available local schools (as in Vellore), within England itself many families who could afford the fees chose to send their children to a boarding school where they could get a better education. In the best of circumstances, the child from abroad had loving matrons or masters to care for them at the school and caring guardians close at hand where they could go for short holidays. In the worst of circumstances, a child might have indifferent schoolmasters and indifferent guardians. The prevailing attitude, however, was that the boarding school system built character and that the benefits outweighed the negatives. Thus, the system was prized enough that families sacrificed so their children could attend.

If possible financially, and travel time permitting, one or both parents would travel to see their children on the short school holidays and would bring the children home during the longer ones. But this option was not available to missionary couples. They had to rely on finding suitable guardians who might be responsible for years at a time. The Harris sisters, Paul's beloved aunties, had served admirably as guardians for Paul and Connie, but in that instance the children lived with them year-round and attended school as day students.

Margaret and Paul did not think Christopher was doing well at Breeks boarding school in India. He needed a change, and they were optimistic about the school they had found for him in England: St. Lawrence College in Ramsgate, a fine Christian school for boys. But no final decision had been made regarding Jean. She had done well at Breeks, but she would have to leave there prior to the family's next scheduled furlough in 1963. Also, it appeared that her potential and abilities might not be fully developed if she stayed at Breeks. The question was which of two less-than-ideal choices should be made: stay nearer to the family but risk that her talents might not be fully developed, or enroll at a top quality school in England but not see her family for five years. Her parents chose what seemed best for Jean, despite the heartbreak they felt over having to leave her.

Living in America, I realize people often think parents only send children to boarding school when they cannot cope with them at home or if a child needs special discipline. That is not the average British perspective on boarding schools. I look back at my own childhood and my parents' loving decision to send us to a first-rate school that gave us all the advantages of an education plus character building. They knew it would not be easy for them or for us, and certainly not inexpensive; but it was the wisest choice they could make for our future. For Paul and me, as for my parents, these decisions were made solely out of love and to provide the best possible chances for our children.

Christopher and Jean entered this new phase of their lives in different fashions. Christopher was happy to be leaving Breeks. Although he had made many good friends there and did not want to say good-bye to them, he was struggling scholastically and was often at odds with some of the staff. He saw St. Lawrence as a chance to start over.

For Jean the need for a change was not as pressing. But she was distressed at Christopher being alone in England and felt she could provide some companionship during school vacations if she stayed. It would mean separation from the rest of the family, and much would depend on the relationship she developed with her guardians. Paul and Margaret struggled to find these guardians for their two oldest children within the limited time they had to do so.

John and Peggy Edmunds kindly offered to be guardians for both Christopher and Jean. The Edmunds were doctors whom Margaret and Paul had known from their University College days. John had been active in the Christian Union, and Margaret had been partially responsible for bringing Peggy to Christ. Unfortunately, the Edmunds were committed to leave for a two- to three-month post in Canada and would have only a few days to become acquainted with their new wards. Despite these time constraints, there did not seem to be any other options nearly as attractive to Margaret and Paul. With deep appreciation they accepted the Edmunds' sincere offer.

Meanwhile, Margaret visited a school in Kent, not far from Christopher's new school, and tentatively enrolled Jean there. But Paul's sister, Connie, proposed another possibility. Her daughters, Jessica and Elizabeth, were already attending the Clarendon School for Girls in Abergele, North Wales. Several of Paul and Connie's cousins had gone to that school, and it had an excellent reputation. Paul went to see it and soon felt confident that it would be the right choice for Jean.

Time was running out, which meant eleven-year-old Jean, along with her brother, had just one overnight visit with the Edmunds in their home, which was to be their temporary home for the next five years. It was not the happy visit that Paul and Margaret hoped it would be.

> We took Jean and Christopher to the Edmunds' home, Hampermill Cottage outside Watford, a place with charming old-world style. Jean loved it and especially loved their dog. A good start, we thought. We had a pleasant visit with our old friends, John and Peggy, and then it was time to leave. The plan was for the children to remain overnight so they could spend a bit more get-acquainted time with the Edmunds.
>
> As we got into the car, Jean came running from the house. Reality had hit. This was to be "home," these were to be her "parents" for the next five years while Paul and I were thousands of miles away. Jean sensed that she would never feel at home here or that she would ever bond with Peggy and John. She clung to me crying, "Don't leave me here. Take me with you back home."

Dr. William Berry, 1932
Margaret's father

Margaret Muriel ("Greta") Berry, 1940
Margaret's mother

The Berry house in Tempe, near Bloemfontein, South Africa

Margaret ("Pearl") the ballerina, age 4

Margaret (r.) and her sister Frieda

Margaret beside an aloe plant at the Tempe house, age 4

The Berry girls, on vacation in
Falmouth, England, 1927
(Left to right: Margaret, Anna, Frieda)

Dr. Berry and his daughters, South Africa
(Left to right: Margaret, Frieda, Anna)

Crossing the Limpopo River, North Transvaal, South Africa
All wheeled vehicles were towed over at a ford by donkey train.

Frieda, Anna, and Margaret in their
Malvern Girls' College uniforms,
Malvern, England, 1932

Margaret, 1932

Margaret, 1941

Paul, Christopher, and Jean, Vellore, India, 1947

Wedding day for Dr. Paul Brand and Dr. Margaret Brand, Emmanuel Church, Northwood, England, May 29, 1943

Mary, Jean, Estelle, and Christopher on the veranda of the Brand home, Vellore, 1950 Ayah Martha is in the background.

The Brands' first car, Kotagiri, 1948
Paul, Jean, Christopher, Margaret

"Aunt" Ida Scudder, Christopher, and Jean, Vellore, 1949. Dr. Ida is receiving birthday greetings and flowers.

INDIA

Dr. and Mrs. Berry and Granny Brand with Mary, Jean, Christopher, and Margaret, Vellore, 1949

Margaret with Christopher,
Estelle, Mary, and Jean,
Vellore, 1951

Trish, Estelle, Mary, Jean,
and Christopher, 1955

"The Wends" on vacation,
Korakundah, 1959. "We had
one car for ten of us!"

On furlough in England, 1952
(Back row: Christopher, Paul,
Jean; front row: Mary,
Margaret, Estelle)

INDIA

Margaret stands on a
rocky outcrop above
the campus and points
at an overview of the
Christian Medical
College, Vellore, 1950.

The Brand children with Gigi the leopard
(Child on the left is Graham Hancock.)

Margaret travels by horseback to visit Granny Brand in the Kalarayan Hills, 1960. (Pauline sits in front of Margaret.)

Drs. Paul & Margaret, 1955

A family picnic in the hills of southern India, 1957

On furlough, visiting friends in England, 1958

Margaret with Trish, Estelle, Pauline, and Mary, Vellore, 1962. The Brand home on the college campus is in background (upstairs).

Jean with Auntie Eunice and Auntie Hope, Ruislip, England.

The Brands with Granny Brand, 1961

Granny Brand traveling
by dohli, 1960

INDIA

Granny Brand on horseback
at age 82

Margaret and the children in England at a
wedding where Trish was a junior bridesmaid, 1963.

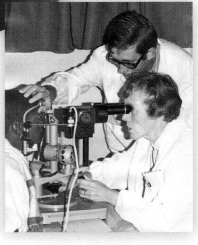

Dr. Margaret, Carville,
Louisiana, 1966.
Behind her
stands
Chaplain
Oscar
Harris.

Teaching a visiting
doctor, Carville, 1971

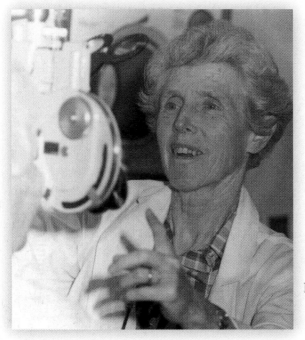

Doing a refraction, Carville, 1971

The Brand family, Carville, 1968

Trish with Simon
the skunk

Riding the horses at Carville

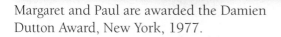

Margaret and Paul are awarded the Damien
Dutton Award, New York, 1977.

Dr. Margaret and her proud husband at
the "Woman of the Year" award ceremony

Margaret receives
the USPHS "Woman
of the Year" award,
presented by director
Dr. John Trautman,
1976.

Mary, Estelle,
and Margaret
model their saris and
Margaret's sling, Vellore, 2004.

Margaret with Dr. Ernest
Fritschi, Vellore, 2004

Aruldoss and Manomani, Vellore,
2004. These faithful family helpers
have been dear friends of the Brand
family for many years.

INDIA

Jean, Mary, Christopher,
Trish, Pauline, and
Estelle, 1984

Paul and Margaret celebrate their 55th wedding
anniversary with all the family, 1998.

Margaret and Paul,
Seattle, 2001

Peggy had never experienced long separation from her parents. She could not understand the misery Jean was feeling, and at the time we mistook the separation from us as being the only reason for Jean's apprehension. In the end, Paul persuaded her to stay for the night.

Furlough was coming to an end. In two weeks, Margaret and Paul and the four younger children would be on board ship heading for India. But first Christopher and Jean had to be properly outfitted, packed, and sent off to their schools. While Margaret finished packing Christopher's trunk, Paul took Jean and her luggage to Euston Station to join the Clarendon School group. There he had to say his good-bye to her. Margaret and the girls hadn't had the opportunity to see Clarendon, so she had made arrangements to travel a few days later to Abergele, visit the school, spend a night with Jean at outside lodgings, and then depart. From Abergele she and the girls would travel by train to Liverpool and meet Paul at the docks. Paul, meanwhile, was committed to giving a lecture at Oxford just before departing.

We drove Christopher to St. Lawrence College in Ramsgate, where we toured the school, met our son's housemaster, and got a feeling for his environment. Then we had to say our good-byes and return to London.

Christopher, who never talked easily about his feelings, was quite stoical. Although he may have felt as strongly as Jean did, he didn't show it. This was gentle on us but must have taken all his strength to hide his feelings.

Next, while Paul prepared to give his lecture at Oxford, the girls and I took the train to Abergele, a pretty little town on the north coast of Wales. After booking in at a small guesthouse and leaving our luggage (the heavy stuff had already been sent ahead to the ship at Liverpool), we went to Clarendon School to meet Jean.

Jean and Christopher fully supported their parents' work in India and understood the sacrifice necessary on the part of all members of the family for such work to be done. They both wanted to spare their parents from painful good-byes. But Jean was overwhelmed by the added fact that she would not see her infant sister for five years.

Jean seemed happy as she showed us her bedroom, which she shared with three other "missionary kids," and took us around the beautiful grounds. We then met her teachers and the principal, and all seemed pleasant and friendly. During the entire time, Jean insisted on carrying ten-month-old Pauline.

Jean was allowed to spend the night with us at the guesthouse, and we all tried not to talk about the next day. But finally she said, "I know you and Daddy have to go. You have a lot of work to do." Then she wistfully added, "But I wish Pauline could stay." Her heart was breaking, as was mine. Neither of us slept much.

In the morning we took a taxi back to the school. All the way Jean clutched Pauline as if she could not bear to let her go. We had little time for the final, painful good byes, as we had to get to the station and catch the train for Liverpool.

The last thing I heard as I got into the taxi was Jean pleading, between her sobs, "Don't go, Mum. *Don't go!*" One of the teachers came out and gently led her back to the school where she had a good cry before returning to her classes. The teachers had seen moments like that many times and understood the heartbreak. But saying goodbye to Jean outside her school that day was one of the hardest things I have ever done.

Margaret had no time to dwell on the sorrow she felt as she and the children rushed back to their lodgings to pack their remaining things and get the family and luggage to the station in time. Adding to the pressure was the fact that this was the only train that could get them to their ship in time to board.

The owner of the guesthouse kindly lent them an old pram (baby buggy) to use as a luggage cart. Margaret would push this, filled with luggage, while carrying Pauline. Mary and Estelle would also carry all they could. They were all ready to go when, suddenly, they could not find Trish.

When Trish did not respond to our calls for her, I sent Mary to check our rooms. Estelle was dispatched to run up the street to a small toy store that Trish had found fascinating. No success!

By this time I was getting frantic. I could see us missing our train and unable to contact Paul to tell him what had happened. Then I thought of the bathroom.

I dashed back upstairs and found the bathroom door closed. I called out, "Trish, are you in there?" A plaintive little voice answered, "Yes,

Mummie, and I can't get out." She had managed to shut the door and lock it.

The bathroom was two floors up, and the landlord did not have a ladder to reach the window. But he was very understanding of our plight. He ran up those stairs like an athlete. Outside the door he called to Trish, "Stand back, little girl. I'm coming in!" And he threw all his tall, heavy weight against the door. The lock gave way, and Trish was free. I was concerned about the broken door, but he told me not to worry—just run!

We had five minutes to catch the train and the station was a ten-minute walk away, up a slight hill. I knew we could not possibly make it in five minutes, not with small children and a load of luggage.

Mary was a good runner, so I told her to run as fast as she could ahead of us and ask the stationmaster to please hold the train as it was so important that we got to the boat in time.

Thankfully, the stationmaster was an amiable fellow. He held the train for us, and we made it to Liverpool, met an anxious Paul who had wondered if we were coming, boarded our ship, and off we sailed to start our third term in India.

Sea voyages provided wonderful times for fun for the family, and they had plenty of it on the voyage back to India—but it was muted. The two left behind were missed deeply, every day.

Chapter 17

A Third Term in India

"I have found a God who cares about me."

B ack in Vellore, after an absence of nine months, the Brands had to read-
just to the tropical climate as they re-opened their house and unpacked
their household goods from storage. Their greatest adjustment, however, was
to the absence of Jean and Christopher.

Paul had to catch up on the activities in his college department and at
Karigiri, and he had to get ready for his trip to the International Leprosy
Association Congress in Tokyo, where in a few weeks he would be reading a
paper on his surgical work. For Paul and for many leprosy patients around
the world, this would have historic significance. But two incidents involving two of his daughters that occurred on the same day consumed much of
Paul's emotional energy.

When the Brands arrived in Bombay after their furlough, they stopped to
visit their friends the Marconis before leaving for Vellore. The year before,
this Italian couple had come to Vellore to direct and produce a film titled
Lifted Hands. Using staff and patients, the film followed the story of a teenage boy from leprosy diagnosis to treatment and rehabilitation, providing an
excellent teaching tool for leprosy missions to use for their educational and
fund-raising activities. The Marconis had brought with them an unusual
pet, a leopard cub named Gigi, which immediately became part of the Brand
household.

Back in Bombay, we visited the Marconi home. Gigi, now a full-grown leopard, was tethered at the front door. The year before, when she was a four-month-old cub, the children were thrilled to have her in our house. Even Trish, who was only three years old at the time, delighted to play with her. Gigi had sharp little teeth, and even at that age her jaws were very strong. It was a struggle to take from her a toy she had chosen to possess.

Gigi, now a large animal, a truly beautiful creature, was quite intimidating. The older girls kept a safe distance back. She was sunning herself on the steps at the ground floor apartment. Around her neck was a strong chain that kept her tethered within a radius of ten feet.

Paul went to ring the doorbell and then stretched out his arm to fondle Gigi. She accepted that, but I could see from where I stood that her attention was on Trish, who had fearlessly gone forward with her daddy. It was a moment of calm before the storm.

Without even seeming to get to her feet, Gigi leapt at Trish and bore her to the ground, crouching, her full weight on the child and her teeth firmly on her throat.

I was transfixed with horror. Leopards strangle their prey, and that was what seemed to be happening right before my eyes. Trish's cry was getting weaker and she was clearly bleeding from her neck. (We realized afterwards that indeed Gigi could have killed Trish in a moment had she meant to do so. She was playing with her like a cat does with a mouse.)

Paul grabbed Gigi's collar to try and wrench her off. She snarled louder and bit harder.

Mercifully, Mr. Marconi, coming down from his apartment to answer the door, looked out and saw the scene. "Let go," he yelled to Paul, "or she'll tear her throat right out!" Paul let go.

Seconds later, Marconi brought a rolled-up magazine heavily down on Gigi's nose, hoping the shock would distract her. It didn't. He then pressed with his thumbs through her tender cheeks onto her back teeth. He had strong hands, and it worked. The leopard relaxed her jaws, and Paul dragged Trish out of the animal's reach, though not before her claws scored down the length of her body. Fortunately the claws were trimmed and the wounds didn't go deep.

Paul helped Trish to her feet, took her hand, and with great relief, but speaking as casually as he could, said, "I think we'd better go in and get you washed up a bit." So he walked her up the steps as if it had been no big deal that his little daughter had been within inches of death!

Keeping her upright was, of course, the best way to slow down any bleeding, as it minimized the blood pressure in her neck. We had no idea, at that point, if the leopard's teeth had punctured a major blood vessel.

As we washed her wounds, applied an antibiotic ointment, and dressed them, Paul kept up a running conversation with Trish about all kinds of inconsequential things, trying to keep her mind off the pain and to try and lessen the trauma. We kept her quiet for the next twenty-four hours and nothing alarming happened.

I don't think Trish realized how scared we all were, nor even how scared she had been! She told her sisters quite firmly that she had forgiven Gigi but did not intend to pat another leopard. When we returned to Vellore she was also heard mentioning to some adults that "little children should never play with leopards unless their mummies and daddies are in the room with them!" For a few weeks after the incident, Trish occasionally cried out in her sleep. When she did, I quickly roused her, reassured her, and settled her down again.

The second incident involved Jean. Shortly after the Brands returned to Vellore, Jean fell when playing in a tree at school, breaking her left wrist and her left arm above the elbow so severely that the bone of the upper fracture tore through the sleeve of her blouse. Her accident occurred the same day as Gigi's attack on Trish, leading one Hindu friend to remark that "it was a most inauspicious day for your family." (In Hindu culture, astrology is used to predict auspicious versus inauspicious days for individuals so that major events such as weddings or even surgery can be scheduled. Though the Brands did not believe in such zodiac predictions, they would agree that the events of this particular day were profoundly unfortunate.)

The school doctor immediately had Jean seen by an expert orthopedic surgeon. With Jean under anesthesia, the surgeon set the fractures, closed the wounds, and placed her arm (with the elbow straightened) in a splint rather than a cast, as swelling in the cast would have risked pressure on muscles and nerves resulting in paralysis. Paul and Margaret received an airmail letter explaining the accident and the treatment, and Paul was relieved that Jean was in the best of hands. He realized that the surgeon, who happened to be a colleague he knew and trusted, had had to make some difficult decisions and that whatever treatment he chose involved the risk of serious complications. After a week or two, the surgeon returned Jean to the operating room where, with Jean once again under anesthesia, he forced the elbow into a flexed position and put a cast on it.

Soon after Jean's second surgery, this trusted and expert orthopedic surgeon died suddenly. The physician who assumed her care was young and inexperienced and did not appreciate Jean's increasing complaints about the pain that was developing in her arm and the numbness developing in her hand. She remained in the hospital, deteriorating daily.

Jean's guardians, the Edmunds, were still abroad in Canada, and Paul was in Japan for his speaking engagement when Margaret received a concerned message from the principal of the school. Miss Swain, a sincere and responsible Christian, had no medical training, but she was concerned that Jean seemed to be doing poorly. Margaret immediately wrote to their old friend Dr. Howard Somervell, a retired orthopedic consultant who was living about four hours' travel distance from Jean's hospital in Rhyll.

As soon as he received Margaret's letter, Dr. Somervell went to visit Jean. He was there as a friend and not a consultant, but he sent his observations to the Brands: it looked as if Jean had suffered some nerve damage due to pressure on the stretched nerves at the swollen elbow and that the involved muscle groups might be permanently injured.

Paul was in Hong Kong when he received Howard's report, which confirmed Paul's worst fears about Jean's injury and its complications. He was devastated that his beloved daughter was having serious problems while he was busy on the other side of the world trying to restore function in other people's hands. Fortunately the Edmunds returned from Canada and immediately arranged for a consultant from Liverpool to examine Jean. The consultant diagnosed the problem as "Volkmann's Ischemic Contracture," a condition that results in permanent paralysis of the forearm and hand muscles. Jean was referred to Professor Herbert Seddon in London at the Royal National Orthopaedic Hospital. Professor Seddon did not think the arm was unredeemable. After he operated and explored the status of the nerves, he gave the Brands a much more hopeful prognosis. He found that the muscles were not permanently damaged and was able to relieve some of the stretch on the nerves.

Although this third surgery left Jean with new scars, she would eventually recover normal sensation and muscle function in her forearm and hand, but she would lose some of the full movement of her elbow and wrist. She needed extensive physical therapy in London, and while she was undergoing this and absent from her school at Clarendon, she was able to keep up with her studies by homeschooling. Peggy Edmunds's mother, Marion, was a widow and a retired teacher who lived with the Edmunds and became fondly known as "Auntie Marion" to Christopher and Jean. The children had great confidence that she understood them, and they confided in her when they most missed their parents. When Jean needed a teacher, she was the perfect tutor.

Jean was able to return to school for the summer term, which ran from just after the Easter break until mid-July. Her arm was still healing, but she no longer needed professional physical therapy. It was a hot summer that year, and the girls at Clarendon were glad to be in their light summer uniforms. But that apparel exposed Jean's scarred arm, and some of her classmates cruelly taunted her into covering the arm with long-sleeve sweaters so that they would not have to see her scars.

While her physical and emotional suffering made Jean a stronger person, her lonely ordeal would forever weigh upon her parents' hearts.

When Jean had her accident, one of the Vellore staff said, "You just go back to England. It may cost you something, but you really should go back."

Believing that God had called us to return to India to complete unfinished work, we did the only thing we could do—we prayed and prayed about it. This time there was no shining vision such as God had given me back in 1947, not even a strong sense that God was nudging us to go back. We made contact with other people in England, former professional colleagues who had been at Vellore, to help Jean with her recovery, and many did. But the marvelous thing is that God brought her through it as only He could, with a stronger faith in Him.

A generation earlier when Jesse and Evelyn Brand had left Paul and Connie in England to return to their work in India, Evelyn had left her children with the promise in Psalm 27:10: "When my father and my mother forsake me then the Lord will take me up." This became a much-quoted verse in the family, and Jean too found it a great comfort. She might have said, "When everybody else lets you down, God's there." She trusted Him then, as she has many times since.

With the two oldest children absent and Jean enduring her struggles so far away, there was a pall over the Christmas holidays. Nevertheless it was necessary to move forward with preparations concerning Mary and Estelle, who themselves were about to go to boarding school for the first time. Mary, now age ten, and Estelle, almost nine, went to Breeks in January of 1959. Following in the footsteps of Jean and Christopher, the girls knew what to expect and looked forward to the experience. Mary thrived at boarding school, her self-confidence balanced with a respect for authority when needed, so that she had no problems with classmates, the classroom, or on the sports fields. Estelle had always been quiet and the least adventurous of the children. And if she was or wasn't unhappy at Breeks, she never let anyone know.

Margaret now had only the two younger children at home—Pauline, a toddler, and Trish, who was now ready for kindergarten. The four older children had been homeschooled by Margaret alone, but there now appeared a new possibility for early education.

A group of mothers, including Margaret, decided to organize an elementary school for staff children on the campus. The number of staff families had grown during the Brands' twelve years at CMC, and with so many children it seemed logical to combine the resources of the families into a single effort. A major benefit of these combined efforts was that their children would not need to be sent to boarding school at such young ages.

Different homes were used for different grades, with each mother agreeing to teach certain grades. Later a committee was formed, a curriculum chosen, and a few qualified teachers were hired. The new school was called Vidyalayam, "place of learning." Parents filled in where needed, according to their skills and experience. Eventually the founders succeeded in building a small schoolhouse, but for some time all the classes were hosted in individual homes.

The teaching of languages posed a few problems. Indian staff were the natural teachers for Hindi (the national language of India) and Tamil (the local language of the state of Tamil-Nadu), but the children who would be going into the British educational system needed to be taught French and Latin. Alison Webb taught French, while Margaret agreed to do the Latin. She would take her Latin textbook to Karigiri and between seeing patients would study declensions and conjugations, vocabulary and common idioms, to be taught to her pupils in the afternoon. Margaret also had the honor of composing the first school song.[1]

❧

With Trish now occupied part of the day with kindergarten and fifteen-month-old Pauline under the care of her ayah, Manomoni, Margaret could return to her research in ocular leprosy. She arranged to divide her time between the general ophthalmology services at Schell, including the eye camps, and the ocular leprosy research at Schieffelin.

The Schell Eye Hospital was always a busy place. Most of the patients were from the surrounding rural areas. Although they were poor by Western standards, they could afford to pay a little for their surgery and medicine, and we found that it was important for their own dignity to allow them to contribute. If they had no money, their family could at least help to feed the family member in hospital. But there were those who had nothing. Hospital policy assured that such patients would not be turned away if there was a medical need we could meet. Ten of our beds on the ward were free, with free food and no fees, and we saved those ten beds for impoverished patients who needed cataract surgery and whose hospital stay was of predictable length, as opposed to those who might require weeks in the hospital. We doctors were responsible for how we used those beds, and we dared not use these scarce beds for patients whom we felt we could not help. On one particular busy morning in the eye clinic, I faced just such a dilemma.

I don't remember her name, so I'll call her Parthi, meaning "Grandma." She sat in front of me, pitifully thin. A dirty sari wrapped around her spoke of hard times. She had been blind for more than fifteen years. Her eye sockets appeared almost empty, so there was nothing we could do for her. There was no reason to keep her in one of our few free beds. I asked the Bible Woman to find the family, make sure they heard the gospel story, and then let the woman be taken

---

1. Today, the song is still sung and the enrollment in Vidyalayam is over one hundred pupils.

home.[2] Gently the BW escorted Parthi away as I picked up the next card from the pile.

When our morning clinic ended, one lonely figure was still in the waiting area—Parthi. She had no family to help her home. They had abandoned her at the clinic, and we had no idea where she belonged. The name of a village was written on her card, but there were several villages with that same name, and Parthi could not seem to distinguish which one was hers. We had no option but to admit her, hoping the family would soon return and take care of her. They did, finally—about a month later!

During that month we got to know Parthi fairly well, and it was clear why the family wanted a rest from her. She was a cantankerous old woman, bitter, always shouting, always complaining. She was a widow. For how long I don't know, but in many Indian cultures being a widow is a mark that the gods are punishing you because you have allowed your husband to die—it was your responsibility to keep him alive. Then she went blind. So there she was: a blind, useless widow, and the community had little patience with her. As she became the object of teasing, she fought back with her only defense, a sharp tongue.

In the hospital the other patients complained about how she wouldn't let them sleep at night. The nurses were getting impatient and said, "Why can't we get rid of her?" But there was no place to send her. I, too, must confess that each time I saw her, still in the ward, I felt angry with her family for leaving her with us. I thought of her as a nuisance, as an obstacle to our real work.

Those words haunt me now. I certainly did not see Parthi as God saw her. But Emily did.

Emily was one of our humble ward aides. She had had little education, earned minimal wages, and had little responsibility. She helped patients get to the washroom and toilet and ran errands. Who she was, however, was far more significant than what she did. She was a sweet and loving woman who loved the Lord and loved people. She had a family of her own, yet she came and spent time with Parthi, and the two became friends—a new experience for poor old Parthi, who began to mellow.

---

2. Bible Women were paid employees who taught the Bible to those who wanted it; they also were loving, compassionate friends to the patients and their families. They were part of the Religious Works department of the hospital.

Physically we had done nothing for Parthi except feed her well enough that she put on a bit of weight, which she could certainly use. But Emily had done something quite special. Because of Emily's friendship, Parthi trusted her. And when Emily shared in her simple way what Jesus meant to her and that He could and wanted to be Parthi's friend too, Parthi really listened.

Parthi's family showed up and took her home. Some months passed before we learned the rest of the amazing story.

One day a group of itinerant evangelists were going through a certain village fifty or sixty miles from Vellore. They had not been there before and were surprised that their coming aroused so much interest. The villagers came running from their homes when they heard the evangelists singing. "Tell us more about that Jesus Swami (Jesus God)," they called. How had they even heard His name?

It was Parthi's village, and the villagers had heard about Jesus from her. When Parthi returned from the hospital, she was no longer a bitter old grouch. The villagers were amazed at the transformation. When they asked what had happened to her, she said, "The gods in this village never cared about me. But I have found a God who cares about me. It's the Jesus God. I heard about Him back there at the hospital."

The end of the story is that twenty-six people became believers and a church was born in that village—all because humble Emily saw Parthi as God saw her. I was thinking that our first job was to help people keep or get back their sight. But this was the real work. It was one of those occasions when God does something wonderful in spite of us!

Many times Margaret saw God use a number of people, including herself, to lead individuals to Christ. One such lost and despairing soul was a young man named Venkatachalam who Margaret met at the Schieffelin Leprosy Research and Training Centre, Karigiri.

During the late 1950s, in a city many miles from Vellore, Venkatachalam had a bright future ahead of him. He came from a high caste family and was a brilliant engineering student as well as a linguist who could read in many languages. A good marriage had been arranged for him, and the wedding would take place after his graduation. Life looked good for him—except that Venkatachalam knew there was a problem. For several months he had noticed a small, pale patch of insensitivity on his arm, and then others appeared on his back and shoulders. He knew it was leprosy. He didn't need a doctor to make the diagnosis. He did not know how he had contracted it, but his main concern was to keep it secret and to get his degree as soon as possible so that he could then get treated and, hopefully, get well enough that no one need ever know. V knew there was a government-run leprosy treatment center just a block from his college, but someone might see him going there. No, he decided, he must wait until he had his diploma. For the present he would wear long sleeves to hide his arms and tell no one.

Then his eyes began bothering him, and his fingers went numb and were becoming clawed. It was not long before fellow students reported to the faculty that he was "a leper."

In those days, leprosy was considered a curse from the gods, a payback for some sin in a previous incarnation. His hopes and dreams crashed. He had to leave college in disgrace. His family, devastated, canceled the marriage agreement. Then they asked him to leave home since they could not live with his disgrace. They gave him money for train fare and told him to go far away, get a job, get treated, and if he got better, then come home. He never saw them again.

He took the money and did as he was told. He had no problem getting a train and going far away. Getting a job was something else. Everywhere he tried he was rejected. One look at his hands, and he was told to move on.

He ran out of money to buy food and became a beggar, wandering from city to city. With little food and nowhere to sleep other than the sidewalk, he soon contracted tuberculosis. He finally arrived at Vellore, where he joined scores of other beggars at the marketplace.

Chandra Manual, our social worker and dear friend, was in the market buying supplies for our work one morning when she heard the chorus of beggar cries trying to get her attention. But she heard something else. It was as if God was saying, "Go to that man. He needs you right now."

That man was Venkatachalam (V). She started talking with him and quickly realized that he was an educated man, unlike most other beggars. But he was extremely sick, his leprosy very advanced. He needed help quickly.

Chandra brought V to the hospital at Karigiri. Because of his advanced

TB he was a danger to others, so he was placed in one of our few private rooms. At last he had a clean bed to lie on, a place where he could wash, food to eat, quiet, and respect. He was treated with Dapsone, the only medication then used for leprosy. Trying to build up his general health was the most important thing we could do.

David was a young man from a Hindu family who had recently come to know the Lord and was very excited about it. At Karigiri he took care of the day-to-day needs of patients in the private rooms and was assigned to care for V. David cleaned his room, brought him food at meal times, and did whatever he could to make V comfortable. He found books and newspapers for him to read. He was a friend to V, who appreciated David but wished he would stop singing and talking about Jesus.

V's eyes were my responsibility, and I saw him in the clinic twice a week. He had bad inflammation in both eyes, probably due to a combination of leprosy and TB. I was deeply concerned but couldn't give him the medicine that would help control the inflammation since it would make his TB worse. I did what I could but was doubtful that I could really save his sight.

One day I was feeling very discouraged about his condition, and I said to him as he was leaving the clinic, "Remember that, no matter what happens (I think he knew that I meant "if you go blind"), God loves you." He turned around, surprising me with his expression of anger and disgust as he spat on the floor. "How can you say 'God loves you'?" He was almost shouting at me. "God has taken from me everything I counted dear—my health, my career, my marriage, my family, my money. I know He has cursed me (one of the terms used for leprosy means 'Cursed of God'). How can you say that He loves me?"

I could do nothing but keep on loving him, just as David continued loving him, caring for his room and daily needs, and telling him about Jesus.

Finally Venkatachalam thought to himself: *You'd better listen to these people. They have a right to be heard.* David was the one who very simply and humbly led him to accept Christ Jesus as his Savior and Lord. Suddenly V felt loved! Night turned to bright shining day for him, and he was a new man.

But his physical condition was still critical. The chest surgeon from CMC said that if they removed the diseased lung and if V survived the surgery (and that was doubtful), he might get a few extra months of life. Knowing the risks, V agreed to have the surgery.

On the day before surgery I went to see him in the thoracic surgery unit in Vellore. He was sitting up trying to read his Bible, but it was obviously a struggle for him. When he saw me, the first thing he said was, "Doc, can you find me a really good pair of reading glasses? I can't quite manage to see this and I must." I told him that I certainly could do that for him, but right then I was concerned to know how he felt about the surgery. Did he realize that he was only a short step from heaven? Was he really ready? Was he afraid of it? When I asked him, he smiled—a lop-sided sort of smile because his face muscles were paralyzed—and answered, "Why should I be afraid? Jesus is here with me now, and if I die I shall be with Him forever."

V came through the surgery with flying colors, and in no time he was back on his feet. As soon as he was well enough, he was baptized in the little lotus pool in the courtyard of the leprosy center at Karigiri. At that time he took the name John, meaning "God is gracious."

All that was in 1963, and shortly afterward we went on furlough. While in England, I received a beautiful letter from John in which he wrote, "I'm so glad I got leprosy. If I hadn't I might never have discovered my wonderful Savior, Jesus."

John lived about six months longer. Really lived, witnessing constantly to his new relationship and joy. Then one night he had a massive hemorrhage and very quickly was with his Savior.

Chapter 18

Life Passages

"Mummy, have we had Christmas?"

By 1959 the Vellore Christian Medical College and Hospital was one of the major medical centers in Asia, with 735 doctors, nurses, and technicians. Fifty members of the staff were from overseas. The campus was home to some 800 students in the fields of medicine, nursing, pathology, pharmacy, radiology, public health, and clinical laboratory.

This CMC community in which the Brands lived and worked was made up of a fascinating variety of religions, nationalities, classes, and ethnic groups. The college faculty, while largely Christian, also included Hindu and Muslim instructors. The Christian staff, from a variety of denominations, included Indians as well as westerners. Visiting physicians and other health care workers came from around the globe. Scheiffelin as well attracted medical workers from leprosy programs and hospitals located on every continent.

Besides the medical professionals there were British business people and their families in the area, and in the mountains the English tea plantation owners and staff, along with retired expatriates from the West. There were beggars from the villages, there were Brahmans of the highest caste, and there were untouchables. There were Indian government officials, politicians, shopkeepers, townspeople, and landowners. Some form of English was spoken in most places, but to care for many patients or deal with local issues, some familiarity with the Tamil language was necessary, and in fact was a requirement of the leprosy mission. The person who became the Brand's language teacher was chosen by the Lord for a special reason.

A young man came to Paul one day. His name was Ardikesavelu (Ardi). He was a former leprosy patient whose disease was inactive but who had been left with some hand and foot paralysis. He sought Paul's help to correct the deformities that had stigmatized him and made it impossible to get a job in spite of his abilities. Paul soon recognized that he would be an excellent Tamil teacher. There was an official "pundit" (teacher) hired by the college, but he had not been a great success. He was out of touch with the ordinary everyday needs of the patients. So while Ardi received Paul's care, he also became Paul's language teacher, paid from Paul's pocket initially but later taken on the payroll of the institution.

The Webbs and I soon became Ardi's pupils too, and he prepared us for the Tamil exam required for missionaries. We had five hours of instruction a week and were assigned a good bit of homework. One of the books required for our study was the gospel of Luke. There were many times when we might stop discussing some point of Tamil construction and instead talk about what Jesus was teaching or doing. Ardi was always very reverent and stated that he too believed in Jesus just like he believed in his Hindu gods. We never seemed to get beyond that point. But we enjoyed his lessons and did manage to pass our exam. Ardi went on to teach others and became a respected member of staff, a big change from the despairing man who had first sought Paul's help.

Forty years later when Paul and I were on a brief visit to Vellore, a young man and his family came to see us one evening. It was Ardi's eldest son. Ardi himself had died but had left a wonderful legacy. The son and his entire family had become Christians. They were obviously deeply grateful for the part we had played in that. The son had a good job, spoke excellent English, and was really eloquent as he expressed gratitude to Paul, in his words, "for lifting us out of the gutter." Their gratitude went, above all, to the Lord.

CMC was an invigorating institution, and Vellore a wonderful community in which to live. But Margaret's extended family members were never absent from her thoughts.

Margaret's older sister, Anna, and her husband, Anthony, were in Nairobi, Kenya, in northeast Africa, with Anna practicing general medicine. She and Anthony left Kenya in 1962, when the country won its independence from

Britain, and returned to Cambridge, England, where Anna obtained a degree in Public Health, training similar to that which her father had obtained years earlier. (Their children, Janet and Ruth, eventually took the same University College Hospital medical course that their own parents as well as Paul and Margaret had attended. Janet attended the boarding school at Malvern, as had her mother and her aunts, Margaret and Frieda.)

Frieda was a nurse and receptionist for her husband, Jim, when he opened a dentistry practice in Bulawayo, Rhodesia (Zimbabwe). Their three children attended school in Africa. Jim and Frieda had built a small apartment onto their home, and the senior Berrys moved from South Africa to spend their last years there with family. On a camping trip in 1959 with Jim and Frieda, Dr. Berry died quietly in his sleep at the age of eighty.

Each of Will Berry's three daughters had become professionals, as he had hoped. And they had become model mothers, raising children as bright and fearless as themselves. He took pride in the accomplishments and the spirit of adventure, similar to his own, being practiced by his extended family of sons-in-law and grandchildren on the continents of Europe, Africa, and Asia.

What stands out most in my memories of my father is his great love for wild things. He objected to my mother bringing cut flowers into the house. He thought they looked far prettier in the garden. He knew the names and the calls of so many birds, the names and often the pharmacological properties of so many wild plants. He loved trees.

He respected other people's point of view, and as my mother would often remark, he was a compassionate person. He gave away quite lavish amounts of money to those in need, and he taught us integrity. "If you promise to do something, make sure you do it" was his instruction to us. He modeled that in his own life.

I thank God for letting me have such a good father and look forward to seeing him in heaven.

The following year another death caused deep mourning in the streets of Vellore. In May of 1960, word came that Dr. Ida Scudder had died at the age of ninety. Her body was returned to Vellore from her retirement home in the hills at Kodaikanal, and hundreds from her medical complex as well as thousands of citizens from the city of Vellore and surrounding villages came to participate in her funeral. Although Dr. Ida never married or had children, she became mother and grandmother and great-grandmother to thousands of people. What she had started as a dispensary sixty years earlier had become a world-famous medical college and hospital, yet maintained her original purpose and mission. Her legacy of "audacious confidence in human potential" and trust in the grace of God would continue.

Paul had the honor of giving the eulogy and address at Dr. Ida's funeral. He took for the text God's words to Joshua after Moses had died: "Moses my servant is dead. Now therefore arise, go over this Jordan..." (Joshua 1:2). Paul and I, along with the grieving CMC family, knew well that there were a lot of Jordans to cross, a lot of people to serve, a lot of work to be done. We all also knew that the God who had led Dr. Ida would lead us too.

Paul and Margaret represented the same combination of pursuit of knowledge, service to the needy, and witness to Christ. Typical of this desire to provide service, Paul accepted an offer from the World Health Organization to spend a few weeks in Geneva, Switzerland, for discussions about leprosy and to write a small manual on the prevention and correction of deformities in leprosy. He was given a first-class ticket and a generous grant for expenses. This was a Godsend, for it meant that there was the possibility that Margaret could accompany him and they could see Jean and Christopher much sooner than they had thought when they left England in 1958. The foursome would holiday together as they traveled from England to Switzerland and would have the opportunity to restore the relationship disrupted by the past two years. Mary would leave Breeks temporarily and come back to Vellore to help care for Pauline who, with Trish and Estelle, would be staying with the Webb family. While in Vellore, Mary would attend Vidyalayam to continue her schooling.

Margaret and Paul landed at Heathrow Airport and took the train to Victoria Station in London, where they were met by the Edmunds and what were now the two Brand teenagers, Christopher, age sixteen, and Jean, age fourteen. Paul teasingly stood on a suitcase so that he could look down on his son, who was now slightly taller than he. The Edmunds generously made room for Paul and Margaret in their home until they left for Europe, and the Leprosy Mission kindly lent them a vehicle for the trip. The Brands, used to driving on the left in England and India, headed for Europe.

We planned our route, packed the car (a brand new Vauxhall), and took the ferry to France. We did not have sleeping accommodations, and regulations prohibited staying in the car, so we tried to catch some sleep just lying on the deck. It didn't work too well. So there we were, in a car we'd never driven before, on the "wrong" side of the road, having to read road signs in French (not our first language!) after an almost sleepless night. It was a recipe for disaster, but the Lord was so good to us, and we had no problems. Christopher, borrowing sailing terminology, said of my driving through Rheims, "Mum 'tacked' through Rheims."

Thankfully our driving skills improved as we found our way across northern France, into Switzerland, and so to Geneva. We stayed in a lovely lakeside hotel where the children and I could swim, browse in the local farmer's market, or just enjoy walking around the quaint streets—it was so wonderful being together. When Paul was able to be with us, we took trips up into the gorgeous Alps, which were bright with summer flowers. We also visited the famous Chateau De Chillon where the poet Byron had been imprisoned.

After Geneva we went to Berne to visit Ciba-Geigy, the drug and instrument company. They wanted to use Paul's expertise in developing new drugs for leprosy. They marketed a drug known as B663. Its generic form, clofazamine, is one of the standard drugs today in treating the disease. The company generously gave both Paul and me several expensive instruments for our work in India.

After our delightful Swiss holiday, we returned to England. Paul shortly left for India, but I stayed on until the children returned to school. While there, we went to Bristol to the home of Dr. Kay Blot, who had been on staff in Vellore for a few years. She knew what an adjustment it had been for the children to come and live in England, and she particularly warmed to Jean. She was about to get married and chose Jean to be her only attendant. What a special time that was!

Being with Jean and Christopher had been a blessing for Margaret and helped to make up for the painful separation two years earlier.

৽

Paul and Margaret decided that Christmas of 1960 would be spent at Granny Brand's wee house in the Kalarayan Hills, some one hundred miles from Vellore. Granny, now eighty-one years old, was still continuing with the missionary work in the hills, which she and her husband Jesse had first started.

The trip to Granny's was as arduous as ever. We traveled by car as far as the road went, then by jeep on the rough track to the foothills. From there we walked, took turns on Granny's little pony, which she had sent down for us, or were carried in a dholi by the sturdy mountain tribesmen. From the foothills the climb was more than three thousand feet, and the distance about eighteen miles. Paul walked all of it. I did most of it. Mary and Estelle also walked a lot, but they were glad to take turns on the pony. Trish, aged six, and Pauline just three, were carried most of the way in a dholi. They looked as if they were in a sack, only their heads showing, suspended from long bamboo poles carried between two men. It was at least a means of transport, though not very comfortable.

We had luggage with us too: camp cots, extra bedding, and clothes for a week. We knew Granny had no access to such things as turkey and plum pudding, so we took those, all prepared and ready just to reheat and serve for Christmas dinner. Everything was packed in "headloads," to be carried on the heads of tribesmen.

Before we left home we had had a small Christmas tree with little gifts for each of the children. They knew they would not receive anything up in the hills. It would be a different kind of Christmas, and they were quite excited.

We reached Granny's on Christmas Eve, exhausted and glad to get to bed. But Granny was an early riser, and hours before dawn we heard her singing in her quavering voice, "Christians, awake! Salute the happy dawn on which the Savior of the world was born."

Even though it was Christmas, we were not ready to salute it at 4:00 a.m.! But Granny's call could not be ignored. We got up and had coffee and hot drinks for the children, and soon the local Christians gathered at the little home to sing and recite Scripture. Most of the celebration was in Tamil.

At 8:00 a.m. we had breakfast, and then there was a ceremony for opening the little thatched-roof school Granny had had built. This was the first school in the area, so people came from all around to help celebrate this historic event. Paul gave a little address, which Granny translated into Tamil, followed by many other Tamil speeches. After the opening, which took a long time, we all sat on the grass and were served a simple meal of rice, dahl (a spicy lentil dish), and vegetables. The servings were generous and the people very happy to get it. Our girls helped serve.

After all the guests had been fed, gifts were distributed. Granny had bought several dozen pencils, hair ribbons for the girls, and little spinning tops for the boys. There was something for everyone. Most of those children never got gifts of any sort, so it was a delightful sight to see their eyes light up with joy and quite a lesson for our girls.

The guests left, and we took a much-needed nap, only to be awakened once more by Granny announcing evening "jebbum" (prayer time). We assembled in her tiny living room, where several people from the nearby village joined us. That little community was mostly illiterate, but they had learned songs and memorized Scripture verses and really wanted to know more about the Christian faith. They had recognized something they needed in dear Granny. Not believers yet but inquirers? Oh, yes! And so we sang on and on.

Then Paul whispered to Granny, "It is getting late. Do you think we can make this our last song and we'll go and heat up the turkey and plum pudding and have our dinner?" She agreed. But in the middle of the last song there was a shout—a call for help from somewhere out in the dark.

Granny seized the hurricane lantern and was out the door in a instant. We heard an exchange in Tamil, and in a few minutes a group of mountain men came in dressed only in loin cloths and carrying a bundle—a hastily made dholi. They laid the dholi down gently, disclosing a young woman who appeared to be dead. Granny was down on her knees in a moment, feeling the woman's pulse, her brow, looking at her tongue. "Typhoid," she said. "She needs fluid." She had seen the illness many times before, and she knew the culture of these people. If a person looked bad enough and might die, that person would be put out of the house so that his or her spirit could get away freely. That meant the person did not get food or water and usually would die.

Granny hobbled off into her small pantry and put together a little buttermilk, lime juice, and honey. Then gently cradling the woman's head on her lap she began spooning the mixture into the woman's mouth as fast as she could swallow it—a very slow process.

Uncertain about the diagnosis, Paul moved the children away, both to give the patient more space and also for their protection. The only light in the room was a small hurricane lantern.

The spooning went on very slowly, but the woman seemed to be responding to it. Judging that the crisis was past, Paul said, "Mother, couldn't somebody else do that now? The children are very tired. We can warm the turkey and give them their Christmas dinner as we had promised, so they can go to bed." Granny turned to him and said, quite fiercely, "Paul! How can you talk about turkey when here's a woman dying! You go off and have your dinner, but I'm going to stay here."

With what light filtered through the doorway into the tiny kitchen, we found the turkey (which was cold), and while the girls and I stood around him in the dark Paul pulled pieces off it and handed them to the children. (The expression "cold turkey" now has its own special meaning in our family!)

The meal over, we put the children to bed. As I tucked her up, Trish said, "Mummy, have we *had* Christmas?" When I mentioned this to Paul, he said, "I hope they will never forget this night as being the most real Christmas they ever had."

Christmas 1960 would be memorable as much for the return trip to Vellore as it was for the events of Christmas Day.

Paul had hardly recovered from the arduous walk up the hills when he had to get back to Vellore and then on to Madras to catch a flight to the States. The children and I would stay on a few days with Granny before starting our journey.

Paul gave money to Granny's postal runner (who would make the thirty-six-mile run down to the plains and back in that one day) to buy chloramphenicol to treat the young woman's typhoid infection. The patient, who had spent the night in the little school building, was alert and feeling better after Granny's treatment but clearly was not out of the woods yet. (In the end, she made a good recovery and went home to her family, who had not expected to see her ever again.)

Then Paul gave me the money for our journey and for housekeeping until he returned from the States. We said good-bye, and he left with a young hill man to guide him. I put the money safely away. I did not have luggage with a lock and key, but thought I'd been smart enough in

concealing it. Granny, the girls, and I then went to a nearby scenic spot
for a picnic.

We were not away from the house more than two hours. Sadly, that
was enough time for a thief to go through our luggage very thoroughly,
finding all but thirty-four rupees. Ah well! At least the postal runner had
the money to buy the medicine. It was the only critical thing.

Granny had a few rupees and gladly let me have those. I figured we
had enough for third-class train tickets plus taxi fare from Katpadi
station to our house in Vellore. That would leave us with ten naia-paise—
not enough to buy food, as just a cup of coffee cost about twenty-five
naia-paise, but a generous friend, Regina Hansen, had offered to give us
our evening meal before taking us to the train. If all went well, we'd be
home in time for a late breakfast.

Early in the day we said good-bye to Granny, who had given us food
for a picnic on the way. At the foot of the hill, a jeep met us to take us to
Regina's house. After an hour's rest there, we had a nice meal, made sure
we had enough drinking water, and loaded up for the ride to the train.
It wasn't to a station as such, no platforms to make boarding easy, just a
place where the train stopped. Regina's driver helped us pile our luggage
beside the track.

The train was due in about thirty minutes. It was a pleasant evening.
Mary had been given a pair of bamboo stilts, which she was eagerly
learning to use. The sun set and dark was coming. So too, we hoped, was
the train.

But an hour later there was still no sign of the train. I was getting
anxious about making our next connection. The children had gone to
sleep, draped across the luggage, while I sat and watched for the lights
coming along the track.

At last it came and stopped, but the passengers on board were asleep
and no one would open a door for us. The children were deeply asleep and
nearly impossible to rouse. Finally the conductor saw my predicament
and demanded a door be opened. From where I stood at ground level, the
open door was above my head. I had to help the children climb up or lift
them up, pass up the luggage piece by piece, and finally climb up myself.
Exhausted, but we'd made it so far!

I then sat anxiously watching for the city lights of Salem. The train
seemed in no hurry to get there. Finally we pulled into the station just

as another train on the eastbound track was leaving. It was the train I had hoped we'd be on! After getting the children and the luggage off the train, I herded my sleepy family to the women's waiting room, which was a lounge of sorts where we could wait until a train came through in the morning. It was quite a large room, already full of sleeping women and children, but the girls were beyond caring about the crowding. They just stretched out and were soon fast asleep (the mosquitoes were not asleep).

I roused them early to get a place on the platform so we could board the train that was to arrive at 6:30 a.m. At 7:00 a.m. there was still no train. Then the stationmaster informed me it would be another hour late. That meant I would miss the connection to Katpadi. He told me not to worry; there'd be a train the next evening!

Indian families prepared for such eventualities, carrying provisions for several days. Or they would buy meals at the large stations where hot food was sold and trains stopped long enough. But I had no provisions, almost no money, and four hungry children. At least we had drinking water!

Mary and Estelle were a great help to me. They, too, were hungry but understood our problem. So when the younger ones even mentioned hunger, the older girls immediately suggested another game to play and distracted them for a while.

At last a train pulled into the station. It would take us as far as Jalarpet, and there we could connect in the evening with a train to Katpadi.

A woman on the train had a basket of custard apples, and I was able to buy two for each of the girls. Custard apples have little juice but lots of sugar in them. Just what we needed. We had a contest: "Who could make theirs last longest?" They all settled down to the serious business of eating their custard apples. But just then we pulled into Jalarpet. When I asked if the Katpadi train had gone yet, the answer was, "No, it's just coming in on Platform 3."

Platform 3 was across the track from us. To reach it we had to walk fifty yards along our platform, then up over a footbridge that crossed the tracks to the other side. We could not afford to hire coolies to carry our luggage, so I had to load up the older girls with the heavy stuff (they did a great job balancing it on their heads in a most professional way), gave little Trish as much as she could handle, issued firm instructions to

Pauline to hang on to the back of my skirt, and picked up all the rest of our belongings.

I hadn't gone far when I realized I couldn't feel the tug on my skirt. I looked back. No Pauline! Then I saw a crowd at the door we had just exited, and from somewhere in the midst I could hear Pauline frantically screaming, "Get back!" to those who were trying to get in or out of the train.

In the rush to gather up children and luggage, I had forgotten about the custard apples, but Pauline hadn't. She had dropped hers and somebody had trodden on it. Now she was desperately trying to rescue what she could off the floor. Though the apple was well mixed with the dirt and a total mess, she refused to abandon it.

I left our stuff on the platform, picked up Pauline—covered to her elbows in a mixture of squashed fruit and dirt—and hurriedly carried her over to the other train, gave Mary instructions to try to find some water and wash her, ran back over the bridge to the first train and picked up our remnants of luggage which, praise the Lord, had not been stolen, and so back to the children anxiously waiting my return.

Finally on board, we discovered there were no seats left, so we sat in the only spot we could find—on the floor in the corridor sitting on our luggage. Thus we rode to Katpadi. Hungry, filthy, dirty, tired? Yes, but all well—and with all our luggage still with us. I was so proud of my little "coolies"!

Then a wonderful thing happened. At the station we saw the father of one of our students. He had come to meet a friend and bring him a gift, a tower of bananas still attached to the heavy stalk cut from the palm. He could not find the friend, so he asked if we could use the fruit. Talk about manna from heaven! What a picnic we had in the taxi all the way home!

⌒⌒

Paul was away for about a month, starting the day after Christmas 1960. During this trip, he visited Sweden and various places in the United States. This time his work was sponsored by the World Health Organization and was specifically focused on the subjects of leprosy and reconstructive surgery. Three incidents during his tour would have major implications in the future for him and Margaret.

In New York, at the World Congress meeting for the disabled, Paul received the prestigious Albert Lasker Award, given annually by the (then called) International Society for the Welfare of Cripples to the person who had contributed most to the disabled. Here he had a chance meeting with Mary Switzer, a senior officer in the Department of Health and Human Services in Washington, DC, which would be of later importance.

Paul then went to Philadelphia and finally to Los Angeles, where he presented a paper at the meeting of the American Society of Plastic and Reconstructive Surgery. Here, due to the interest of the eminent University of Pittsburgh plastic surgeon Dr. William White, a plan was formulated whereby several prominent reconstructive surgeons from the United States would go to Vellore to spend time both teaching as well as learning. This would result in Margaret's being hostess to some of the most prominent surgeons in America and would create life-long relationships between the Brands and the American surgical community. Finally, Paul stopped at Stockholm, Sweden, where he secured generous grants from the Swedish Red Cross, which would provide a new operating room at Karigiri and would start leprosy control programs based in Karigiri that extended far into the future.

Paul returned a few weeks later and we all talked our heads off as we shared the experiences we'd had since the morning he left us at Granny's mountain cabin. He brought with him the Lasker award, a beautiful silver-plated replica of "The Winged Victory of Samothrace," and was pleased about the wonderful encouragement for his work that he'd received throughout the tour. About ten surgeons, leaders in their field of plastic and reconstructive surgery, had heard Paul speak and had been inspired to volunteer to come to India, work with him, and share their expertise. Each would pay his own way, stay for three months, and then pass the work to the next. It was to be a wonderful experience for us all.

Chapter 19

Receiving Honors and Guests

"Far be it from me to interfere with Her Majesty's 'good pleasure'."

Early in 1961 Queen Elizabeth II and Prince Philip visited India, her first visit since India's independence in 1947. Paul had met Prince Philip two years before when the prince had visited Madras. Now the queen and the prince were coming to Madras as part of her tour of India, and British Commonwealth citizens in the region were invited to attend a reception, with only a few invited to actually be presented to the queen.

Two years earlier there had been quite a lavish party for Prince Philip when he was visiting India alone, and we had been invited to the function on the magnificent grounds of the British High Commissioner's residence. The prince strolled informally among the thousands of guests and stopped here or there quite randomly to speak with individuals. One of those stops was beside Paul, and they got into a conversation. The discussion soon turned to leprosy, hands, and reconstructive surgery. The prince showed intense interest and Paul found his highness to be "a nice fellow."

This time the party would be even grander, with the presence of both the prince and the queen. The guests would include members of the Commonwealth countries and, of course, Indians. A select few of the attendees would be invited to be presented to the queen. The dress code was quite explicit: National dress for the Indians and formal evening attire for the westerners—which meant floor-length dresses and elbow-length gloves for the women and tuxedos for the men.

All the British and Commonwealth staff in Vellore were invited, but not Paul and me. We were a little surprised but not at all envious. We watched (I have to admit, with some amusement) the frantic efforts of the others to find clothing fit for the occasion. That meant borrowing from American colleagues in most cases.

Then, about ten days before the event, Paul got a phone call from the office of the British High Commissioner in Madras, asking whether or not we were coming. Paul answered that we had not been invited. "Not invited?" was the alarmed response. "But you are to be presented!" (Apparently the invitation was so special that somehow it hadn't made it to the post office along with the rest.)

Now we were the ones frantically searching for something to wear. Paul had no tuxedo, and I had no floor-length dress. All the evening clothes available had been lent out, and Vellore had no fashionable dress store. Even if it had, to spend money buying such things was unthinkable. What were we going to do?

Then dear Ruth Myers came to my rescue. She was a microbiologist and a lovely, humble Christian, concerned about our crisis. Seeing my predicament, she offered me her black velvet dress. Ruth had had polio as a child, and, as a result, one of her legs was shorter than the other. To camouflage this, her dress hems were cut parallel to the floor. Her dress fit me, although the hem looked a bit strange—ankle length on my right side and mid-calf on the left. Someone else lent me a pair of evening shoes, and I found a pair of gloves—not elbow length but at least gloves.

For Paul we borrowed a pair of dark pants from one of the students. They were much too long, but I could baste them up during our ninety-mile car drive from Vellore to Madras. We then borrowed a light sharkskin coat from an American colleague, and I would shorten the sleeves of that too on our journey. We might look like a couple of gypsies being presented to the Queen of England, but this was our one opportunity, and we didn't want to miss this occasion.

With the Gaults, an Australian couple, we set off in our car for the ninety-mile journey. We were about halfway there when the car died. Our efforts at resuscitation failed, so we stood by the road hoping to thumb a lift. Finally a bus came by and we flagged it down. Once the driver heard we were on our way to meet the queen, he wouldn't stop for any more passengers—it became our very own express bus. He knew we wouldn't get through if we didn't hurry because the roads into the city would soon be closed. He kindly delivered us to the house of Dr. Somesakhar, who was to take us on to the party.

Dr. Somesakhar was a well-known practitioner and had several friends who owned tuxedos. When we arrived at his house, he led Paul into a room where he had about fourteen suits hanging, waiting for his selection. Paul was soon outfitted grandly enough to meet anyone. He looked great. I was the one who looked like a Cinderella who hadn't met her fairy godmother.

The grounds at the High Commissioner's place were beautiful, the grass perfectly manicured, the flowerbeds breathtaking. There were about nine couples being presented, and we were lined up alphabetically, which meant we were second in line. We were briefed on all the proper protocol and etiquette involved in meeting the queen. If she wished to speak to us, her assistants would first announce our names. Then she might say, "How are you, Mr. and Mrs. Brand?" We would bow or curtsy and respond, adding, "Your Majesty." If she continued the conversation, we were to address her as "Madam." The bowing and curtsying also had to be done to protocol. The men should take the queen's fingertips and bow over her hand, and the ladies should do a full-bend curtsy, also touching only the queen's fingertips.

The sky had darkened and the bandstand and dais were floodlit when the queen stepped to the front as the band, splendid in their immaculate uniforms, struck up "God Save Our Gracious Queen." How beautiful, how regal she looked! *I'm so glad to be British,* I thought.

I stood in the line, a little nervously, mentally rehearsing the protocol for the big moment. In my younger days I had loved ballet dancing and knew then how to do a perfect curtsy, but this was different. I was wearing someone else's shoes (with high heels) and standing not on a firm surface but on grass with its irregularities. And I was hoping the queen would not notice my unfashionable hemline or my short gloves.

No more time to rehearse. Queen Elizabeth and Prince Philip were now talking to the first couple in line. Our turn next. Our names had been announced! The queen had asked how we were. Paul had done his bow, and I started my curtsy. But as I reached full knee-bend, I felt myself going over on one ankle. All protocol left my mind. I grabbed the queen's hand and hauled myself up. I was so horrified by what I'd done that I totally forgot about "Your Majesty" and" Madam." By the way I addressed her, we might have been sitting across the kitchen table from each other.

Queen Elizabeth asked us what we were doing in India, and I replied that we were working at a hospital in Vellore. "What do you do there?" she continued. I answered, "Teaching" and hastily added, in case she thought I was teaching English, "We teach medical students." "Well, of course" was her response. Not a very satisfactory finish. After she'd moved to the next people in line, I felt like saying, "Let's ask her if we might do all that over again so I can get it right."

But our interaction with Prince Philip was very different. He remembered meeting Paul two years before and asked him a pointed question about getting jobs for patients who had had hand repairs but still bore the stigma of leprosy. He and Paul chatted animatedly, and the queen looked back several times waiting for him to catch up with her.

⁓

As the summer of 1961 approached, an anonymous donor gave money to the Leprosy Mission to pay the airfares for Christopher and Jean to fly to India during their summer break, which was from mid-July to early September. This was the first time the younger siblings had seen their brother and sister in three years.

For me this was the highlight of the year—even bigger than our visit with the queen! Jean was sad but not surprised that Pauline ignored her at first and would have nothing to do with her. Thus it is with many missionary families when siblings are separated for years. Mary remembers, after being away in boarding school for a few months, that Trish said to her when she was doing something upon her return, "Do you think you should be doing that without asking *my* mummy first?" Fortunately these times apart did not leave a permanent scar on our children's relationships. And in this case Pauline was soon accepting Jean's offer to play with her.

Another major event that year was Paul's acceptance in July of the appointment of principal of the medical college, an entirely new layer of duties to add to his activities. This included overseeing the building of a new out-patient department on the hospital campus, for which his training in archi-tecture and construction came in handy. He enjoyed the work but hardly had time for it. At the same time Margaret's household responsibilities expanded as she found herself entertaining the chiefs of plastic surgery of several major American universities who individually began coming to Vellore as they had promised.

In just six years the Schieffelin Leprosy Research and Training Centre at Karigiri had become a world center for leprosy, dedicated to both research in the pathology of the disease and state-of-the-art treatment by medication, surgery, and rehabilitation. It had established an aggressive outreach surveil-lance program that enabled them to find people afflicted with leprosy early and hopefully arrest it before they developed the complications of the dis-ease. Their program became a model for the rest of the world, and the exper-tise of the Karigiri staff now attracted medical professionals from near and far for both short courses and long terms. One component of this exciting work was new insight into the complexities of ocular leprosy, and Margaret had become the main teacher.

Yet despite the professional heights to which Paul and Margaret were as-cending, their simple lifestyle remained unchanged. They lived within the yearly budget granted them by the Leprosy Mission and happily made do with whatever clothing and furniture were available.

The prestigious visiting surgeons from the States seemed to relish the sim-pler lifestyle they found in India. These visitors put up uncomplainingly with mosquito nets, cold-water showers, and the Brand children practicing the piano, which was located in the guest room. On one occasion two visiting surgeons were there, and when the very tall member of the pair returned one day without the other, Pauline asked Dr. Dave Robinson, chairman of the Department of Plastic Surgery at the University of Kansas, "Where's that boy who was with you?" referring to Dr. Erle Peacock, another department chairman.[1]

Paul and Margaret respected and admired their guests, as they did anyone who sacrificed to contribute to the betterment of mankind. But awards for doing so meant little to them. This was no more apparent than when Paul,

---

1. Years later, Mary's husband, Jim, who was training to be a surgeon, found that some of these pillars of American surgery and authors of texts he was studying were known to her as "Uncle Erle" or "Uncle Peter." (In India "uncle" and "aunt" are terms of respect.)

in the summer of 1961, found himself being honored by Queen Elizabeth with the title of "Commander of the Order of the British Empire" (CBE), one rank below knighthood. Had Paul been in England he would have been summoned to Buckingham Palace for the investiture, to receive the title with due ritual. Since he was too busy to attend, the whole matter seemed of little consequence to him. In fact, he forgot even to mention the award or the upcoming presentation to Margaret. She learned of his receiving such a distinction when checking his pockets prior to sending his dirty clothes to the dhobic (washerman).

Paul's shirt pockets were his filing cabinets. But on washdays, when I had to clear them out, I sometimes discovered a letter or two that needed answering. I would then jog his memory. While doing that job one day, I came upon a letter from the British High Commissioner in Madras. It was in reference to the upcoming yearly Queen's Honors List and said, "It is Her Majesty's good pleasure to confer upon you the rank of Commander of the Order of the British Empire." The rest of the letter implied that they wished to know if Paul was willing to receive it (not everyone wants to be recognized like that).

Knowing Paul as I did, I should not have been surprised that he hadn't remembered to mention it to me. That evening when he came in, I asked him about the letter. Had he read it? Had he responded? Well, yes, he had. What had he said? Rather shyly he replied, "Far be it from me to interfere with Her Majesty's 'good pleasure'."

We knew we could not go to London for the investiture, but the British High Commissioner had authority to act for the queen in his office in Madras. Paul felt comfortable with that arrangement; he could just go and pick up the insignia some day when he happened to be in Madras.

A year later, in October or early November of 1962, when Paul had a meeting to attend in Delhi and was returning through the Madras airport, he arranged to stop at the High Commissioner's office on his way home. I wanted to be there for this exciting and momentous occasion and planned to take Estelle with me. Paul tried to discourage me. "There's nothing to it," he said. "I shall just go in, receive the citation and insignia across the desk, and be on my way home. Don't bother to come all that way." Undeterred, I planned to drive to Madras, meet him at the airport, and go with him to the High Commissioner's office.

Paul was to land in Madras on a Monday, but my plans changed abruptly on the Friday evening before when I began to feel ill. By Saturday I had high fever and horrible pain in my muscles. At first I was afraid I had come down with polio, but one of my physician colleagues thought it was a severe attack of dengue fever. Although this diagnosis was less frightening, he warned me not to do anything vigorous for three or four days. A visit to Madras was out of the question. That was disappointing for me and for Estelle, who had been looking forward to it. Dear Alison Webb stepped in and offered not only to take our car and pick up Paul but also to take Estelle with her and to represent the family.

While in Delhi, Paul had stayed in a rather run down, but affordable, hotel. (An important fact to know, as you will soon see.) Alison and Estelle met him at the airport, gave him news of my illness (I was less feverish by then, so Alison could also reassure him about my condition), and they set off for the High Commissioner's residence (the same one where, the previous year, we had met the queen), where Paul assumed he would "run in" and pick up his award.

The place was decorated with flags and bunting and was bustling with chauffeur-driven limousines arriving and letting off fashionably dressed guests such as the mayor with his retinue and all sorts of elite professionals. A band, resplendent in their uniforms, was playing.

"What's this?" a puzzled Paul said to Alison. "Have we come on the wrong day?" But she had figured it out and responded, "Don't you see? It's all for you!" Horrified, he tried to straighten his crumpled suit and tie. Alison too felt very inadequate for the occasion. Only Estelle, wearing one of Mary's hand-me-downs, seemed calm and poised (as Alison related to me later).

Inside the High Commissioner's palatial home a crowd had already gathered, lining the marble entrance hall in the center of which was a long red carpet leading to the stairway. One of the aides informed Paul that the High Commissioner, dressed formally, would come down the stairs and meet Paul at a small landing where the investiture would take place. The HC would unroll a scroll, read the citation (which had been signed by the Queen and Prince Philip), roll up the scroll, hand it to Paul, then hang the medallion around his neck. (The medallion was in the form of a gold cross with a facsimile of King George V and Queen Mary, who had instituted the Order.)

Paul would have to walk that red carpet alone, all eyes on him in his crumpled suit. Just as he was about to start, Dr. Somasekhar—the Indian doctor who had arranged for Paul to have a tuxedo for that earlier ceremony when the queen came—stepped forward and took something off his lapel as he whispered, "You don't need that." It was a bedbug, which had doubtless been his traveling companion since he left the hotel in Delhi!

As the last year of their third term ended and the furlough of 1963 approached, the Brands had three major issues to consider. First, Paul's responsibilities had expanded beyond India. In addition to his multiple roles at Vellore, he had also become an international leprosy and rehabilitation consultant. Increasingly he was being asked to spend time working with leprosy programs in Africa, Asia, and South America, with sponsoring organizations headquartered in America, England, and Europe. India was not the most convenient base for such constant global travel.

Second, if the Brands should leave India, what professional opportunities might be available to Margaret? She was recognized by her peers as an authority on ocular leprosy and had done pioneering work in understanding the disease and the best treatments for its various manifestations. But she was not a qualified ophthalmologist in any medical system, Indian or British. To practice her skills fully in England would require her to do formal training and pass examinations. At the age of forty-three, with six children to raise, the idea of going back into prolonged medical training was not very appealing.

Finally, Mary and Estelle would likely be left in England at the end of the furlough to start boarding school. The Edmunds were no longer available to act as guardians. Hence Margaret and Paul would have to find new guardians not only for Christopher and Jean but also for the other two girls as well.

It was a time of much mental and spiritual turmoil for me, with many questions and no clear answers. Would we be leaving India? Would I say goodbye to my professional career? Or would we return to the work that had become so much a part of me? And what about Mary and Estelle? Mary wanted to go to Clarendon boarding school in Wales, as Jean had done. Estelle didn't. If we left India, should we settle in England? I scarcely knew how to pray about all this and felt quite depressed. The post-viral fatigue I developed at just this time did nothing to help my decision-making.

Looking back, however, I realize that God was leading us in His gentle way.

Chapter 20

Leaving India

"Our times are in His hands."

One potential concern over leaving India—that Paul and Margaret's work would continue—was not an issue. During their sixteen years there they had seen CMC become one of the premier medical training facilities in Southeast Asia, abundantly staffed by a superb Indian faculty. The leprosy center at Karigiri had also become a vibrant and strong facility and was in the hands of excellent Indian administrators and staff. Dr. Ida's dream to train Indians for continuing God's work in South India had been fulfilled.

Paul felt that he had trained enough people and that they could carry on the work without him. Although I hated the thought of leaving India because it was now home to me, Paul and I finally decided that we should return to England.

Paul did not have a job or position awaiting him in England, although the Leprosy Mission was happy to support him as a consultant. He did have a one-year tour scheduled, which would literally take him around the world in his capacity as leprosy consultant with the Leprosy Mission and the World Health Organization, ending back in Vellore for a few months.

Paul planned to return yearly to Vellore for perhaps three-month visits, and it was thought that Margaret would visit as well. But they would not, as a family, return to their College Hill household. They would never again be full-time citizens of the campus community, with little children at Vidyalayam, older children at boarding school in Ooty, patient lists assigned to them at Schell and the hospital clinics, research projects to work on at Karigiri, or students to address at chapel on Sunday or Bible classes Wednesday mornings. They must say farewell to faithful Indian friends and coworkers like Aruldoss and Manomani. It was a leave-taking that signaled the end of a major period in the life of the Brand family.

Although they were a family of eight, the Brands did not have a great deal to pack. Most of their furniture was owned by the college and would be left behind. They did have books and papers, cameras and photos, china, a few Indian items such as paintings and vases, personal items that would bring back sweet memories of those years in Vellore, and, of course, clothes and toys belonging to the children.

Granny Brand came to help with the packing, and although she was now eighty-four years old, she assisted Margaret with the chore of sorting through things accumulated over fifteen years by six children. This process was sometimes difficult, as Granny did not want to discard anything; she had a way to fix or use every item, no matter how tattered. Margaret was comforted to know that nothing they tossed out would be wasted. A short line of people appeared daily to see what Granny might have for them. There was one item, however, that Granny wanted no one to have.

Farewell parties were held, gifts given, and good-byes said. Friends and colleagues prayed with us, asking the Lord to help us in our travels and future choices. Among the many loving farewell gifts we received was a brass statue of the Hindu god, Krishna (the one with several arms). The person giving it thought it would be a wonderful reminder of India, as the statue is commonly seen in Hindu homes and is thought to bring all sorts of good luck.

When Granny saw it, she said, "You must not keep this. You can't even keep it in your house tonight!"

She had been fighting idol worship all her missionary life—people thinking if they had something like that in their home it would bring good luck. I agreed with her, although I felt bad about the person who had given it in love. We found a Hindu family who was very glad to have it.

On the day we departed for Bombay to meet our ship, dear Granny bravely waved us off at the train station. She was confident of seeing Paul and, perhaps, me again, but I think she suspected that it was indeed a final good-bye for her as far as the children were concerned. This was a sad moment for her.[1]

Part of the departure preparation included helping Alison Webb since she, along with her children Philip and Clare, would be traveling back to England with the Brands. Alison was pregnant, and John did not want her traveling alone. He still had urgent work to finish before he could join them. Their two older boys, Michael and Andrew, were in boarding school in India and needed to finish that term. John would fly home with them later.

> We had a pleasant voyage on the *Cilicia*, the same ship that had taken us to India in 1958, and docked in Liverpool in April 1963. Then we took the train to London, where we received a joyful welcome by Jean. (Christopher would be with us before long.) She had had a small job cleaning the chemistry lab at Clarendon School and had saved all her earnings. With that she bought me a wristwatch and Paul an electric blanket.

The family settled once again in Pilgrim Lodge at Kew until a more permanent residence could be found. Easter break was quickly upon them, with Christopher and Jean gathered with the rest of the family to catch up on their experiences since they had last seen one another and make plans for new school assignments when classes resumed in May.

As the mother of this complex brood, Margaret had much to do. But shortly after arriving in England she was struck by a recurrence of the tropical illness that had first manifested itself with fever, fatigue, and muscle pain the previous year, at the time Paul received his CBE award from the queen, and which at the time was diagnosed as dengue fever.

> Settling into life in England was tougher than I had anticipated. I felt incredibly tired, had a low-grade fever at night, a lot of muscle pain, and clinical depression. Some people thought this was entirely psychosomatic. I would get so incredibly tired, and in the night I would have intense pain

---

10. Paul continued to see his mother almost every year when he spent time at Karigiri or Vellore, and in 1974 Jean visited her grandmother when she was in India. But for the rest of the children and myself, this was the last time we saw Granny.

in my legs. I was afraid I would end up with muscular dystrophy and felt a real burden on the family, and on Paul in particular as he tried to cope with everything that was my responsibility.

I was taken to University College Hospital (our old alma mater) for tests, which gave no answers and no conclusive diagnosis was made, except the reassurance that I would get better. And gradually, over the next few months, I did.

A few years later I heard from a family in India of a mysterious epidemic that had hit many of our colleagues soon after we had left the country. Their symptoms were just what I had experienced, and it turned out that the diagnosis was a new viral illness called Chikungunya, which was transmitted by the bite of a mosquito. Since this disease was unfamiliar to doctors in India and England in 1963, they could not correctly diagnose my illness.

With Margaret so incapacitated, Paul threw himself into the challenge of laundry, cooking, and organizing the children to work as a team with chores and assignments. Alison also helped immensely in the effort. Trish and Pauline, with Philip and Clare, were enrolled at St. Luke's School, within walking distance from Pilgrim Lodge. Jean, with cousins Jessica and Elizabeth Wilmshurst, whose parents were still in Nigeria, had come from Clarendon School for Easter holidays to welcome the family. Jean helped her father with some of the household management, put together a trunk of used uniforms and necessary personal items for Mary, and with the cousins began educating (and terrifying) Mary about her new school. Mary felt that she was entering a higher level of civilization, surrounded by proper English ladies, having to worry about everything from etiquette to keeping nylon stocking seams straight.

Estelle was enrolled in the PNEU-based Miss Lambert's School for Girls, a day school at Paddington, which meant a daily commute by train. She too was entering a new life, moving to a high society world where, after coming in from their limousines, the girls would greet Miss Lambert with a curtsy. Estelle could learn to curtsy, but she would not have any chauffeur bringing her.

Once the holidays ended, Christopher resumed classes; Jean and Mary left for Clarendon; Estelle began her daily commutes into London; and Trish and Pauline started their daily walks to St. Luke's.

It was always a joy to bring the children back to England, since the youngest ones could view with fresh eyes what were familiar sights for the rest of the family. On one excursion to the center of London to see the Houses of Parliament, the children noticed the great clock, Big Ben, and Paul explained how during World War II the nine o'clock chiming of Big Ben signaled to the nation that it was time for a moment of prayer. Trish, aged nine, asked, "Who winds Big Ben?" (those were the days before quartz mechanisms and batteries). Before Paul could answer, Pauline, then six, responded, "God does, of course!"

This was a moment of clarity for me, and a precious reminder from a little child that "(Our) times are in His hands" (Psalm 31:15).

How impatient I can be and wonder why God takes so long to answer prayer, to perform on His promises. How often I need to remember that He is the one who "winds up" my Big Ben! His timing is always right!

During the summer break of 1963 Margaret and Paul planned a wonderful holiday camping trip across Europe. Their car, a Vauxhall Victor station wagon lent by the Leprosy Mission, pulled a "pop-up" camper. Besides the eight Brands, the entourage included two of Christopher's school friends. Paul made it clear that "Mummy is not to lift a finger," and with so many willing young people in the group, assignments were easily handed out. It was a relaxing respite for everyone as they camped at eight different sites over two weeks in France and Switzerland and provided a wonderful opportunity for the family to become re-acquainted after so much separation.

After a satisfying holiday, the family returned to Pilgrim Lodge refreshed and invigorated. Margaret, especially, appreciated a return of her energy.

That fall all of the children returned to their schools except for Jean, who wanted to be home for a while to help take care of the younger children and to take a few courses at the local polytechnic college.

Paul found himself in the unusual situation of working full-time with multiple duties and engagements and correspondence associated with such demands, yet without an office or secretarial assistance. He hired a part-time secretary, Joan Hedges. She coped with his correspondence and also helped take care of the children as the need arose. Part of her work involved completing arrangements for Paul's ambitious year of world travel. This was to begin in September 1963 with a trip to Rio de Janeiro, Brazil, to attend the International Leprosy Association Congress. To his delight, Margaret was able to accompany him while Jean stayed with the children. He told Margaret to bring a few slides along in case there was time for her to introduce the subject of the care of eyes in leprosy. Paul was dismayed that her work had never garnered the attention that his had, and he was determined to change that if possible.

> **Paul was moderator of the Rehabilitation session at the International Leprosy Congress. Several speakers went way over their allotted time. Paul tried to rein them in, but to no avail. In the end he had only five minutes to present his own material, all new and important. But he insisted that I take some of that time to talk about eyes. I showed two slides and spoke about corneal ulceration and the awful consequences of blindness to a person without sensation. It was an historic moment. In subsequent international congresses, eye care was on the agenda.**

Paul and Margaret visited several leprosy rehabilitation programs elsewhere in South America, including Venezuela, and then traveled on to the United States, where they visited the only leprosarium in the United States, a research center and hospital managed by the U.S. Public Health Service at Carville, Louisiana, south of Baton Rouge. They also spent a night in New Orleans with an American hand surgeon, Dr. Dan Riordan, who did some work at the Carville facility. It was evident that he and Paul shared a common bond with their interest in reconstructing the hands of leprosy patients.

This was Margaret's first visit to the United States, and from Carville they headed north to several cities in the Midwest, where they had opportunities to build on the friendships established when various surgeons had spent time with them in Vellore. Paul was called on often to speak about his work, and he took those opportunities to introduce his audiences to Margaret's work as well. Sometimes the pair were involved in as many as six or seven speaking engagements in one day.

They then traveled to the East Coast with engagements in New York City, New England, and finally to Canada and Montreal. On the way they were able to stop in Connecticut, where Margaret visited extended family she had never seen.

In New England I met for the first time one of my mother's older sisters, Aunt Kathleen, and her children, Craig and Betsy. How special to feel connected with them!

We talked about New York, which I had scarcely seen. They had a friend who regularly visited the city, and he offered to show me around, so we took the train in together. He didn't talk much and seemed always to be in a hurry. He told me just to stay close and follow him. I did, since I was terrified of losing sight of him for even a moment. But how embarrassing when I followed him right into the men's restroom! That's one of my chief memories of New York.

Paul and Margaret reached Montreal in early November. After a final few days together, she flew back to England, while Paul's itinerary continued to take him around the globe. (He would not return to England until the following July.) From Montreal he traveled to California before heading across the Pacific. At Stanford University he was scheduled to speak on a Sunday morning in the university church. As it happened, that Sunday was just two days after the assassination of President John F. Kennedy, and, in spite of his appeals at how inappropriate it was for him to be in the pulpit, Paul found himself having to find words of consolation for a grieving American congregation.

In Los Angeles, with a seemingly bored talk show host not particularly interested in leprosy, Paul caught the host's attention by remarking that the awful thing about leprosy patients was that so few had pet cats. When the interviewer asked why that should be a problem, Paul calmly explained that without cats there were rats, and the rats would eat insensitive fingers and toes during the night. The host, now on the edge of his seat, was in no hurry to cut short the interview.

Paul continued westward to Australia, where, among other things, he looked at a position offered to him in Sydney. He traveled on to New Guinea, Malaysia, and Thailand. Finally he landed in India, where he spent several months at Vellore and Karigiri. He made it back to England in time for the summer holidays of 1964. Looking ahead, Paul envisaged working one-half year in India and the other half in England for the indefinite future, but Margaret's future professional career was uncertain. More long separations seemed likely.

Both Paul and I recognized that we were into something far bigger than we had ever imagined. While this was challenging and exciting in some ways, it needed careful handling. Separations can put great stress on marriages as well as on parent/child relationships. But help is available.

Some of our separations occurred in the days before the era of easy telephone communication. There were no e-mails, no cell phones to bring instant contacts. But detailed, regular, satisfying letters made a huge difference. Paul was a master letter writer. We read and re-read his as a family. I felt mine to him were a bit loaded with the various parenting problems I was experiencing, but he was very thoughtful and never judgmental in his response. He enjoyed the light, funny stuff too.

There is no doubt in my mind that our relationship to God was the main reason for our separation being bearable. We knew we were doing it as part of the work He had allowed us to undertake, and we knew we were upholding one another all the time. The children too felt they could play a part in this. (Paul was the first one mentioned in their prayers.) We made a point of studying the same scriptures each day and exchanging insights from time to time.

In retrospect, I know we grew spiritually in those difficult times, and we were basically at peace. But what a celebration when reunion came!

⁓

Margaret had returned to Kew in mid-November after an absence of nearly two months. The trip had been a blessing to her and Paul since they had not been alone together for years. Yet it was also wonderful to be home with the children, especially with Christmas now approaching. Margaret was well aware that even with Jean's increasing expertise in meal preparation, as the mother of the family she needed to learn or re-learn how to cook. While in India she had managed the kitchen in terms of supplies and menus, but Aruldoss, who was superbly trained in Western cuisine and able to cook for high commissioners if need be, did the actual cooking.

Many times people ask me how I managed to raise six children and do homeschooling, work as a doctor, do research, prepare and lead Bible studies. It sounds an incredible achievement. But I have to point out quickly that I had help with all the household stuff. Back in England I soon realized how spoiled I had been with Aruldoss to do the shopping and cooking and his wife, Manomani, to take care of the children—washing the diapers and other small items, cleaning the house, and generally keeping things neat—and the dhobie (washerman) to do the general laundry. Now, one thing that was hard for me was learning to cook. I seemed to be unable to predict just when I'd get a meal on the table. I thought I'd never get the hang of it.

For Christmas 1963, our first back in England after many years, Alison Webb and I planned to fix a turkey dinner together. We consulted our recipe books and thought we had everything under control. I had read of a way to get a really delicious tender bird by slow cooking it. I did the arithmetic and had it all ready to go in the oven at the appropriate time. I had stuffed it, skewered it, tied the legs in the proper ways. It should have been perfect.

We planned to eat around noon, but noon came and dinner was not ready. I must have set the oven improperly, and the turkey was not done. We kept our hungry families happy with snacks for a while, not wanting to spoil their appetites. But dinner got postponed and postponed, and it was around 6:00 p.m. when we finally ate. It was good, but everyone was so hungry by then it would not have mattered what we served.

We ate leftovers for several days, until finally turkey soup seemed the best way to finish them off. Paul had given me a blender and, never having had one before, I was excited to try all the tricks it promised me. With that blender, nothing, absolutely nothing, would get wasted. It was a missionary's dream! I would make a fabulous turkey soup, both saving money and making a nutritious meal. And the blender would do it all! There was just one small problem. The blender couldn't cope with the string I had used to truss up the turkey—and apparently I had used a lot. With every mouthful it seemed Mary pulled another piece out of her mouth. She wasn't at all discreet about it either. She kept us quite helpless laughing about it. I wasn't allowed to forget turkey soup for a long time.

I really missed Aruldoss and India and having people take care of the cooking. But, as it was with ophthalmology, I made a start and I learned.

Someone else I soon missed was Alison Webb, as early 1964 saw the return of the Webb family to India. This marked the end of a very special era for our families. Our combined holidays and other social events now would be few and far between but much appreciated when they could happen.

⥾

In late spring of that year, Mr. Newberry Fox, the general secretary of the Leprosy Mission, approached Margaret with the idea of providing the Brand family with a home of their own. He and others at the mission were enthusiastic about purchasing a home for the family in the London area. After looking at several possible locations with Mr. Fox, Margaret favored a semi-detached (duplex) house at 8 Colebrooke Avenue in Ealing. Its main advantage was that it was near a good school for Trish and Pauline. Once Paul returned from India, the decision was finalized. The Brands would move after they returned from their family summer holiday in Ireland.

The Leprosy Mission purchased the Colebrooke Avenue house and paid for some essential remodeling, leaving the Brands with the fun of redecorating and furnishing it. This was a dream come true for Jean, who was excited that they finally had their own home, even if they didn't own the title deed. With her talent for choosing color, fabric, and design, she set about decorating the new house. The family scanned the advertisements in the paper each day, searching for secondhand furniture. They bought a few new pieces, but most came from auctions and newspaper ads. Finally the day came and the Brands moved into their new home. But something was still missing.

Pauline had written to Paul while he was still in India, expressing an urgent longing for him to come home. He doubtless felt very touched to think she was missing him so much. That was until he read her last sentence. "We can't have any pets here. We've got to get into our own home, and we can't do that till you come back so please come soon!"

As soon as we moved into our home on Colebrooke Avenue, the children reminded him of the need to get a puppy or kitten. We got both: Pixie, a four-month-old Scottish terrier, and Rani, a two-month-old Siamese kitten. Great rejoicing!

⥾

The start of the 1964 school year found Trish and Pauline looking very smart in their new school uniforms. Jean had decided on a career in nursing and enrolled in the nurses training program at St. Thomas's Hospital, known as The Nightingale School. Christopher was attending a tutorial school to improve his physics. He was also working at a local hotel doing various jobs and brought home his entire salary to help the family budget. Mary returned to Clarendon and Estelle to Miss Lambert's.

With all of the children now in school, Margaret began working two or three afternoons a week in the outpatient clinics of the Metropolitan Ophthalmic Hospitals. She was usually at home when the children returned from school. But occasionally she had to be away overnight when she did deputation work for the Leprosy Mission, in which case Christopher and Jean supervised the household. Generally there were no surprising incidents, but one in particular has stayed with Margaret.

> Paul was out of the country, and I had to go to Birmingham to address a fundraising meeting. Afterward, I was put up for the night in a local hotel. I remember how cold it was, and I also remember the vivid dream I had that our house on Colebrooke Avenue was on fire. It was so disturbing it actually woke me. What a relief that it was just a dream!
>
> In the morning I took the train back to London and walked home from Ealing Station. As I turned into Colebrooke Avenue, I immediately looked along the row of houses to number 8, relieved to see that the house looked quite normal. That dream was still in my mind.
>
> I hadn't brought my key, so I knocked at the door. Pauline opened the door a crack, took one look at me, and immediately shut it again! "Pauline," I called, "aren't you going to let me in?" From inside came a little voice, "You're going to be so cross with me!"
>
> "Why?" I asked. "You didn't burn the house down." She opened the door and said, "Mum, how did you know?"
>
> What had happened was that she and Trish had decided to move into our big bed, which had an electric blanket (the one Jean had lovingly given us when we arrived back in England). They had turned the setting on high and had not been asleep long before they were too warm. They didn't wake enough to switch it off but simply pushed the blanket further down the bed, where the blanket eventually self-ignited and began to burn the bed! They went to tell Christopher, who was sleeping in the next

room. He was too sleepy to understand their strange story and, assuming they had had bad dreams, sent them back to bed.

Meanwhile, the bedding was smoldering, the smoke getting heavier.

Next they tried Jean, who awoke, quickly sized up the situation, and wisely opened the window, threw out all the bedding, and let the fire burn itself out on the grass below. The two youngest Brands were sent to finish the night in their own beds!

But Pauline couldn't get over it—how did I know about that fire?

The Brands had established a permanent home in their native country with a comforting certainty regarding their professional careers and the children's schooling. They had no idea how dramatically their lives would soon be altered.

Chapter 21

Expanding Horizons

"Come to Carville."

In 1965 Paul had another full year of travel commitments. At the same time, he was being offered two major positions in England: a post leading to chairman at the Royal National Orthopedic Hospital and the chair in orthopedics at his alma mater, University College Hospital. Either position would be a crowning achievement in one's career. Neither, however, would allow him time for the work that he could not abandon: consulting on programs in leprosy and rehabilitation in India and elsewhere in the world and continuing with his leprosy research.

One of Paul's trips that year was to Venezuela, where he was to do a survey for the World Health Organization. He would be gone for about ten weeks, and on his way there he planned to visit the National Leprosarium in Carville, Louisiana, once again. While at Carville, he gave several lectures on the work he'd done in India. At the conclusion of his presentation, he was approached by the director, Dr. Edgar Johnwick, who said, "It is apparent to me that your leprosy patients in India have a better rehabilitation program than my patients in America. I can't accept that!" He then went on to offer Paul the position of Chief of the Rehabilitation Branch at Carville. The U.S. Public Health Service, he said, would do anything Paul wanted in order to have him take the position.

Paul had several concerns. What about being allowed to work in the States with his foreign credentials? Not a problem. What about a place to live? There were staff houses on the grounds that his family could use. What about time to travel for foreign commitments? As much time as he wanted. And what about Margaret? Here was perhaps the key to the decision: Dr. Johnwick promised that Margaret could be head of the eye department.

Paul was introduced to some of the wonderful staff at Carville, such as Chaplain Oscar Harris and his wife Juanita, and the Brubaker family, ex-Peace Corps volunteers who had worked in Nigeria and who had children similar in age to some of the Brands. Chaplain Harris drove Paul around the Baton Rouge area some thirty miles away, pointing out the housing, the shops, and the fine schools and state university. He explained that transportation was available for the children to be taken from the leprosy station to school. To further tempt him, Dr. Johnwick spoke of a boat he owned that he planned to sail out into the Gulf of Mexico; Paul and Margaret could accompany him on some of his trips. Paul had dreamed of just such an adventure all of his life. Dr. Johnwick also mentioned that Paul's daughters could even have their own horses at Carville if the girls happened to be interested.

Before Paul had even departed Carville, Dr. Johnwick phoned Washington and confirmed that all he promised was possible. Paul then sat down and made a tape on a reel-to-reel wire recorder, which he sent to the family, describing this offer. Dr. Johnwick hoped to have an answer as soon as possible, but Paul emphasized that he needed the input of seven others before he could respond.

> Carville looked like a wonderful opportunity, both for Paul and for me, but what about the rest of the family? What would they think about it? Paul mailed us the wire reel recording, describing the offer and the area. We sat around and listened. And listened. To say it wasn't very clear was a masterly understatement. We played it over and over, trying to decipher the critical words. Paul had gone on to Venezuela by then, and a telephone call to him to clarify details would have been costly, perhaps even impossible. So we had to try and figure it out ourselves. Should we go or should we stay where we were?
>
> Christopher, who was now twenty-one and trying to improve his knowledge of physics so that he could pursue entrance into a medical college, had already decided that regardless of what the rest of the family decided, he was going to America.
>
> Jean was understandably troubled. During those five difficult years of separation, she had been sustained by the hope that one day the family

would all be together and in a real home. And that, indeed, was how she viewed that little house on Colebrooke Avenue which she had just finished furnishing and decorating. Also, she was in the middle of her nursing training at the Nightingale School. How could she leave all this?

Estelle was comfortable either way, and to Mary it wasn't going to be a big deal. Furthermore, she had heard somewhere on the tape that it might be possible to keep a horse. That was a strong incentive to go to Carville!

Trish and Pauline would fit in with the American system, but having just gotten them into a prestigious school in Ealing, I felt embarrassed at the thought of taking them out so soon.

For myself, I was excited about the thought of going to America. This seemed a great opportunity for all of us.

Aside from personal implications for each of the family, there was the matter of the house. The Leprosy Mission had generously provided for them and would be understandably distressed if the house were not being used as expected. Fortunately Paul's cousin Dr. John Harris, along with his wife, Elsie, and their children, were due to return for a one-year furlough from their work in Africa. They would be happy to use the house during their year. Even better, Jean could continue to have a room there, a place to come when she was off-duty from the hospital. Estelle, who had only one year left before she would take her O Levels, could live with them and commute to her school in Paddington daily until she took her national exam in July.[1] Mary, who had at least another two years at Clarendon, could regard it as her British base between boarding school and Carville. The house at 8 Colebrooke Avenue could remain "home" for several of the children for one more year at least. Beyond that, there was no clear plan.

Paul returned to a bewildering set of questions from his waiting family as they exhaustively discussed all sides of the issue, positive and negative. They prayed, asking the Lord to guide them in this most difficult of decisions. And in the end, Paul and Margaret decided to accept the offer. They would move to the state of Louisiana in the United States in January of 1966.

The Brands' decision to move to the States did not sit well with the Leprosy Mission, which had sponsored them for the past thirteen years, including

---

1. The O Level exam was a national exam. O Levels are comparable to tenth grade in the U.S., and in many instances was the level at which young students not intending to go on to university would leave grade school and go to a trade school.

the purchase of the house at Colebrooke. They had no spokespeople of the fame and caliber of Paul and Margaret to promote their cause and help raise funds. It did help that this new post would allow Paul to return to Karigiri frequently, one of the mission's premier facilities and projects. Eventually, however, the initial dismay was put aside, and over future years and up to the present a warm relationship has continued.

❧

In early January of 1966, Margaret, Trish, and Pauline boarded the plane for America, a first-time experience for the girls and a grand beginning to their adventure. Upon arriving in New York they were to change planes and fly on to New Orleans, where Paul, who had gone on ahead for some speaking engagements, would meet them.

In typical Brand manner, Margaret's return to the United States was more dramatic than planned. Lunch was served on the flight over the Atlantic, and the menu clearly said "lobster canapé." Margaret was violently allergic to shellfish, but her mind was occupied by the tumult of other things. She took a bite and immediately recognized her mistake.

> I suddenly realized what I might have just eaten, and when I asked the flight attendant if it was shellfish, she answered quite proudly that, yes, indeed, it was Massachusetts lobster. I asked her if she had any antihistamine and she said no. I knew in a few hours the allergic reaction would hit me, and sure enough, as we were landing in New York, I had to head for the bathroom. When we entered the airport I was still feeling awful, and I made a beeline to the restroom as soon as I could. Eleven-year-old Trish had to take charge to get us through immigration and customs.
>
> Between this and my earlier experience touring New York, that city and restrooms are forever coupled in my memory!

In 1966, most Americans would have been surprised to learn not only that the disease of leprosy still existed but also that there was actually a facility for leprosy patients within their own country. As the Brands drove the eighty miles from the New Orleans airport to the Carville leprosy center adjacent to the Mississippi River, Margaret and the girls enjoyed the new sights and looked forward to this next phase in their remarkable lives.

Chapter 22

Settling in at Carville

"Where ya'll from?"

The U. S. Public Health Service leprosy facility, located on a 330-acre plot thirty miles south of the Louisiana state capitol of Baton Rouge, was well off the beaten track. Reaching it required turning off a four-lane state highway onto a two-lane parish (county) road and then onto an almost single-lane road that meandered through the small African-American neighborhood of the community of Carville and dead-ended at the Mississippi levee. On one corner at this T-intersection was the ancient Carville general store, owned by the Carville family after whom the town was named. Turning right one then drove two miles down a narrow road with the river levee looming on the left. Massive oaks lined the right side of the road, and beyond them fields with grazing cattle. A short driveway leading off the river road led to the gate of the fenced facility. Continuing on the river road beyond the facility led only to swampy, uninhabited bottomland.

Immediately inside the entrance gate was a guardhouse, which was manned at all times. No patient could leave without a doctor's permission, and the guard politely checked each vehicle that entered. If unauthorized visitors asked to enter and look around, they were referred to one of the official guided tours that were arranged each day. The guard was also a source of information, able to inform visitors about the facility and its work.

Within the compound and to the right of the gate stood a majestic old building that dated from ante-bellum days (pre-Civil War) and was the original plantation house on the property. The mansion had been renovated and remodeled to house the administrative department of the Public Health Service Hospital. Further to the right were the two-story hospital buildings with wings extending at right angles. Nestled between the spaces created were a white clapboard Protestant chapel and a red brick Catholic chapel. Ancient live oak trees hovered over the buildings, providing welcoming shade during the hot Louisiana summers.

To the left of the gate extended a residential street, one of two running parallel for about a city block, and along these two streets were individual houses, dating from the 1920s to the 1950s, where the staff lived. Down the first street was the large one-story house that the Brands would occupy.

The one-story, four-bedroom house assigned to the Brands was originally scheduled to be demolished. It was the oldest of the staff quarter homes and needed more frequent repairs than the others, but it proved perfect for the Brands' needs and allowed them to reside on the station, which was their preference. On two sides were screened porches, and all the windows had wide, deep awnings to keep the interior cool, although this also made the interior of the house somewhat dark. In the days before air conditioning, the shades along with the high ceilings would have been helpful in the searing Louisiana heat. During their occupancy, the Brands were made more comfortable by window air conditioners in several rooms.

Behind the staff houses and the hospital buildings at the front of the grounds were open fields and meandering lanes, one leading to a small man-made lake stocked with fish—and the station's resident alligator. There was a cemetery, a two-story Bachelor Officers Quarters, and, further back, some old barns where horses could be stabled. The facilities included a nine-hole golf course, a swimming pool, and a tennis court for the staff to use. Near the hospital buildings was a similar golf course for the patients, as well as baseball diamonds and a set of small bungalows for patients who were life-long residents.

While Carville treated and housed those who suffered from an often-misunderstood and disfiguring disease, it was not a depressing place. Huge oaks draped in Spanish moss lined the manicured paths and streets, and modest but exquisite landscaping was provided for each of the staff houses. The street leading to the Brands' house was flanked by giant azalea bushes, which provided a blaze of magenta and other bright colors in the spring. Because Carville was a Public Health Service Hospital funded by federal money, everything was well maintained. And because of its location in the South, the climate and setting were similar to Vellore.

This site, however, had not always been so welcoming. In the 1890s the Louisiana legislature, under pressure to clean up the fetid conditions of a "pesthouse" in New Orleans, declared that those with leprosy would be deposited at this spot. Thereafter, leprosy patients were transported upriver on coal barges from New Orleans. Early residents had no fresh water and were crammed into abandoned slave cabins next to swamps infested with malaria-carrying mosquitoes and poisonous snakes. Two years after this leprosy colony began, nuns of the Daughters of Charity of St. Vincent de Paul order assumed nursing care, with the facility managed by the state of Louisiana. There was much work to be done, including fencing the station, but because of the fear of leprosy among the surrounding populace, most of the work had to be done by the sisters themselves.

Then, a horrific tragedy brought about changes. In the early 1900s, a young Chinese man who was thought to have leprosy was locked into a box-car in one state and sent by rail to another. That state refused responsibility for someone with leprosy and sent the boxcar on to the next state. When the car was finally opened, the man was dead. Recognizing that the individual states and their health departments could not be trusted to care for such unfortunates with this disease, the director of the American Leprosy Mission brought this sad story to the attention of the U.S. Congress, which passed a bill bringing the care of leprosy patients under federal jurisdiction. With the highest incidence of leprosy in the United States being in the South, it was logical for the government to purchase the Carville site for a national center, and it eventually became a part of the U.S. Public Health Service (USPHS).

In 1966, when the Brands came to Carville, the USPHS itself was a vast and busy division of government health services. Its domain included several Public Health Service hospitals, all located at port cities such as Seattle, New Orleans, San Francisco, and New York and responsible for providing care to Coast Guard and Merchant Marine members and their families. USPHS also included the Indian Health Service, which provided medical care to Native American reservation sites. And with the Vietnam War in progress, many bright young men were fulfilling their military draft obligation by bringing their medical skills to the Public Health Service. The surgeon general of the United States was the chief officer responsible for this complex system.

Until 1945, leprosy patients at the Carville facility were forbidden to see relatives or spouses, to fraternize with patients of the opposite sex, to use telephones, or to leave the grounds unaccompanied, and until 1946 they were banned from voting. For decades, in fact, newly admitted patients who were married were advised to divorce so that their spouses could move on with their lives. Guard towers and barbed wire atop the chain link fencing didn't disappear until the 1950s, and the jail on the grounds for housing "escapees" wasn't closed until 1954. Fumigation or sterilization of outgoing mail had been stopped only a few years before the Brands arrived.

Yet in the area of leprosy research Carville had made an invaluable contribution to the treatment of the disease: the discovery in 1941 that the sulphone antibiotic drugs could arrest the disease. This was one of the most significant contributions ever made in the field of leprosy, and credit for this work goes to Dr. Faget, then director of Carville. For the first time in history, patients could be offered treatment, not just support, and Carville was established as the most advanced center for leprosy research in America.

When the Brands came, there were still many patients who had spent the majority of their lives as residents of Carville and many with tales of bad experiences in the "old days." They might be bacteria-free, thanks to sulphones and other drugs, but the deformities caused by the disease had left them marked for life. While their stories reflected the often sad realities of the disease, some did have their amusing aspects, as Margaret learned from one of her patients.

I first met "Harry J." when he was being readmitted for care of his eyes. He had previously been a patient for several years, during which time he and his wife (who loved him but was advised that their marriage was over) divorced. She had remarried.

In going through the readmission formalities, Harry J. was asked for "next of kin." He thought for a moment and then gave a name. When the nun admitting him asked what the relationship was, he thought hard again and then answered, "I guess I'd call him my husband-in-law." The next of kin he was referring to was the husband of his ex-wife.

When Harry J. had previously been at Carville, he had received the sulphone medicine, and his disease had gradually remitted and finally he was discharged. He had no home to go to but knew people in New York, including his ex-wife. He had no intention of disrupting her life with her new spouse, but he did want her to know that he was out of hospital and in the New York area.

Sometime later, he received a letter from her saying that she needed help. Her husband had had a stroke and was bedridden. She had to get a job and earn a living for both of them and couldn't stay home to look after him. She wondered if Harry could come and take care of him.

Harry J. went to live with them, and as he cared for his ex-wife's husband, the two men developed a close friendship. It was not surprising, then, when Harry had to return to Carville for treatment for his eye problems, that he named his "husband-in-law" as "next-of-kin"!

Not many weeks later, we heard that the husband had died. And sometime later we learned that Harry J. and his wife were happily remarried.

Carville was filled with stories—some beautiful and with happy endings like Harry's, others poignant and moving like "Tom's."

If patients were too sick to attend the eye clinic, I would go to their room to treat them. In Tom's room, on the nightstand by his bed, I noticed a beautiful picture frame and in it a photograph of a lovely girl in a wedding dress. The photograph had obviously been cut from a newspaper.

When I asked Tom who she was, he told me she was his daughter, his only child. A friend happened to see her wedding picture in the newspaper and sent it to Tom.

"Tom," I asked in astonishment, "you didn't go to the wedding?"

"Oh no," he answered, "she thinks I'm dead."

I tried to get his permission to trace his daughter and reunite them, but he insisted it was better left as it was.

"Joe's" story had a happier ending. When Joe began having serious eye problems as a result of his Hansen's disease, he began traveling to Carville every few weeks from his home in Florida. It was a long journey, but he refused to see a local ophthalmologist because he didn't want to tell him about his disease.

Joe's daughter and her two children lived with him and his wife. His wife knew Joe's diagnosis, but his daughter did not because Joe was afraid that if she found out, she would immediately take his precious grandchildren and leave for fear they might "catch" the disease. When he came for his check-ups, he told his daughter that he was going on a business trip to New Orleans and gave a phone number (one of his friends) where she could reach him.

I could see that this "double life" was doing Joe no good and pleaded many times with him to tell his daughter the truth. He resisted for weeks, but finally did it. Next time I saw him, he looked different, unburdened. And with good reason. When he told his daughter the truth, she said, "Dad, I knew something was wrong and I was afraid you were running from the police. What a relief that you've only got leprosy!"

By coming to Carville, Paul was in a perfect position to build upon his accomplishments in the field of leprosy. As a result of his last tour of the States and with major reconstructive surgeons from the U.S. spending time at Vellore, Paul now found himself with many friends among the leaders in American reconstructive surgery, and they welcomed him as a colleague. In fact, his reputation in the field was at that time better known in America than in England, and along with his new responsibilities at Carville, his commitments to Vellore, and consulting for the World Health Organization, he could now move among the major universities and surgical associations in the States, participating as guest professor or speaker.

Unfortunately, the staff surgeon at Carville, perhaps understandably, was intimidated by Paul's presence, and the politics of the situation made for a difficult start. Dr. Johnwick, the director of Carville who had first offered Paul the position, had died unexpectedly of a heart attack before the Brands arrived. The incoming director, who had not met Paul, was persuaded by the staff surgeon to re-write Paul's job description and title. Paul would not be in charge of both surgery and rehabilitation as expected but would have responsibility for rehabilitation alone. The offer for Margaret to be head of the eye department still stood.

The staff surgeon insisted that Paul not do any surgical work at Carville but confine himself to the role as Chief of Rehabilitation. At that same time, Paul was getting offers for prestigious positions such as Chairman of Orthopedics at Stanford University medical school and a similar position at Loma Linda University, and we began wondering if we had made the right decision. Had there also been an opportunity for me to continue ocular leprosy work at either of those hospitals, we would very likely have left Carville after that first year. Eventually, after about three years, a wise assistant director intervened, got the USPHS department in Washington involved, and Paul was given the responsibility for which he had come to Carville.

As head of the eye department, Margaret was the first full-time ophthalmologist Carville had engaged. Dr. Jimmy Allen, who was Chairman of the Ophthalmology Department of Tulane University Medical School in New Orleans, had a keen interest in leprosy work and had given much of his valuable time to work at Carville but was limited by his other responsibilities. He continued to come once or twice a month as Margaret's consultant. He also had her appointed an Assistant Professor of Ophthalmology at Tulane so that students, residents, and others could study with her and get credit for that training.

Because Margaret was not board-certified in ophthalmology, she did not do cataract and other intraocular procedures; those Dr. Allen performed on the days he came to Carville. But he was glad to entrust her with any nighttime emergencies, which saved him a long trip from New Orleans.

Margaret's new job included being put into the on-call rotation, which made for an unusual first day of work.

> After a brief period of orientation in the workings of Carville and of my department specifically, I started my new post. One thing my orientation had not included, however, was information about the duty called "Medical Officer of the Day (MOD)." It was a simple system. The ordinary office hours for all personnel were from 8:00 a.m. to 4:30 p.m. After those hours, one of the doctors would be on duty to take care of all emergencies. A list of MODs was posted at the guardhouse, and the guard called up the assigned doctor if needed.
>
> I was still very jet-lagged and had gone to sleep early when the phone rang. "Is that Dr. Brand?" the voice asked. "You are the MOD tonight, and you are needed over in the recreation room. One of the patients has armed himself and is running amok. Would you come over right away and subdue him?
>
> I thought I must be dreaming. I had no idea what a MOD was, where the recreation room might be, how a patient could get armed, and with

what. But even if I had known, what good could I possibly be in that situation?

I turned helplessly to Paul. He took the phone, and the upshot was that someone else—one of the tough male physicians—was called.

Like a refrain, the words came back, "You'll learn, please start."

The Brands had arrived in the middle of the school year, and one of the first priorities was to enroll eleven-year-old Trish and eight-year-old Pauline in school. The nearest public school was the kindergarten through twelfth grade school in the town of St. Gabriel, which was the "white" school. (This was still the days of segregation.) Several children of staff members living on the hospital grounds attended St. Gabriel's, and the school bus included the leprosy center as one of its daily stops. Black students went to Sunshine School, which was further away. For Trish and Pauline, who had just left the posh Notting Hill School for Girls, it was quite a culture shock to find themselves in an American public school in the Deep South.

Another part of the new culture the Brands faced was the language of America and of the South. Though the English-speaking Brands were in an English-speaking country, certain words had different meanings, and the difference between Louisiana and British accents could make communication difficult.

It was our first week in Carville. We needed an iron, so off we went to Baton Rouge, our nearest major shopping center. We went to a dime store, where their prices were in an affordable range, and checked the line of appliances, looking for an iron that had some sort of guarantee. We couldn't find one, so finally Paul went to the cashier with an iron and asked, "Does this iron come with any sort of guarantee?"

He may as well have asked how to get to the moon. She just looked at him in astonishment. So I went over to try and help her understand. Still no answer. Then came her question: "Where ya'll from, Boston?" She wasn't being flippant. It was a serious question. "No, we're from England."

Again that look of astonishment. "From England!" We might as well have come *from* the moon. She set the iron down and turned to the other sales clerks as she bellowed across the store, "Come on over y'all, come and hear these people talk!"

We felt like "Exhibit A" as we tried unselfconsciously to tell them we had come to work at Carville. That made sense to some of them. They then began questioning us about leprosy, which gave us the opportunity to do some educating, so the trip was not wasted. We also brought home a cheap iron—with no guarantee, but it served us well.

At Pauline's school a teacher, a dear lady, Miss Sadie, was quite intrigued with her British accent. "Oh, Pauline," she said, "I hope you never lose that lovely accent." It took Pauline a moment to figure out what she'd said. Then, in a very clipped British accent she responded, "I'm going to lose it just as fast as I jolly well can."

Pauline had to learn that if you need to correct a mistake in your writing, you don't use a "rubber," you use an eraser. And if your want to keep your feet dry in wet weather you wear rubbers, not "wellies" (Wellington boots).

Gradually we all learned American terminology.

While the Brands' accents were foreign to their neighbors, the reverse was also true. On one occasion Margaret thought it was nice that one of the workers at Carville was going to go "hunning," which she took to mean gathering honey in the woods. She was quickly informed that he was looking for rabbits, not bees.

The approaching Easter holidays meant that Mary and Estelle would be coming for four weeks to visit and to see Carville and their new home for the first time. The girls were asked to bring several items with them, most notably Estelle's special pet, a Siamese cat named Rani, and fishing poles. So on their first trip on an airplane, they were by themselves, and their carry-on luggage included a portable kennel with a cat inside. From London to New York and New York to New Orleans any number of people must have wondered what these two were up to, traveling with a cat and fishing poles. Mary and Estelle kept hoping that someone would ask so that they could casually mention that they were on their way to a leprosy colony.

Estelle and Mary saw Louisiana at its best in April with gentle rains, cool evenings, azaleas in bloom, and spring returning life to the fields and bayous. They were left to entertain themselves, however, since the Easter holiday in the States was no more than a long weekend (as opposed to a few weeks in Britain) and their younger sisters were at school all day while their parents were working. The two resorted to spending time at the hospital, watching their mother work, meeting patients, playing with the hand-pedaled wheel-chairs parked along the outdoor walkways, and visiting with the lab animals. In the States, both of them were old enough to drive, since age sixteen, not age eighteen as in England, was the legal requirement, and they were happy to take advantage of this difference between the two countries' motoring laws.

During the subsequent summer holidays, Mary and Estelle once again returned to Carville, along with Jean, and their first summer in the States was a glorious time for the family with everyone together again. In September of 1965, Christopher, who had spent some time touring the U.S. on his own (by bus), enrolled at Louisiana State University at Natchitoches, about two-and-a-half hours' drive from Carville, and came home to Carville for vacations.

Exploring a new place had always been a favorite family pursuit, and now they had the Louisiana bayous, plantations, and a variety of unfamiliar flowers, shrubs, and trees as well as birds and other wildlife such as armadillos, skunks, possums, and alligators. There were the cities of Baton Rouge and New Orleans some distance away, and the grand old Mississippi River just outside the front door. They could take a ferry across the Mississippi near the Carville General Store and on the other side drive south to Land's End where the road did, in fact, end. There were strange foods, unusual dialects, Cajuns, African Americans, and Southern high society. And there was this foreign American culture to learn. Television, radio, coinage, music—everything was different. Ironically, at a time when the Beatles' "British invasion" of America was in full swing, the young English Brands didn't have much familiarity with what the young Americans were so excited about. Popular culture had never occupied their time.

With Carville now the base of operations for the Brand family, Paul was free to continue his trips abroad under sponsorship of organizations such as the World Health Organization and the Leprosy Mission. The USPHS encouraged him to embark on these overseas leprosy projects, representing America's commitment to the problem of the disease worldwide.

The Africa Leprosy Rehabilitation and Training (ALERT) program in Ethiopia required that Paul make an initial trip of two or three months, with subsequent ongoing trips of support. His task was to train an orthopedic surgeon, Dr. Luther Fisher, in the area of reconstructive hand and foot surgery for leprosy patients. India also required frequent visits, increasingly confined to Karigiri rather than Vellore after he joined the board of Karigiri in 1971. He also visited Venezuela to follow up on the work he had started there in 1965. Paul was in constant demand both at religious conferences and medical conferences. His secretary at Carville found herself filling his calendar two years into the future, booking flights and hotels throughout the United States and around the world.

> On one February evening at home, Paul answered the phone. He was being invited to speak at a weekend event in October. I heard him ask, "October? Which year are you talking about?" His question apparently surprised the caller, for Paul went on to respond, "I'm sorry, but all my weekends in October this year and next year are already booked."
>
> I, too, was getting more invitations to speak. And we were both enjoying the home side of this new adventure. We were both working full time but without the domestic help we had had in India. Shopping required a thirty-minute drive to Baton Rouge, so it became a much-anticipated weekly family outing on Saturdays.

At Carville Dr. Margaret was receiving salary and benefits befitting her stature. No longer was she considered the "honorary ophthalmologist" as she had been at Karigiri. As she had done there, she began a longitudinal study, eventually lasting twenty-two years, which followed specific leprosy patients with ocular disease. She examined the eyes of these patients every three to four months, recording small changes that gave clues to the mischief the mycobacteria were causing on a chronic basis as well as what effect aging had on patients with ocular leprosy. At Carville she could photograph her findings, which greatly enhanced the value of the study.

Another benefit was that in Dr. Jimmy Allen she found a wonderful colleague with whom she could share her insights. He brought his years of knowledge to the problems they were treating but always was ready to listen to Margaret's view and recognized her extensive experience with ocular leprosy.

Margaret's situation at Carville was convenient in many ways. She could walk the two blocks to the eye clinic, spend half or full days at work, and by late afternoon be home with the children and the rest of her domestic responsibilities. She found that even her cooking skills were improving. Like her mother before her, she began making her own bread, using a recipe of her own design. With whatever time might be left, she worked on the overwhelming amount of correspondence she maintained with absent children, extended family members, and friends abroad. Paul embraced computers early on, but Margaret stayed with her trusty manual typewriter.

In the evenings we would occasionally watch a television program, but not often. Paul did most of the vegetable gardening, while I did the flowers. I knitted a great deal and wrote letters to the absent children. Weekly correspondence was important to all of us. Letter writing, which was something I enjoyed and looked forward to, was a big part of our recreation. I would write part of the letter and Paul would write a part of it. Whenever possible, Paul and I did not open a family member's letter without the other one being there to enjoy it at the same time.

Margaret had never forgotten the importance her childhood letters held for her father and saw personal correspondence as the most crucial element in maintaining a sense of family among her scattered children. Though the children might not write to one another, they were loyal in writing home, and Margaret undertook the Herculean task of typing up each child's letters as they arrived and sending carbon copies to the rest. The fact that the writer would frequently get his or her letter back with corrections in the margin by "Ed." (editor) didn't diminish their desire to continue writing home. For decades everyone in the family received a packet from "Mummy" with their siblings' letters stuffed inside. It was a brilliant and successful plan, and as a result, none of the children felt uninformed or alone. On the contrary, this effort only reaffirmed how deeply their mother loved them and how much they were in their parents' thoughts every day.

Carville was a small community, and Margaret and Paul made many life-long friends there. The couple that became closest to Paul and Margaret were Oscar and Juanita Harris. Oscar was the hospital's Protestant chaplain and Juanita the pianist, organist, and choir director of the Protestant chapel on station. Their faith was as pure, strong, and uncomplicated as the hill missionaries in India, and with these two the Brands found a common bond. Oscar rejoiced at having such a family in his congregation, and the Brands rejoiced in celebrating with him every Sunday that they could. Margaret joined Juanita's choir, and over the years the Brand children participated during the times they lived at home. While many of the staff at Carville attended the church, this station community was a government facility, not a missionary group. But this church family of Oscar and Juanita's—later led by Pastor Ray and Wanda MacPherson—with a loyal group of faithful patients, along with the Catholic chaplains such as Father Kelly, Father Jerome, and Father Reynolds, and many of the nuns working at Carville, provided a marvelous population of witnesses.

During the Brands' first years at Carville, the Brubakers lived across the street from them. Dr. Merlin Brubaker was the director appointed after Dr. Johnwick died. The Brubakers were about the same age as the Brands and had also had experience overseas. Merlin and his wife, Polly, had four children: Judy, who was Mary's age, and three younger boys, Jon, Jimmy, and Joel. Judy Brubaker had a horse, Black Gal, and Trish yearned to have one, too. Daily she scanned the advertisements in the newspaper and eventually found a little Welsh pony for sale.

Peanuts was past his prime but still an active healthy little guy, just right for Trish. She totally lost her heart to him. We spruced up the old barn behind our house and made it into a comfortable home for Peanuts and Black Gal. The kids spent every weekend cleaning the barn, cleaning tack, and exercising the new friends. When Mary became the proud owner of a lovely mare, Kumari (a Hindi word meaning "Princess"), and a horse called Big Boy, we had horses enough (owned or rented as needed) for anyone who wanted to ride when the long school vacations came around.

Horses were not the only animals in the family. The Brand menagerie provided delights for everyone. There was Rani the cat and her kittens, Honey the collie and her puppies—and Simon the skunk!

Judy Brubaker's boyfriend found a tiny, orphaned baby skunk in the forest—its mother had been shot—and brought it to the Brand girls. The little skunk still had its eyes closed and had to be fed by eyedroppers and baby bottles. The girls named him Simon, and early on he accepted Mary as his surrogate mother, trailing after her in a comical way. Honey the dog was terrified of him, having experienced firsthand what these creatures could do. Rani the cat tried to put him in his place, but he was unperturbed.

As Simon grew and developed the typical skunk posture—head and shoulders low to the ground with rear-end sticking up—he began to resemble the shape of a particular style of French Citroen automobile. Therefore, befitting his full-grown size, he received the full-grown name of "Simon Citroen Deux Cheveaux." Early on he was taken to a vet to have his spray mechanism removed, but he was not aware that he could not spray. He would go through the motions: head down, tail stiffly up, moving backwards towards his supposed foe while drumming his front feet on the ground. Any animal with skunk experience, like Honey, lost no time in getting out of range. It was amusing to the family but not at all funny to her.

We enclosed a small tree and the shrubs around it, hoping Simon would find that a nice home. He did for a while but then got bored and dug his way out. Then there was no telling where he might roam.

He was an ecumenical skunk. One time it was the Catholic chapel (the confessional box no less) that attracted him. On another occasion it was the Union Protestant Church. He nearly gave Juanita Harris a fit. She was practicing the organ and spotted a tail projecting out from behind the drapes on the platform. Before she called an emergency crew to come and catch him, someone suggested she might try calling the Brands first. When she did, we discovered Simon was missing. Mary went to the church and called his name. He came at once, glad to be found and snuggling up under her chin as she carried him back to his quarters.

On another occasion he found his way into the ladies restroom in the recreation building. That too gave several people a shock. Once again the Brands were alerted, and Pauline and I went to check. Sure enough, it was our wanderer. Again, it was so apparent that he felt lost and was delighted to be retrieved and carried home under Pauline's chin.

Our experiences with Simon gave me new insights into God's sense of humor!

Simon, Honey, Rani, horses, children, flowerbeds, vegetable gardens, correspondence to and from exotic locales, music-making, a parade of new staff and visitors, choir and violin practice, sewing, bread-making, putting up preserves, keeping the marmalade supply ahead of the demand—the Brand household was a joyful bustle of a house, a most wondrous gift from God.

Some of our most joyous occasions were our Sunday evenings together as a family. Generally we worshiped with the patients in the Union Protestant chapel on Sunday mornings. But in the evenings we would gather in our living room, and if we had guests they would join us. We had acquired some music books called *Youth Praise,* a nice blend of traditional and contemporary melodies. Someone would play the piano and sometimes I would play the violin. In unison or harmony we sang and sang.

Paul would lead us in a devotional and then came prayer time. Everybody had suggestions for prayer needs and everyone would pray. Those family members absent at that moment got special mention.

Unforgettable evenings! Looking back on those years, those times were some of my greatest joys.

I have often been asked about Paul's and my spiritual walk. Whether we prayed together, and did we find that absolutely necessary?

Paul and I prayed together all our married life. At the very beginning, on the night of our wedding, we knelt together and read from the Psalms. We started having a devotional time together at night because that was the time we were less rushed. When Paul was away on his travels, I continued my nightly prayers—and I had a lot to pray about with six children!

When the children were at home, once breakfast was finished I would hand the Bible to one of the kids and ask them to read a few verses before they would head off to school and I to work. I would then pray a short prayer. We always had a devotion, usually led by Paul or me, whenever a family member was returning to their home after a visit, or if the family was about to travel. In our house we called these short prayer gatherings "jebums," a Tamil word we learned from Granny Brand.

By the end of their first year at Carville, Paul and Margaret agreed that this was the best place in the world they could have chosen. In the summer of 1966 Estelle left England and came to Carville, where she then attended eleventh and twelfth grades at the university lab school at Louisiana State University (LSU) in Baton Rouge. She, like sisters Trish and Pauline, had to adjust to a style of education and a culture quite different from that which she had left, but, as was true for the rest of her family, she was able to adapt without difficulty.

I think those were the happiest years of Estelle's education. She made many new friends and joined in extracurricular activities such as drama and singing with great enthusiasm. This was a joyous surprise to us as she had been a bit shy to express her own talents.

In July 1967 Mary, too, joined the family at Carville. She had completed her final A Levels year at Clarendon, which meant that she was ready for university. After years of short home visits, she could now live at home for the indefinite future, commuting to the LSU campus in Baton Rouge to begin college. She and Judy Brubaker became fast friends and eventually both went on to study nursing together. Christopher was now studying zoology at LSU Natchitoches. He thoroughly enjoyed living in America and the opportunities it offered, as well as such sports as kayaking and scuba diving.

Only Jean remained in England. When she attended the Keswick Convention, an annual Christian event in England, she felt called into mission work. After she completed her nurses training in 1968, she enrolled at London Bible College to pursue a bachelor of divinity degree.

Although Jean could only visit Carville infrequently, her presence was felt in the clothes she helped her sisters make, the curtains hanging in certain rooms, and especially in a special project one Christmas.

Paul and I were at work one day, a week or so before Christmas. Jean had come from London and was helping put up decorations. Back in India the children had learned an interesting way of making paper chains, and Mary was quite an expert in this, so she created something special for the celebration.

Jean had other ideas. She found my ragbag containing scraps of fabric from various dressmaking projects. With just a pair of scissors, a needle

and thread, glue, and some bits of pretty-colored foil or wrapping paper and ribbon, plus a lot of creativity, she went to work.

When we returned home that day, we were welcomed into the living room and there found four newly created banners: Joseph and Mary and the manger, complete with the ox and donkey; the shepherds, dozens of sheep, and a bright light shining on them; angels with aluminum foil trumpets flying through the star-lit night sky; and the three magi with their gifts (also from various colored foil).

More than forty years later, those banners are still my main decoration for the special season. Needless to say, they are handled with great care!

Paul and Margaret's extended families were still far-flung. Paul's sister Connie and her husband David had retired from their mission work in Nigeria and were living in south London. Paul's mother, Granny Brand, was still in India, and Paul's return visits to Vellore and Karigiri allowed him ongoing personal contact with her. Margaret's mother was in Buluwayo, Rhodesia, living with Margaret's sister Frieda and her husband Jim. Margaret's sister Anna and her family had left Kenya and settled in Cambridge, England.

In 1967, Margaret's eighty-year-old mother began suffering failing health, and in late February Margaret traveled to Africa to see her mother for what would be the last time.

My sister Frieda wrote that if I wanted to see Mother while she could still recognize me, I should come soon. The weather in Rhodesia (now named Zimbabwe) was pleasant, the flowers beautiful, and as always it was great to be with Frieda and Jim. But the great disappointment was that my dear mother didn't know who I was or, really, who she was. She spoke to me very deferentially, addressing me as "Dr. Brand." I would try to get her recalling incidents of our childhood in South Africa, and she remembered those but could not make the connection between her little girl Pearl and the person she now called Dr. Brand. After a week I had about one hour with her when she knew who I was, and she felt so bad that she had not recognized me until then. Only one hour, but thankfully I had that.

Looking back on those days when we sat together, I am reminded of something else for which I am truly thankful. It reassures me that we shall meet again.

I was telling Mother about experiences at Carville and, in particular, about a Chinese patient called Harry Fong. Because of leprosy and then a stroke affecting his whole right side and speech, he could not speak or show any facial expression. He had only half of one finger left out of his ten digits. He felt truly distanced from us all.

I had never known Harry in better times. And I'm ashamed to say I had not made the effort to do so now. I was too easily affected by his apparent unresponsiveness and had not thought enough about the helplessness and loneliness inside him.

Harry was wheeled to the eye clinic every few weeks. He had scarred corneas but was not otherwise deteriorating. His sight was poor, but he could read large letters. I would make a note in his records and let him go back to bed.

Chaplain Oscar Harris told me that at one time Harry came to worship but had given up on that after his stroke.

One morning Oscar came to tell me that Harry was dying. I was busy in the eye clinic, but suddenly Harry became the most urgent concern for me. Was he ready to go? Did he know the Lord loved him? If so, had he ever told anyone of that? I excused myself from the clinic.

I found a large piece of strong paper and on it wrote in three-inch letters: THE LORD IS MY SHEPHERD, writing the word MY in red. I took the paper to Harry's room. He seemed asleep, but I bent close to his ear and asked him if he remembered the Twenty-third Psalm. I started to repeat the psalm, and he seemed to understand. Then I showed him the words on the paper and, pointing to the red letters, I asked him, "Harry, is Jesus *your* shepherd? Do you know He loves *you*?"

While I told Mother about Harry, I watched her face. She was listening intently and suddenly interrupted. "And did he?" she asked with real concern. I answered, "Let me tell you."

Harry could not speak a word, but he could grunt. He could scarcely control his hands, but he had enough strength to make some movement as he sort of jabbed with his half remaining finger toward the words, especially the word MY. And even though his face could show little expression, at that moment he seemed radiant. I just knew he was trying to say that Jesus was indeed the one he trusted.

I hung the text on his I.V. pole and returned to the clinic. Several other people visited him as the day went on, and each one was impressed that Harry was grunting and jabbing at the message on the paper. It was his testimony.

Harry went to be with *his* Good Shepherd the next morning.

As I finished the story, my mother looked at me and then said, with great relief, "I am so glad." I could tell she meant it. That was her testimony!

My mother died of pneumonia in September of that year and was buried in Buluwayo. My father had been buried in South Africa, in Bloemfontein.

As the end of 1967 approached, so did the end of the Brands' initial commitment to the Public Health Service. They had to decide whether to renew their contracts for another year. The Public Health Service had been true to its word in allowing Paul almost unlimited leave in order to travel throughout the States and the world, and Margaret had her own eye clinic within walking distance of the house. Four of the girls were living at home, and Christopher was nearby. They had made good friends both on the station and in Baton Rouge.

By this time we knew Carville was a good place for us to be. Paul was becoming excited about the opportunity to devote time to research, especially starting a quest to find a substitute for the sensation of pain, which our patients had lost due to leprosy.

Paul was convinced that insensitivity was the key to the chronic ulceration of feet that leprosy, as well as diabetic, patients suffered. He wanted scientific evidence to show the world, and he wanted to find a substitute for that precious missing piece. Carville was surely the place for such research. But he needed help, in the form of personnel and equipment, and those were not in the budget.

Paul and Margaret renewed their contracts with the USPHS, not knowing that the budget for Paul's research section was about to change dramatically for the better.

Chapter 23

Trust and Triumph

"I can't see. My battery's dead!"

When Paul received the Lasker Award in 1961 in New York from the World Congress Meeting for the Disabled, he became acquainted with another recipient at the ceremony: Mary Switzer, Commissioner of the Department of Vocational Rehabilitation for the Department of Health, Education, and Welfare (HEW) of the federal government. As the two waited backstage for their moment in the ceremony, they discussed the work that had brought them together, and Mary found in Paul's work a level of insight and innovation in the area of rehabilitation that had not been seen in this country. She did not forget their conversation, and when she later learned that Paul was now on the staff of a U.S. Public Health Service facility, which meant she now had the authority to financially support his work, she came to Carville with an entourage. By the end of the visit she had made a commitment that would propel the Rehabilitation Branch at Carville to world-class status.

> Mary, who herself had accomplished good things for disabled people in the States and was highly respected by other leaders in Washington, was most interested in Paul's work. When she and her assistants visited Carville and Paul laid out his hopes and plans, Mary took them right to heart. Before she left she had promised him the most generous assistance imaginable.
>
> Mary's visit was very exciting for Paul as he saw the possibility of

realizing a great dream. With Mary Switzer backing him, he could ask for anything he needed. She had total confidence in his using her assistance wisely.

Put into the spiritual perspective, I understand better what Jesus meant when He said, "Whatever you ask in my name, that I will do that the Father may be glorified in the Son"(John 14: 13).

Dr. Margaret also benefited professionally in many ways from her new position at Carville. In 1967 the Public Health Service sent her to the Panama Canal Zone to lecture and hold clinics for the military medical staff there on tropical diseases of the eye. She enjoyed visiting a new place and especially enjoyed one task they allowed her to perform.

After my professional responsibilities were over, I was given a tour of the famous Panama Canal control room. I was awed by the array of buttons —such little things but with such potential power. While I was in the control room, one of the gates had to be opened to let a large ship through. As I waited to see that happen, I was shocked to hear them ask if I would like the honor of pressing the button. My next thought was, *Suppose I press the wrong button?* Of course there were plenty of competent people standing around to make sure I didn't do that.

With one little finger on one little button I made a huge canal gate swing open. It gave me an awesome sense of power—but only for a few minutes!

Margaret's staff appointment at Tulane Medical School allowed her to connect with colleagues in the ophthalmology department there, but more importantly to work with residents in the training programs. Her lectures on ocular leprosy became part of the department's curriculum, and residents would travel to Carville to spend time with her, which was a benefit to her as much as to them. And in 1968 she presented a paper on ocular leprosy at the International Leprosy Association meeting in London.

Although Margaret was being invited to present scientific medical papers at meetings and to lecture to residents and other physicians, she also saw a need to educate other health care providers on a much more basic level. Some of those brave souls worked in remote areas where specialists were often unavailable. Yet there were simple things they could do if they received instruction. Over the next twenty years Margaret would see a gradual realization of her dream to educate people in remote places who had responsibility—but lacked expertise—for preventing blindness in leprosy patients.

> I realized when I was in the Canal Zone that even though the doctors there were good internists or family practitioners, they didn't see the eyes as being part of their responsibility and had no training in this for their leprosy patients. And such lack of training was not limited to the Canal Zone doctors.
>
> One doctor visiting Carville from Colombia, South America, lamented the ignorance of the average leprosy doctor in his country concerning eye problems. As we discussed what might be done, it became clear that training was the obvious need. "When you don't know what you will do with what you might find, you don't go looking for it," he said. "So, the simplest solution is to ignore the eyes altogether."
>
> Clearly there was a need for more eye training for all categories and levels of health care providers. Seminars and workshops are a good way to achieve this, but for the lone worker in an isolated area, literature can make the difference between total helplessness and the ability and confidence to give the care and advice that could prevent a grave situation from becoming disaster, at least until more experienced help is available.
>
> It was to these ends that the book *Care of the Eyes in Hansen's Disease* came into being. What began as a series of articles in the patient-published Carville hospital newspaper, *The Star*, became a booklet on the basics of eye care and treatment in leprosy, which was distributed without charge throughout the world to rural and village workers. One of *The Star* editors was Emmanuel Faria, himself a leprosy patient. He understood the helplessness of someone with insensitive hands and feet who developed blindness. He urged me to write, then painstakingly edited my efforts and saw to it that they were put into a usable form for distribution.

Dr. Margaret's insights and experience also provided valuable lessons for other surgeons and consultants. For patients who had lost the ability to blink because of nerve damage, Margaret began using a "muscle transfer" operation, something Paul had introduced to revolutionize the treatment of paralyzed hands. This technique moved working muscles into an area where the normal muscles no longer worked. For the eye, Margaret used a portion of the temporalis muscle from the cheek, which is connected to the jaw and normally used for chewing. Transferred to the eyelid, this meant that whenever the patient chewed, biting down hard, he would also blink. There was no need to re-train the brain to get the muscle to work in its new position (as was necessary in hand surgery), but there was a need to train the patient to remember to chew frequently. Chewing gum would seem to be the obvious solution, but one rarely bites down hard enough in chewing gum to close the eyelids. Success would depend a great deal on how much pain sensation remained in the eye. Patients who had enough corneal sensation to tell when their eyes were getting dry would increase their chewing to alleviate the discomfort. But patients who could not sense eye pain simply forgot to use their new "motor," leaving their eyes at risk.

☙

In the 1940s the only drug effective in treating leprosy was the antibiotic Dapsone. It was soon used worldwide, and hundreds of thousands of patients benefited. But by the 1960s leprosy bacilli were showing resistance to the effects of Dapsone. Patients in whom the disease had been well-controlled began demonstrating a relapse to active disease states.

The surface of the eye is relatively cool compared to the rest of the body; as such, it is hospitable to the mycobacteria, and hence it was not surprising that the first signs of relapse appeared in eye structures. Margaret was able to spot these signs by using the high magnification of the corneal microscope and immediately informed the primary physician, in many instances a dermatologist, so that the patient could be put on a different medication. Not every doctor, however, accepted Margaret's diagnosis of relapse showing up in the eyes. Some of her colleagues—including experienced dermatologists—felt that the old ways of diagnosing the disease and then monitoring its progress were infallible. They wanted to rely upon finding the presence of bacteria in the skin as detected by the traditional examination of "skin scrapings." They did not need an ophthalmologist telling them when a patient's disease was relapsing.

We were seeing an increasing number of patients whose disease, though controlled well for months, was showing signs of fresh activity.

Obviously Dapsone was no longer helping them. And in the eye, the disease took a rather aggressive form, especially if that individual had experienced "red eye" (from inflammation inside the eye). Because of this, it was important to detect any relapse as early as possible.

I examined every patient at least every three months, using a corneal microscope. During one of these exams I noticed suspicious changes in the cornea of one particular patient, who was otherwise very fit. I went to his attending physician and said, "I suspect the disease is active." Confidently the doctor said, "Nope. The skin scrapings are all negative."

When I saw the patient three months later, I found more of the same, so I went back to the doctor to express my growing concern. He remained confident and reassured me that if there was need for anxiety he would be the first to know it through the skin scrapings.

Three months later, I was back once more, this time not just concerned but alarmed. The doctor was obviously irritated with me. Couldn't I take his word for it? (To be honest I couldn't, not when someone's eyes were at risk.) To appease me, he arranged to do a biopsy, which would reveal more than superficial skin scrapings.

The results of that biopsy showed that, indeed, the patient's leprosy was once again active, and I suggested starting him on a different anti-leprosy drug—clofazimine (B663)—right away. The doctor was humble and quite appreciative of learning something new about leprosy and eyes, and from then on he sought my opinion on many occasions.

Drug resistance is such a constant problem with infectious diseases that pharmaceutical companies continually research new drugs. Ciba-Geigy manufactured clofazimine for this very reason. The drug did have one disadvantage, however. Because it was derived from a type of dye, it changed a person's skin color to a reddish-purple as long as he or she was taking it. This was not a serious matter when the individual's skin color was already dark, but for light-skinned people this discoloration was a major problem. And for patients already physically stigmatized by their disease, this side effect was unacceptable. Only the fear of something worse befalling them, such as blindness, overcame their opposition to the drug.

For Dr. Margaret, worldwide recognition of her work meant nothing in and of itself. Her sole concern was to study and accurately report her findings, hoping to benefit and better the treatment of both her patients at Carville as well as leprosy patients throughout the world.

Margaret also was blessed by the insights she gained into the human condition from her many wonderful patients. She never ceased learning from them, both medically and spiritually.

One elderly patient, Julian, had no sense of touch. He was quite blind in one eye, and the sight in his other eye was threatened because his eyelids did not function well. Julian was also coincidentally somewhat deaf and depended on a hearing aid—a rather bulky, battery-operated device that lived in a sort of box that dangled from a cord around his neck and often got in the way when he ate. His vision depended on his hearing and his hearing on his vision. Whenever these were at their worst, he would become agitated and paranoid, afraid that people were going to harm him.

One Friday morning I performed eyelid surgery on Julian, hoping to protect his remaining eye. The surgery went well, but I had failed to warn him that he would probably have a bit of post-operative swelling, which would make it difficult for him to see properly for a day or two.

The next day when I went to Julian's room to check on him, the poor man was terribly upset. The eyelid swelling was bad, although the eye behind it looked fine and I was sure that once the swelling subsided he would benefit from the surgery. But, since his hearing aid batteries had died, Julian couldn't hear me as I tried to explain all this. He was quite sure he was now totally blind. I tried speaking loudly, close to his hearing aid. He knew I was talking to him but could not hear what I was saying. Repeatedly and desperately he shouted, "I can't see. My battery's dead!"

What a lesson this was for me as I thought about how dependent my spiritual sight is on my spiritual "battery." I'm sure that if I allowed the Spirit to keep my "battery" charged the way it should be, my insight into people's real needs and problems would be far clearer and I would be of more help to them.

Jose, from Puerto Rico, was another remarkable individual. Jose had advanced disease, which was resistant to Dapsone. He had grossly infected hands and feet and severe inflammation with advanced cataracts in both eyes. He had lost sensation over ninety percent of his body, including his hearing (medication related) and his sense of smell.[1] Jose spent his days lying in a fetal position, without sense of touch, sight, hearing, or smell. He only knew there was someone "out there" during the day when food was put in his mouth. He could distinguish salt, sour, bitter, and sweet—that was all. He had enough vision to know when the light went on in his room. But at night, in the dark, he must have wondered whether he was alive or dead.

More than a year passed before the clofazamine got his active disease under control. His eye inflammation also improved to the point where it was safe to consider cataract surgery, which might restore some of his vision. Since we could not communicate with Jose, however, we could not get his legal "informed consent" to operate.

With the help of the Puerto Rican police we contacted a sister who was legally responsible for him, and she gave us permission to do the surgery. But how could we tell him that we planned to operate and that he would need to lie still? We couldn't. We could only pray and trust the Lord for the rest.

Jose relaxed and cooperated just as if he could hear. He seemed to be at peace, as if he knew we were trying to help, not harm, him. Dr. Allen and I did the surgery, and Jose regained about forty percent of his vision, which was a better outcome than we had dared to hope for, considering how bad his eyes had been for so long.

When Jose recovered from the surgery, it was as if he had awakened from a coma. He was part of the world again. He began attending chapel regularly. He could not hear, but he could see people, and when the moment came for us to greet each other, folk would come and give him a hug. To him that hug meant as much as anything else in the service, and he responded with a lovely grin.

Jose knew how to read, and he now was able to see large letters held in front of him. I made a card on which I wrote the words "Jesus loves you, Jose. Do you believe that?" He studied the letters for a minute, then bellowed (he had no idea how loud his voice could be), "YES!" That was his testimony.

---

1. Certain drugs can cause loss of hearing. Doctors have to be very cautious and aware of this possible reaction and keep checking the patient's hearing while they are on that drug.

Hope is a significant factor both in the tolerance of suffering people and in their recovery. And the absence of hope can be devastating.

Maria, a dear little woman from Puerto Rico, was one of my first patients at Carville. She had "red eye" but was doing fairly well with treatment. Her eyesight was slowly improving, and her spirits were high. She was planning to go home to her family for Christmas. She had not seen them in several years.

Then one morning she came to the clinic looking dejected. Her eyes looked bad, really bad, and nothing seemed to help. She deteriorated quickly. I could not understand why until I learned that she had received a letter from her family telling her that there would not be room for her and that she should not come home.

Poor Maria! Rejection was not a new thing for her, but somehow this news was more than she could bear. Her sight went, her health went, and she died a few months later.

Dr. Margaret had created an arsenal of tools with which to help her patients and prevent blindness. She had helped to establish the guidelines most appropriate for treating ocular leprosy, which included medications, surgery, surveillance, and patient education. She knew what effects hope and despair had upon the response of the patients. But one of the most difficult aspects of patient care was dealing with the person's attitude.

We had one patient at Carville whom I shall call Vera. She was in her mid-fifties and had had the disease for a long time. She had lost her eyebrows and her eyelashes and felt very self-conscious. She was always beautifully dressed and was very particular about everything. But she wouldn't go out, wouldn't leave the station. She thought the public would notice that she didn't have eyelashes.

Buses would take patients on shopping expeditions or on other ventures, and Vera's friends, who were not self-conscious about their appearance, gladly participated in these public events. But Vera would never go. She penciled in her eyebrows, but she couldn't solve the problem of her eyelashes, so she refused to be seen in public.

Then she came up with the idea of solving this problem by adding a hefty line of industrial-strength mascara across her eyelids. This was not easy for her to do. She wore glasses, but she had to take her glasses off to do her makeup, so she couldn't see clearly when she looked into the mirror; everything was blurred. Vera also had poor corneal sensation, and her hands weren't very flexible, which meant she couldn't control the mascara brush very well. As a result, she would run the brush and the mascara partially onto the eyelid but also right across her corneas! If she had had normal corneal sensation, she would have been in agony; she would have stopped right there. But she didn't—so on she continued and completed the line all the way across on both eyes. She was pleased with the result, and out she went, content now to meet the public.

A few days later Vera showed up in the eye clinic with red, weepy eyes. Under the corneal microscope I was amazed to see small dark spots tattooed across the swollen cornea and other tissues. When I realized what she was doing, I was horrified and warned her about the consequences. Vera's eyes recovered, but she came back a second time with the same problem. Again I warned her that this must stop.

I knew that Vera was an intelligent individual, and when she returned a third time I was quite frustrated. Again I warned that she might develop corneal ulcers and might become blind. Yet I could see that she was still not taking me seriously. I was at a loss as to how to express myself in terms that would get through to her.

As I started to admonish her, she pulled her head away from the microscope, put her hands on her hips, and defiantly said, "Doc, you don't understand. It's more important how the world sees me than whether or not I can see the world!"

What a sad and terrible priority to have, I thought. I was about to respond in this manner when the Lord tapped me on the shoulder and said, "Don't be so judgmental. Aren't you too often concerned about your own image?" He wanted me to see that I had no right to judge Vera so severely and that I could best communicate with her by loving her, as He loves her, and with the love He shows for me.[2]

◌

---

2. Vera did finally listen and was at least careful enough to safeguard her eyes.

In 1968, with the Brand family now permanently settled at Carville, Trish announced that she wished to attend Clarendon School in the UK as Jean and Mary had done. Over the past three years in America, Trish and Pauline's upbringing had been considerably different from what the older children had experienced in India and England. The younger girls' religious foundation at home was solid as ever, but outside the home, attitudes and lifestyle were looser.

From her first day at St. Gabriel, when she was only eleven years old, Trish had been popular with the boys, some much senior to her. While I'm sure she enjoyed this popularity, she began to realize that she wasn't being challenged academically. She scored "A's" effortlessly, and this began to influence her thinking.

One day, to our surprise, she shared some of those thoughts. "I am having a wonderful time at school," she said. "I have lots of friends and everything is easy. But I do want to make something of my life, and I don't think it is going to happen here. I need a different sort of education, perhaps at a girls-only school where there'll be fewer distractions. Could I go back to England and go to Clarendon School?"

Clarendon not only had high academic standards but also strict rules of conduct. Did she really know what it would mean to her? we asked. I reminded her that there would not be any boys at Clarendon, and they couldn't even visit without permission.

"I've thought about that," she answered, "and have decided that boys aren't everything!"

We contacted Clarendon School and, yes, they would be glad to accept her. She would need to be tutored in French, but aside from that she would fit in with her age group. Jean would act as Trish's guardian in England, knowing how to cope with travel arrangements, managing her allowance, and dealing with uniforms and other clothing requirements. This included sewing proper name labels on to every one of Trish's clothing items, even each of the requisite twenty-four handkerchiefs she must bring. It was a lot of work, but Jean took it all in stride, happy to have one of the family near her again.

Mary also left home in the fall of 1968 but only to relocate to New Orleans. For her second year of the four-year nursing degree program, she and Judy

Brubaker moved as roommates into the nursing student dormitory near Charity Hospital in downtown New Orleans. Her workload was hectic, but her proximity to Carville allowed her and Judy to return frequently on weekends to see their families—and their horses.

Estelle had completed high school and graduated from the LSU lab school feeling somewhat better prepared for college. She decided that she wanted to become a teacher, but rather than continue in the States she chose to return to London and enroll in Southlands Teacher Training College in Wimbledon. She would later return to Louisiana to finish college.

By mid-summer 1968, Jean had completed her three-year nursing training and planned to enter the three-year Bachelor of Divinity degree program at London Bible College in the fall of 1969. In order to qualify for entrance to the Bible college, she spent the intervening months taking A Levels correspondence coursework. While working on her correspondence courses, she supported herself with a variety of jobs, not unlike her Grandpa Berry had done as a young man in Paris. She eventually planned to return to India where she might work for churches while using her nurse's training in some capacity.

Meanwhile, the household at Carville settled into a period of relative quiet, with only Paul, Margaret, and eleven-year-old Pauline (and the pets) residing there. Christopher had enlisted in the US Army and was stationed in Thailand; Jean, Trish, and Estelle were in England; and Mary returned only one or two weekends each month.

Paul and Margaret enjoyed these years of one-on-one time with Pauline. From early childhood Pauline had demonstrated a passion and talent for creative pursuits. She enjoyed music, becoming skilled at playing the piano. Like her siblings before her, she joined with her mother in singing in the choir of the Protestant chapel. But her primary love was writing, both stories and plays.

By the time Pauline reached seventh grade at St. Gabriel's School in 1970–1971, desegregation had been implemented in the local school system, with black students being bussed to her school. Her school experience became difficult at times.

I was aware of the feelings against blacks among some of our Caucasian friends in Carville, and when Pauline began seventh grade in the newly desegregated St. Gabriel's, I encouraged her to make friends with some of the black students. After a few weeks she had become

friends with a particular girl, and I suggested Pauline invite her friend to spend a Saturday night in our home and then go to church with us on Sunday. She did this, and the girl accepted. As I listened to some of their conversations, however, I realized we were living in two different worlds and wondered if we would ever be able to bridge this gap.

In eighth grade Pauline began attending Sunshine High School, which had formerly been the all-black school in the area. As a white student she was very much a minority. She wanted to try out for the volleyball team, but several of the older black girls trapped her in the locker room and threatened her that she had better not try out "or else." She was roughed up and only rescued because a friend ran to find a teacher who had a key to unlock the doors of the changing rooms.

When several of the black male students heard about what had happened, they offered to be Pauline's guardians, and for a while they did accompany her as her "posse." Then, a month or so after the locker room incident, she was standing in line (the only white person) to try out for a school talent contest, hoping to play a piano piece. Just before her turn to take the stage, the gang of black girls (whose talent was a dance routine) threatened that she would be sorry if she auditioned. Pauline went in anyway, but her nerve failed her, and she left without even sitting at the piano.

Having experienced firsthand the backlash of violence that initially erupted in area schools at the start of desegregation, Pauline's already existing interest in Clarendon intensified. She was also eager to spend time in England and experience the boarding school life her sisters had told her about. She finished the school year at Sunshine and went to Clarendon the next year.

On December 18, 1974, Paul's mother, Granny Brand, died at the home of Dr. Ernest and Mano Fritschi in Karigiri. She was ninety-five years old, and until her last weeks had continued to travel and work on one or another of the range of hills, including the "hills of death" where she and her husband Jesse had started their ministry some sixty years earlier.[3] Thankfully Paul

---

3. In the Tamil language "the Kolli Hills" means "hills of death," called this because of a lethal type of malaria prevalent there. These hills in southern India were all between 3,000 and 5,000 feet in elevation.

had just visited with her in October, and he and Jean together had seen her earlier, in March of that year.

Granny's body was taken to a chapel at Vazhavanthi in the Kolli Hills—a chapel Jesse had built years before—and after a service there she was laid to rest next to Jesse in the presence of a sorrowful multitude. Her work was finished, but her legacy lives on.

"Trust and Triumph" were the words Jesse had had inscribed inside her wedding band, and that was the motto she and Jesse lived by. It was an appropriate motto for Margaret and Paul as well.

Chapter 24

Inspiring People, Interesting Places

"Aren't you going to pray for all of us?"

During her twenty-one years at Carville, Margaret enjoyed both personal and professional growth. She received invitations to either preach at churches or to speak to women's groups about her work and family. On one notable occasion she was invited to meet the governor's wife at their mansion in Baton Rouge. The governor's daughter was a student at LSU and had met Margaret at a Christian student meeting on campus.

Dr. Margaret increasingly brought her expertise to foreign locales, much like Paul had been doing in his work. She traveled as a consultant to Ethiopia, Brazil, Turkey, China, and, almost annually, to India. Most of her travel experiences were uncomplicated, and the politics of the countries she visited did not interfere with her missions. But this changed in the troubled atmosphere of Addis Ababa, Ethiopia, where a Communist revolution had just taken place.

The All Africa Leprosy Training institution (ALERT) had been a great success. Its initial supporters included members of the royal Ethiopian family and the government's Ministry of Health. Doctors, health care workers, and students from nearly every country on the African continent had undergone training sessions there under a variety of sponsorships, including the World Health Organization.

There were many reasons for Paul and others to have chosen Addis Ababa for the site of such a program. Ethiopia was one of the most stable African countries under the leadership of Emperor Haile Selassie II, who was also head of the Ethiopian Orthodox Church, one of the oldest Christian churches in the world. His own granddaughters had attended the same Clarendon School for Girls that the Brand girls were attending. Also, the quality of hand surgery at ALERT was such that the queen sent one of her young granddaughters to the leprosy hospital for repair of a lacerated tendon in her hand.

But politically everything changed in 1974 when Communists took over the government, murdering officials, putting members of the royal family— including the emperor's granddaughters—under house arrest, and driving many Ethiopian professionals out of the country. Yet the new regime recognized the value of the ALERT program and even increased government support of the institution. The leprosy facility and its staff were spared any harm.

On trips in 1968 and 1973 to conduct seminars on eye disease, Margaret encountered no problems. She easily obtained visas, paying a fee at the airport when she arrived. But in 1978 her experiences were drastically different.

The Communist revolution was in full swing. Many of the international institutions were closed, but the Marxist government wanted ALERT to remain open. It was a sort of showcase to the world to demonstrate that the new Ethiopia was concerned about the handicapped.

The head of the training branch at ALERT was Dr. Felton Ross, an internationally recognized leprosy expert. He invited me to teach another eye seminar. He assured me that the government was not interfering in the work of the hospital, that everything would be arranged with the immigration authority so that entry into the country would be no problem.

But when our plane touched down in the early hours of that morning in 1978, I was aware of a tense atmosphere in the airport. There were armed troops everywhere. No familiar faces. It was somewhat unnerving.

I carried some Ethiopian money in my purse, expecting that I would buy my visa as on earlier visits. But I could find no visa booth; moreover, no one had told me that not only was the money bearing the image and inscription of the emperor no longer valid currency, it was a liability just possessing it. But I had little time to think about that before I was hurried into the immigration room. My stress level was rising!

The officials were not rude but were politely hostile! They asked questions such as, "Why did you not get a visa before leaving the States?" "How do you have this illegal money?" "Why are you here?" I told them about ALERT and Dr. Ross and the eye seminar for leprosy workers. They softened a bit. In the end they let me go on to Customs, but they told me they would keep my passport until they had verified my information. They returned it a week later.

As soon as I got out of the building I found Dr. Ross, who had been waiting for me, not allowed inside to be an advocate. He was sorry to hear of my experiences but not surprised. He had done all he could to facilitate things for me. But those were not normal times.

It did not take long to see that the mood at the airport permeated the entire city and its populace. Dr. Margaret's experience was nothing compared to the dangers the average citizen faced as armed adolescent "soldiers" roamed the countryside.

No one dared speak. No one trusted his neighbor. Children were tortured to make them betray their parents. Any little criticism of the new Marxist regime could bring imprisonment or, in many instances, summary execution. Schools were not safe. Children might leave home in the morning but not return. They too had faced an execution squad. Their bodies were taken to the city refuse dump and left there. Parents would hurry to the site to look for their children. Not only were school children at risk of death themselves, they were forced to enlist and be trained to carry a gun.

I had arrived on a Thursday and was comfortably accommodated in the guesthouse at the ALERT compound. On Sunday, Jos Anderson, a Danish doctor who with his wife Karen were long-time friends of ours, offered to take me to church with them. Churches used by expatriates were allowed to stay open, but not those of Ethiopian Christians. I noticed as we were driving down the main street that all along the roadsides were young teenage boys carrying rifles and wearing red headbands.

There was a jeep ahead of us. To my horror I saw one of those boys lift his gun, take aim, and shoot at it. The driver was killed and rolled out into the road. There was nothing we could do. Dr. Anderson just pulled out a bit, and we passed that sad scene. We then came to a roadblock, an identity checkpoint. And there I was with no passport! Another unnerving moment!

Dr. Anderson was obviously an experienced traveler in this sort of situation. He explained to the fellows manning the checkpoint that I was an important doctor who was needed for the leprosy work. When they heard "leprosy" they relaxed and waived us on. How glad I was to be associated with leprosy work. That association was my safe passport.

⌒

Dr. Margaret has made several trips to Brazil. Rio de Janeiro has special significance because it was at the meeting of the International Leprosy Association there in 1963, when Paul gave her the podium, that ocular leprosy began to garner the attention of international leprologists. Subsequent trips have included other areas of the country. Her fondest memories pertain to three special individuals: Dr. Bill Woods, Linda Lehman, and Hannelone Vieth.

Bill Woods was commissioned by his church in Belfast, Ireland, to do evangelistic work in the Amazon delta and basin. Faithful to his calling, he was preaching the gospel but felt uneasy about the lack of health care for his people. He asked his church back home if they would sponsor him to go to medical school in Brazil. The church was willing to give him leave to study but could not afford to pay him more than his regular stipend.

By this time Bill's Portuguese was fluent, so off he went to Rio de Janeiro, got accepted in a medical school, and became a student. To pay for tuition he and a friend built and sold houses. This young part-time student, part-time builder graduated and then completed a residency in ophthalmology. With this training accomplished and with the assurance of his loyal troop of prayer warriors backing him, he felt ready to face the Amazon again.

I had been invited to read a paper on "Eye Problems in Leprosy" at a conference of ophthalmologists in Manaus, the capital of Amazonas State. The time allotted was twenty minutes, but they had not told me that I should allow about half that for the interpreter! Dr. Woods was my interpreter. He did his best and so did I, but precisely ten minutes into my material the chairman thanked me and announced the next speaker.

It was hard to accept that I had come all that way to read half a paper! I felt quite discouraged. But not Bill. He could think of all kinds of good reasons why I had come to Brazil, quite apart from reading that paper. We saw many patients together, looked at dozens of bad eyes, discussed what we might do to help them. We operated together. I may have taught him a few things. And he taught me—not just surgery but things of eternal value. Bill's quiet persistent faith and his irrepressible sense of humor, never taking himself too seriously but always serious about God's work, have been a great example to me and all who know him.

Margaret flew south from Manaus to Sao Paulo and traveled from there by road to Bauru, a significant training center for leprosy workers of all kinds.

In Bauru I met up with my dear friend Linda Lehman, an occupational therapist who had spent time with us at Carville. We had the joy of sharing a room, sharing a lot of laughs, sharing some sad moments, and prayer together. I also met the medical director, who was an experienced doctor, but he and I had quite a difference of opinion about the drug clofazamine. He adamantly refused to consider using it, insisting that none of his patients would accept the skin discoloration.

I examined the eyes of some of those patients and was shocked to see their condition. The disease was out of control, and if they did not get effective treatment very soon they would be blind. So I went back to the medical director and shared out of my experience. He still was not convinced, but I was told later that he had started to use clofazamine. I think that may have been part of the reason why I had to go to Brazil.

From Bauru Linda and I traveled to Bambui, a small town with a community of dedicated Italian nuns who took care of a leprosy colony. At that time Linda was the occupational therapist for the community. She was anxious to do what she could to save the sight of several of her patients. We spent many hours examining them and talking about measures that might safeguard their eyes. Her equipment was meager, but the nuns assured her that they could ask their order in Italy for items and they would get them. So we prepared a request list. A local ophthalmologist came to some of our discussions and began to get interested in the problems. I could see better days ahead for those patients.

Another good friend and colleague with whom I became re-acquainted in Bauru was Hannelone Vieth. We had first met at Carville where she worked with me in the eye clinic. She was of German background, and her basic training was nursing. She and Linda became close friends and professionally skilled as they worked together producing eye care training material in Portuguese for leprosy workers. Hannelore soon learned to use a corneal microscope and could quickly screen several patients, identifying those who would need to be seen by a visiting ophthalmologist. That doctor then became interested, whereas before he pleaded he was too busy to come and work with leprosy patients.

Sometime during the 1990s when I had been conducting a seminar on "Eye Care in Leprosy" for a group of Indian doctors in Karigiri, one of the participants was heard to remark, "I am not sure how much I learned, but I surely caught fire." I am so proud of both Hannelone and Linda! I feel I had a part in both of them "catching fire" concerning eyes in leprosy.

In 1984 Margaret and Paul were invited to visit Turkey under the sponsorship of the World Health Organization. Paul had gone the year before and had a delightful time as guest of a marvelous Turkish hand surgeon in Istanbul. He and Margaret were asked to return to the leprosy hospital in Istanbul as lecturers and consultants.

We were delighted to accept the invitation to visit Istanbul. By the time it came, Paul had become acquainted with a wonderful young lady, Ayse, a physical therapist, who had spent time with him in the hospital in Addis Ababa. I too had been acquainted with a young Turkish nurse, Tulay, who spent time with me in the eye clinic in Carville. Both these people were outstanding intellectually as well as in personality. And they had both "caught fire." It was a joy to work with them.

Ayse invited Paul and me to her home for a meal. Her family members were, as are most Turkish, devout Muslims. The following weekend we went to Ephesus for a little sightseeing and invited Ayse to accompany us as our interpreter. We stayed at a hotel in Izmyr, and it was at a zoo there that I discovered that the name *Aslan*, made so dear to readers of

C. S. Lewis's Narnia stories, is Turkish for "lion." We took the bus over to Ephesus and had a great time following the various tour guides around the places that would have been known to the apostle Paul.

Back in Izmyr on Sunday we decided to have our own little prayer and Bible study in our room. So we told Ayse what we were going to do and invited her. She was happy to join us.

Paul gave a brief but compelling little study from St. Paul's letter to the church in Ephesus. Following this we were going to pray. We asked Ayse if she would like us to pray for anyone special. We knew her dad was not in good health, so we were not surprised when she named him. We held hands and Paul led us in prayer. At the end there were tears in Ayse's eyes.

On Monday we were back in Istanbul at the hospital. Ayse and I went to the cafeteria for lunch. Before eating I bowed my head to thank God for my food. There was a little tap on my arm. It was Ayse. "Aren't you going to pray for all of us?" she asked. I was totally taken aback. Not only was prayer before meals not a Muslim custom, but also the room was full of men—Muslim like her. How could I, a Christian, a woman, be so audacious as to offer prayer for them? But Ayse was looking for my answer. So I simply said, "I will if you want me to."

Ayse is quite petite. But she stood up and, in a commanding voice, announced, "Dr. Margaret is going to pray for us all." Talk about absolute astonishment on all those faces! But Ayse wasn't through yet.

I had started to pray when I felt another tap on my arm. "We aren't holding hands!" It says something for the respect all those fellows had for her. Quite meekly they put down their knives and forks, stood up, and shuffled around to grasp their neighbor's hand. And only when all that was done could I pray.

I didn't know how to pray—should I pray in the name of Jesus? I certainly gave God thanks for Jesus and what had been done through Him. And it wasn't a very long prayer! Afterwards one of the men came to me and said, "We should do this every day. Perhaps we would begin to love one another and then we would really work together." That was just an incredible moment of opportunity. For eternity? I would like to think so.

I spent much of my time with Tulay in the eye department. She had a good friend who was an ophthalmologist who would come and see the patients that Tulay had screened and do any surgery needed. Turkan

Saylan, a fine woman doctor, was the director of that institution. Dr. Saylan offered to take me sightseeing, which included a visit to a museum that for centuries had been a mosque, and before that, St. Sophia's church built by the Emperor Constantine in the fifth century. When the Muslims overran the city, they removed all the Christian symbols, replacing them with Islamic ones. I was noting that on the huge doors of this church, cum mosque, cum museum, there must have been two large crosses nailed into the wood. Those had been removed, but the imprints and the nail marks remained. There would have been efforts to erase them, but, as I pointed out to my friend, you cannot erase the cross.

Two years later while in Karigiri to teach a seminar, I had a remarkably vivid dream about those doors and the marks of the crosses. In my dream I was one of a huge flock of sheep that was being herded down a steep ravine. It was gloomy and frightening. The rocky walls were unscalable, the flock too dense to allow me to turn back. There was only one way—forward. But when I looked over the flock ahead I could see there was no way through. I knew what would happen. We would reach the end, an impenetrable wall. There we would go down while others, pressed on by the sheer mass behind them, would trample us to death and in their turn also be killed. Death was inevitable.

Then something happened. Even as I looked over the sheep ahead of me I saw him, a shepherd perhaps. He was up at the front, against the wall. Then I saw him raise his arms to the side, as if on a cross. The wall changed. It became a huge door. It opened and we could see beyond into the most beautiful pasture. There was a glory about it. Along with the other sheep, I streamed through that miraculous door. As I did, I noticed the marks on it, just like the marks on the door of the church in Istanbul. Again, a cross.

I heard a voice calling, even shouting. Jesus said, "I am the door." The words were repeated over and over. They woke me. It was my own voice, shouting triumphantly, joyously! There were no other guests there, so my voice echoed through the empty house. And those words have echoed in my mind many times since then. Especially do I hear them along with the words we sing from the *Messiah*, "Where O death is now thy sting?" For me they have banished that sting (1 Corinthians 15: 55).

Another experience during my time in Istanbul was special enough that I used it in an address I gave in Las Vegas in 1985. I had been named one of two recipients of the "Woman of Distinction" award given by the Alpha Delta Kappa society, an honor society of women educators. (The other honoree that year was Chief Justice Sandra Day O'Connor of the United States Supreme Court.) I was actually invited to deliver the keynote address and scarcely knew how to address such an elite group. I had no experience with the teaching profession other than my homeschooling work. But since everyone likes stories, I told the story of a visit I made to a hospital ward in Turkey.

I was in a ward to examine one of my patients, and as I inched my way between the beds I noticed the patient next to my patient get up. She did not have problems with her eyes, but I could tell that her hands had been badly damaged by insensitivity. Also, she had hardly anything in the way of feet, so she kind of stumbled around. She came to me, her face aglow and her arms outstretched, with no hands or fingers, and embraced me. In her Kurdish language she said, "I love you. You are my sister." The other people there said it was not unusual for leprosy patients to consider each other their "sister," but it was quite unusual to do this to a stranger. This was such a tender moment—that a woman of a different faith, a different language, a different background, would see me as her sister.

As I related this episode, there was a murmur of response in the audience; but I felt that they themselves were somewhat reserved, still strangers to each other. As I finished my remarks, I told them that this was an experience available to all of us and said, "Why not turn, right now, to the one next to you, give her a hug, and say 'I love you. You are my sister.'" That broke the ice. The audience erupted. Those few words were probably the best part of my keynote address.

⟨⟩

One of the most significant international trips for the Doctors Brand was traveling through China soon after it opened its borders to visitors from the West in the 1980s. Subsequently they were invited to consider helping found a leprosy research and treatment facility in China similar to those at Addis and Karigiri.

We were invited to attend the ceremony at the opening of a rehabilitation center for leprosy patients in Guangzhou, formerly known as Canton. It was not only a rehabilitation center that was opening; China itself was opening and wanted the international community to see it.

The list of invitees was impressive. We were welcomed at the airport with a band, and the buses taking us to our hotel were gaily decorated. We were royally treated and made to feel very important. The hotel catered to international guests, and every need was met.

During the Cultural Revolution, which was not too long before our visit, English had been a prohibited language. Consequently few people could speak it. But English was now being taught from kindergarten up. When we went to a store or any public area, little children would shyly come up and try to engage us in conversation. Generally they would run out of ideas after one or two sentences and would giggle and dash off to their moms.

The group of visitors, mainly physicians and spouses, were taken to see some well-run leprosy clinics. It was clear that early case detection and monitoring of treatment was being handled well, but the management of chronic cases with deformities was a different story.

Both Paul and I were asked to give lectures on our subjects at the university in Guangzhou. We had our slides and were assigned an interpreter. The audience was told to come. I have no idea what impression my carefully chosen words had. Chinese people don't betray emotion before strangers. But I admit once or twice I wondered if the interpreter was translating what I said or what he thought I ought to have said. He seemed to make a long paragraph out of my simple six-word sentences.

The Chinese were determined to demonstrate their hospitality through feasting, and Margaret and Paul faced a series of banquets as part of their itinerary. For two people who subsist on small quantities of simple foods, this was a challenge.

We were guests at five banquets. At the time of the first one, Paul wasn't feeling well so I went alone to represent the Brands. I was seated with nine other people, none of whom could speak a word of English.

There was no way I could communicate. I was handed a menu, written in beautiful calligraphy, but in Chinese. No help there!

I am not good at using chopsticks, so was slow at eating. I had scarcely managed one course before my plate would be whisked away and a new plate of food put in front of me. I was congratulating myself on getting through four courses, thinking that surely was the end of the meal, but no. It was barely the start. There were ten more to come! I could identify some of the food items but not all. I had to take a lot on faith. At least I could tell if there was shrimp in any of it, so I didn't get sick.

One course consisted of some type of small bird. Two were served into my bowl, heads and beaks still intact. Happily the wings and feet were gone. I watched my table companions to see what one did. It seemed very simple. They picked the bird up by the head using chopsticks. The body then dangled, and it seemed that one would swing it into one's mouth. I tried to do just that, but unsuccessfully. I was feeling quite full anyway.

It was a real relief when a dish of rice appeared. I had been told that it is always the last course.

Most memorable to Dr. Margaret was the opportunity to meet some Chinese Christians, and one visit to a service at a church formed an especially warm memory.

One of the nice things about this visit was getting to know a man from one of the three "self" churches: self-propagating, self-supporting, self-governing. These are the officially allowed churches. "Self-governing" means that you can govern your own church as long as the government agrees with how you govern. In spite of the restrictions, there are many fine Christians in the church, and when they can get hold of Bibles they treasure and read them—probably much more earnestly than most Christians here in the West.

We were allowed to go to one of these churches on a Sunday. We couldn't understand anything that was being said, but there was no missing the message on the worshipers' faces! There was one old lady who was sitting on the same pew with us, her face beaming. She had spent at least fifteen years in prison. She was released after eight years on condition that she no longer teach people to believe in Jesus. But how could she not tell the story? So, back in prison again for another seven years. But now she was free and was able to worship as long as she was in one of the three "self" churches. The thing that was most noticeable about her was her joy—no bitterness at all. She was just radiant.

The service concluded with the singing of a hymn. We recognized it as "O come, all ye faithful, joyful and triumphant" (it was near Christmas time). The words were different but the tune the same. Today when I sing that carol I think of those Chinese Christians. They had had their faith sorely tried. Based on their experience they had no reason to be so joyous or beaming.

Would I have the right to sing it their way? I wondered.

Margaret and Paul returned to China in 1989 when the attitude toward westerners had reverted to one of suspicion and mistrust and the government seemed less concerned with impressing foreigners. This frustrating atmosphere was exemplified in the Brands' experience trying to teach the group of doctors assigned to them. Despite the situation, they found among patients who had undergone amputations a testimony to the courageous character of some of these unfortunate people.

In 1989 Paul and I were asked to lead a weeklong seminar on correction of hand and foot problems and in prevention of blindness in the disease. Doctors representing the leprosy program, from every province in the country, were brought to Nanjing, to a well-equipped hospital where the seminar was held.

Paul was to teach on deformity prevention as well as hand and foot reconstructive surgery. I was to teach on eye problems and how to correct them. Paul took with him several instruments, expecting to have in his audience doctors who had some surgical experience, even if not in hand surgery. He also expected to have access to good operating facilities.

The first "road block" we encountered was lack of surgical experience. One or two of the trainees had done amputations, but the rest had no surgical skills. There was little or nothing on which Paul could build, at least not in a week. The second problem was that all the teaching was to be done in a classroom with transparencies and blackboard drawings. We would not have access to actual patients, let alone have one admitted to the splendid operating facilities in the hospital where the seminar was held. How could we teach effectively without patients, without operating facilities?

After some pressure and cajoling we were given permission to go to one of the leprosy hospitals in the region. The doctors who attended the course came along, but we soon realized that they were reluctant to get near the patients, let alone touch any of them. We understood later that no one wanted to work with the disease. But if a doctor had displeased his supervisor, he might be assigned to one of the leprosy hospitals as a sort of punishment. It hardly endeared him to the job!

As they did everywhere they traveled, the Brands tried to witness for Christ by their behavior even though they might not be able to do so in word from a pulpit. Paul describes in his words how his action at one hospital hopefully gave the Chinese a clear message by example:

"It soon became clear to us that our trainees were truly afraid to touch a patient. Thus it created a deep impression on them when I took a bad foot in my own ungloved hands and gently examined it. It was my usual practice, and I did it without thinking.

There was one patient whose feet were very bad and would probably soon be amputated. He came in looking so sad. I explained to him through the interpreter what I thought could be done for him and what he could do by resting the feet. I told him that even if the feet had to come off we would try to find some kind of prosthesis for him. He started to cry, and I immediately did what I would have done naturally at Karigiri and that was to put my arms out and give him a hug. Immediately there was a collective gasp in the room. I'm sure those doctors will never forget that!"

The frustration the Brands felt over the attitude of physicians toward patients was compounded by the lack of resources they encountered.

As I had planned for that trip I wanted to make sure we could use our time well, so I had requested certain things. Eye examinations are best done in a darkened room with a bright well-focused light on the eye itself. I asked for dark curtains to be hung over the windows. I asked for flashlights. (I would take a few with me, but knew that flashlights could be procured easily in China.) I asked for access to a sink so that I could wash my hands between one patient and the next. That was as much a teaching point as any other for my seminar. I had also asked for some basic medications that are easily available and not expensive.

When I arrived, the director was apologetic: not one of my requests could be met. They had no resources.

With so many patients to see, I would like to have been able to sit down occasionally, but there was no chair—no furniture of any sort. One thing, however, was plentiful: patients who heard that an eye doctor actually wanted to see them. The interpreter informed me that no eye doctor had ever come to see them before and that they had had no eye medicine. It was heartbreaking for me to see how many of those dear people were needlessly blind. I was concerned about one young woman in particular. She had redness in one eye. It was not a serious matter and could easily be treated with medication; but it needed treatment or it would become serious.

As I was about to finish the clinic, I saw her standing near the door, weeping. I asked, through our interpreter, why she was so sad. Her condition was not that bad and the pain was not a problem. She simply said, "Everyone coming to this hospital goes blind and it starts with a red eye. Now it's my turn." I inquired of the director if he could get the medication she needed. His answer: "We can get no medication. Only the army can get it. We may find someone in the army who could help us. Otherwise we do without!"

Paul and I came back to our hotel that evening feeling very pessimistic. What had we accomplished, and what would it take to change things? But things can change, as I learned when I had the opportunity to return to this area in 1995.

Not everything about that trip was negative. The hospital on the whole seemed clean and the patients were adequately fed. And we saw among the patients examples of courage and ability to improvise.

They obviously did not own much, but one thing each did own was a small, three-legged stool. It was touching to see how protective and possessive they were of them. They kept the stools tied to their person by a piece of string worn round their necks. Thus they would always have a place to sit down. But more importantly, for the many amputees who had just one leg, the stool acted as a prosthesis. They would kneel on it, step on the sound foot, move the stool, kneel again, and thus "walk" quite quickly. Their attitude was wonderful.

God probably had many reasons for sending the Brands to China. They may never know most, but one purpose they do feel certain about. It was to meet their social interpreter in 1989.

One of the greatest blessings to us from this trip was the interpreter we were assigned. Every morning our "social interpreter," Lily, would meet us at our hotel and go with us throughout the day. We never went anywhere without her. Those were our explicit instructions. We were not sure whether she was there just to see that our needs were met or that we stayed within legal boundaries. Either way, we began to bond with this lovely young woman.

We surely needed a social interpreter. So few people on the streets or in stores could speak English. We were in China for two weeks. Most of that time we were occupied by the seminar, but we were instructed that we were to do some sightseeing in the last two or three days. Sightseeing had not been on our agenda. We would far rather have spent that time in the leprosy hospital. But protesting was useless. Our train tickets had been bought (we were allowed to pay for those) and reservations made, so off we went.

The itinerary was not too ambitious, and it was interesting to see something of the countryside, to visit famous historical buildings, and to watch the ladies doing the magnificent silk embroidery in Sou Zhou. Everywhere we went I was impressed by the cleanliness of the streets and buildings.

Lily was discreet and initially left us to ourselves much of the time. When she realized that we welcomed her company, however, she then joined us at meals and on other occasions. On one of our train journeys we found a quiet corner of the compartment and were able to have a private conversation. Lily asked us what we knew about Jesus. She had many questions and was clearly more than casually interested. She asked if we could send her a Bible, an English one? Then, could we send a Chinese one for her husband? And could we send her other books to help her understand more about God and about Jesus? Or, could we send her books about our work?

Our answer was yes to all of those, but where should we send them? China was still uneasy about importing Bibles and any Christian literature. She gave us a relative's address to which we might mail them, as we would cause her all sorts of trouble if we mailed them to her address at work.

After we were home, we sent off a package. Then we waited.

After a few weeks we received a letter. The package had arrived, and Lily was almost lyrical in her expressions of thanks. We looked forward to more letters and were not disappointed. The Lord was teaching her. She had found other Christians and was learning from them.

I was invited back to teach another workshop in 1995, and once again Lily was my interpreter. Paul was not with me on that trip, and Lily asked if she might share my room. It was a great joy to us both! We were able to have Bible study and prayer together every evening. She was hungry for every bit of help the Lord would give her.

Christian churches are open on Sundays in China (they may not open any other time), and we planned to go to a service together. The service would start at 10:30. Lily wanted to be there before 10:00 in order to find a seat. We were there in good time, but the sanctuary was already full. The people pushed up closer and made room for us. Many people were standing the whole time holding their children.

The service lasted two hours. I thought of the congregations back in the States. Most would get restless after an hour. These Chinese Christians seemed quite sorry when the worship service was finished. Even then not many left the building. They would be there until required to leave at closing time.

Following the service, Lily took me by bus to a different part of the city where we went upstairs to a third-floor apartment. It was the home of the leader of a small underground church. These were not legal in China and were subject to severe persecution, but they probably accounted for more than fifty percent of the Christians in the country. The apartment was a small single room, with a simple one-burner stove as the kitchen, a sink with water available, and a small flush toilet for the bathroom. It was sparsely furnished, mostly with mats to spread on the floor. But it was immaculately clean.

Our host fed us all a meal of eggs fried on his one-burner stove. It was delicious. Then they sang. I recognized some of the melodies, if not the Chinese words, and it was truly lovely to listen to the singing. Lily translated for me, and I felt so privileged to be in that group of people who cared for their relationship to God far more than they feared for their lives.

That 1995 seminar was a great encouragement to me. Compared to our earlier visits, there were more faculty, including Dr. Ebenezer Daniel, who is one of my most valued colleagues, now working in Karigiri; and also Dr. Paul Courtright, another good friend and colleague. But even more significant was the attitude of the participants. The fear we had seen before was not there. The patients who were brought from a leprosy institution about twenty miles away were welcomed, and the doctors examined them very professionally. There remains a lot of reservation about admitting such patients to the general hospitals for surgery, but I think that too will change.

Margaret's expertise in ocular leprosy, acquired in a rudimentary clinic at a fledgling leprosy hospital in south India, had become a major contribution to the preservation of vision among patients throughout the world. She had been able to share her knowledge with trainees passing through Carville, as well as students on five continents. Equally important, she had been able to share her vision of God and her love of Jesus Christ with even more people around the world.

Chapter 25

A Life of "Retirement"

"Grammy, why didn't you die?"

Paul decided to retire from his post at Carville in 1986. He was seventy-two years old and busy as ever with speaking engagements on leprosy, orthopedic surgery, rehabilitation, and religious subjects. The complexity of his schedule hadn't changed nor had his workload. But as had been the case in India, many of the projects he had started were now being continued by staff he had trained. Also, through the friendship and assistance of author Philip Yancey, Paul had become involved in writing Christian books, a new path that was far different from his scientific publications.

Margaret's chosen date for retiring her position with the USPHS was the following year, 1987, at the age of sixty-eight. She too had less to do at Carville and had staff trained who could continue her program. She found as well that she could continue her mission for ocular leprosy education through travel and speaking.

In preparation for leaving, Dr. Margaret was able to secure an ideal replacement for herself in Dr. Van Joffrion, an ophthalmologist and a missionary who had been working with leprosy patients in Madagascar. At her instigation, he applied for her position at Carville and was accepted. She knew that the eye clinic would be in good hands.

The Brands were not the only ones moving in a different direction. Ironically, the very success achieved by leprologists throughout the world in the early detection and treatment of leprosy to prevent chronic problems resulted in the demise of Carville. Though there had been no decline in the number of new cases, these patients were now diagnosed and treated early in outpatient clinics, before the advanced eye and extremity problems developed. Thus, a residential hospital for chronic patients was no longer needed.

The research branch continued its vital mission but was moved to the LSU School of Veterinary Medicine in Baton Rouge. Gradually the majority of the chronic patients at Carville were moved elsewhere,[1] and in 1999 the federal government returned the facility to the state of Louisiana to be used as a center for at-risk youth, managed by the Louisiana National Guard.

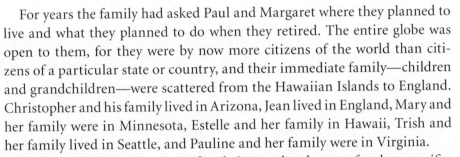

For years the family had asked Paul and Margaret where they planned to live and what they planned to do when they retired. The entire globe was open to them, for they were by now more citizens of the world than citizens of a particular state or country, and their immediate family—children and grandchildren—were scattered from the Hawaiian Islands to England. Christopher and his family lived in Arizona, Jean lived in England, Mary and her family were in Minnesota, Estelle and her family in Hawaii, Trish and her family lived in Seattle, and Pauline and her family were in Virginia.

Paul and Margaret's criteria for their new locale were few but specific. Proximity to a major airport was a necessity. They would continue to travel extensively, returning yearly to India, along with assorted responsibilities for Margaret on the board of the American Leprosy Mission and Paul with the Christian Medical and Dental Society, as well as innumerable speaking engagements. They wanted a climate more temperate than the heat of Louisiana, and they needed computer Internet access.

Increasingly Seattle, Washington, looked like a good choice. They had become familiar with the area during their visits to Trish, who was a resident in anesthesiology there. The climate was moderate, and the greenery was similar to Britain, with the sea and the mountains adding their own allure. This location put them within reasonable distance of Hawaii to the west and England to the east. In addition, Paul would be welcomed by friends at the University of Washington as well as at Seattle Pacific University. If he were

---

1. Some of the patients—about thirty—elected to stay there since it was the only home they knew. A nurse lives there with them and can refer them quickly to a hospital in Baton Rouge if need be.

interested he could consider an appointment of some type to either or both institutions.

Trish and her husband, Mike, were living in West Seattle, where the shoreline hills overlook Puget Sound. Terraced streets and houses extend down the hillside to the beach road. Across the water of the Sound are islands and the snow-peaked mountains of the Olympic range, with ferries constantly running from downtown Seattle out to the islands. A short drive from West Seattle brings one to downtown toward the north and the airport to the south. While walking their dog around their neighborhood, Trish had noticed a small white bungalow on one of the terraced hillside streets below their own house, directly overlooking the Sound. "If that house ever goes up for sale," Trish told Mike, "it would be the perfect house for my parents."

One day Trish noticed a man putting some furniture on the lawn of the little bungalow and tacking up a "for sale" sign. When she asked him about the furniture, he said, "Actually it's the house we're selling."

Trish inquired about the owner's asking price and down payment. Immediately, without even asking to see inside the house, she took out her checkbook and wrote a check for the amount he mentioned. She was so sure that this was to be our house. Then she called me and jokingly said, "I've just bought you a house!"

The owner later told us that other inquirers came later that day and offered more than Trish had agreed to pay, but the owner said no, he had accepted her check and would honor it.

Paul flew up the next weekend and felt the view alone was worth it and that we must somehow make the house suitable to our needs.

Trish and Mike set about finding an architect and a builder to remodel the bungalow. They were put in contact with a wonderful Christian contractor who went on to create the perfect home for Paul and Margaret, and Jean contributed her creative input to the final design. The yard space around the house had plenty of room for a vegetable garden, flowerbeds, fruit bushes, and fruit trees. Best of all, bird feeders could be placed just outside of the dining area's picture window.

No matter how appealing their new home looked, however, Margaret and Paul faced the difficult task of saying good-bye to longtime friends. They also had to decide what to do with twenty years of accumulated possessions.

I think the worst part of leaving Carville was leaving so many good friends, like Ray and Wanda MacPherson, as well as many of the patients. When they gave me a going-away party, it was very hard for me not to be in tears.

Packing seemed a daunting task. We had so many books. We gave many away but still had sixteen boxes of them. Other boxes were filled with papers and mementoes from around the world. We had a little porch sale and got rid of a lot of our things that way.

While movers and shippers carried their belongings across the nation, Margaret and Paul took to the open road in their small station wagon, meandering at leisure from Louisiana to Seattle without deadlines or timetables. For two people so used to harried schedules with an overwhelming list of commitments, the trip was a time of refreshment and relaxation.

We had a little Honda station wagon, and we took nine days to drive from Carville to Seattle. We didn't plan ahead. When we had done enough driving, we found a place to spend the night. We played tapes— Garrison Keillor and a lot of music—and read books to each other as we drove. We visited Carlsbad, New Mexico, and the Grand Canyon and other smaller beautiful canyons. We had lovely weather, and when we finally reached Seattle just before Thanksgiving 1987, we felt we were making a new beginning.

Margaret and Paul moved in with Trish and Mike until the renovations on their house were completed, which took about a year. They would move into their new home just before Christmas in 1988. Meanwhile, they set about filling another requirement. Unlike most people settling into their "quiet golden years," both Margaret and Paul had a voluminous amount of weekly correspondence to manage as well as complex schedules to arrange and travel arrangements to make. They hired Crystal Olpe to give them part-time secretarial help.

But the Brands' new start was marred by a frightening incident.

About a week after we'd arrived, I elected to take Trish and Mike's dog, Sugar, a healthy, vigorous boxer, for a walk. What happened next is speculation, as I have no memory of the events of the accident and only spotty memories of the rest of that day. Sugar must have decided to chase something. Evidently I had her on the leash, but it must have slipped up over my hand onto my wrist, and I could not pull it off fast enough. I must have fallen face down, and Sugar probably dragged me several feet on the rough road.

Meanwhile, back at the house, Paul was worried. Why was I gone so long? He had no idea where to start looking for me. Then the doorbell rang. When he opened the door, there I stood, disheveled and bloody, clutching the leash but no dog (Sugar found her own way home a little later).

I said to Paul, "I don't know who I am or if I live here, but perhaps you can help me."

Paul almost went into shock. He brought me into the house, and he and Trish washed off some of the blood. Trish called Mike, who was a resident at University Hospital, and he told them to bring me over and they would do a CT scan and see if I had any serious brain injuries.

Paul and Trish took me to the hospital, where they did a CT scan. Evidently they asked me to stop talking during the procedure, but although I tried, I couldn't stop. I was talking nonsense, repeating it over and over. The neurologist who examined me gave me a list of words that I was to repeat back to him in an hour or so. I remember lying in the ER, desperately trying to recall even one of them. I felt like I was a little girl who had not done her school homework and there would be serious consequences. His opinion: "I don't think there is permanent brain damage, but I can't guarantee she will be perfectly normal again."

Strangely, my memory loss was selective. I could accurately recall my nine-digit Social Security number but had no idea how old I was. I knew my date of birth but couldn't recall what century we were in.

After a couple of hours in the ER, Trish thought her dad needed a cup of coffee. She had never seen him look so depressed. Not surprising. I had asked him the same five or six questions over and over again. The prospect of a wife who talked non-stop, saying the same thing all day long, must have indeed been depressing. He needed that coffee!

Then, around six o'clock in the evening, my memory began to improve. There was a fervent "Praise the Lord!" around my bed.

A kindly dentist came in and took care of my chipped front tooth. He told me that the material he was using was temporary and that I should get it replaced as soon as possible. (That was over eighteen years ago.)

I had various other superficial injuries and bruises but none serious. Full of praise, my family took me home.

Within a day or two I was functioning well again, but I was worried because I was to go to India soon. How could I teach? At first I couldn't even understand the eye booklet I had written, but I had to believe that things were going to come back as they were coming back in other areas. By the time I went to India at the end of February 1988 and was back in the eye clinic in Karigiri, my memory had recovered.

Toward the end of her time at Carville, Margaret had begun traveling to Karigiri for a yearly three-week visit to help teach an ocular leprosy course for health care providers. As part of its mission Karigiri offered a variety of educational courses for everyone from village medics to physicians. This effort, begun in 1986, would become an annual trip for her—sometimes alone and sometimes with Paul. On their way to or from India they visited Jean and other family and friends in England, or they occasionally went by way of Hawaii and visited Estelle and her family.

In 1986 we had our first combined special course for doctors, for which I was joined by Dr. Timothy ffytche, a retinal specialist from London. This one-week course on ocular leprosy became an annual event, and Tim would use his entire annual vacation leave to come to India. We limited our classes to about sixteen participants. Doctors who had little eye training but were dealing with leprosy patients came from all over India and from neighboring countries such as Myanmar and Thailand.

When I would first return to India after being in Seattle, where I had little or no interactions with leprosy or with ophthalmology, I found myself needing to get familiar again with the eye clinic. Even the Tamil language sounded odd to me, and I sometimes tried to use Spanish— which didn't help at all! Then within a day or two everything would come back and it was truly like I hadn't left. I began to appreciate more and more the marvelous gift of memory that the Creator has given to us.

Schieffelin, like Carville, has undergone changes. Carville closed as a leprosy center in 1999, its research section transferred to Louisiana State

University in Baton Rouge. What began as the Schieffelin Leprosy Research and Training Centre in 1955 has evolved into what is known locally as "Karigiri Hospital." From 17 beds it has grown to 150. The little one-half-room eye clinic started by Margaret is now a full-fledged department serving the general ophthalmology needs of the surrounding population. Schieffelin provides services in the areas of leprosy, dermatology, general medicine, maternal and child health, and community care. Its operating rooms deal with a wide variety of surgical procedures, far beyond the eye and extremity problems of leprosy. And similar to one of Dr. Ida Scudder's original contributions to her Vellore community, Schieffelin opened a school of nursing in 2001.

Margaret and Paul were pleased to see that the most advanced leprosy cases, which were responsible for their entrance into the field forty years earlier, no longer filled the wards and clinics. But they were not happy over a developing tendency by some governments and organizations to assume that the disease was all but eradicated. There are as many new cases yearly as before, and the methods by which the disease spreads or is contracted are not yet understood, yet the World Health Organization has drastically cut funds in their leprosy program. The successful fight against leprosy has been primarily due to the well-staffed surveillance programs and well-monitored drug treatment programs that are carried out in outlying villages and rural areas. But if those programs are discontinued, there could be a resurgence of the disease without the institutions and expertise to deal with it.

⁓

In 1993 the Brand family gathered in Montana to celebrate Margaret and Paul's fiftieth wedding anniversary. All of the children, along with their spouses and children, were able to attend. As an anniversary gift for their parents, Mary, Jean, and Pauline created a unique and meaningful patchwork quilt. The quilt was a complex masterpiece, with each square having several photos imprinted onto it—some squares pertaining to Paul and Margaret, others to individual family members. The creation required weeks of effort, from sorting through boxes of photos, to converting the chosen photos to iron-on formats, to sewing the patches together.

That quilt is one of my most prized possessions. Paul used to say, "If this house were to catch fire, what would you rescue first?" And I would say, "the quilt," because it represents all of the members of our sweet family speaking to us.

The quilt includes photographs of things each member of the family would like to have remembered, photos of Paul and me in our younger days, the families at various stages. Each person has a square, and all the squares are arranged around the center panel, which contains our wedding photo. Along the edge of the quilt are little messages written on the fabric with special pens—a sweet assortment that somehow captures for me each person in a way that a photograph can't.

Even the presentation of the quilt was special. On one of the reunion days Paul and I were sent out of the room. The girls spread the quilt out on the living room floor, and the entire family gathered around the perimeter, each standing by his or her square. Then Paul and I were summoned.

When I saw the quilt and the family gathered around it, I burst into tears—tears of joy. Paul was quite speechless and tearful himself. This was the first time anyone besides those who had put the quilt together had seen it, so the rest of the family seemed just as stunned as we were.

Truly, the quilt belongs to all of us. And, like the quilt, the story of my life would not be complete without the story of all of us.

᠌᠌᠁

In 1995, Paul and Margaret were guests of a group of Christian physicians and dentists on a cruise in the eastern Mediterranean when Paul suffered a small stroke. They were to be the "faculty" on the trip, which included both lectures and sightseeing, visiting several Greek islands and ending in Turkey.

It was mid-morning in the beautiful city of Thessaloniki in Greece. Paul and I were walking back to our cruise ship after touring a museum and a church dedicated to one of the early Christian martyrs. Without breaking stride and in a somewhat casual voice, Paul remarked, "I think I am having a stroke." I looked at him, thinking he must be joking. Then I realized that one side of his face wasn't moving as well as the other, although nothing else appeared unusual. Back on the ship while having lunch, Paul had some difficulty controlling his lips and tended to dribble. My own diagnosis was a facial paralysis (Bell's Palsy).

We took our naps, and when we awoke I noticed his speech was very slurred. We talked to one of the other doctors in our group, and he advised us to see the ship's doctor.

The ship's doctor was concerned but did not have the resources to treat Paul on the ship. In no time she was on the ship-to-shore phone making arrangements to transfer him to a hospital.

Paul's speech might have been slurred, but his mind was sharp. "Just a minute," he interrupted her, "is there a neurologist on duty at the hospital?" She relayed his question and the answer came back, "No, not until Monday" (it was Saturday afternoon and most staff go off for the weekend). Then he asked if there would be any English-speaking doctor on duty. Again, a negative answer. That being the case, Paul saw no purpose in being admitted to the local hospital, especially since we would be in Istanbul in less than twenty-four hours, where we knew many doctors and could get a neurological consultation. So he thanked the doctor and signed a form saying he was "going against medical advice," which freed her of all responsibility.

We left the ship's sickbay, sent a telegram to our friends in Istanbul, and went to share our news with the Christian physicians' group. They expressed concern and then formed a prayer circle around us, and several prayed for the Lord to intervene in His own way. We both slept well that night.

On Sunday morning Paul's status was about the same, and he was able to deliver his lecture just as planned. He stopped once to ask if they could understand his slurred speech. "Sure," they answered, "go on."

In Istanbul a neurologist saw him and made a favorable diagnosis: Paul had suffered a lacunar stroke, which means a small, limited area of brain damage with a very good chance of recovery. He provided some good advice and sent us on our way.

The cruise ended there, and we took the plane back to England, spent a few days with family, then traveled home to the States. By the time we got to Seattle, Paul's speech seemed normal. Praise the Lord!

In 1996 Margaret and Paul were in Karigiri when another health crisis arose with no clear answer apparent. Margaret relied once again upon her faith and the faith of Christians with her.

I was at Karigiri teaching at a paramedical course, and Paul was there chiefly to participate in board meetings for the medical college. Due to shortage of faculty staff, I was alone with about thirty paramedical students who didn't know how to examine eyes.

At the end of a long and exhausting day, I returned to the house where we were staying. Paul and I were supposed to go over to the college, about forty minutes away, where he was to give a major lecture at a dinner meeting. I found Paul, still in his casual clothing, slumped over in a chair in the living room. His mouth was open, and he seemed disoriented. I asked if he was going to change his clothes, and he answered, "What for?" He had totally forgotten about the speech and the dinner, and he looked as if he didn't care whether we went or not.

I called our friend Dr. Ernest Fritschi at the college (CMC) and told him I thought Paul wasn't well enough to go to the dinner but that he had the speech written out and someone else could read it. Paul wanted to talk to Ernest, so I handed him the phone. Paul was entirely confused, and his words made no sense. When I took the phone again, Ernest told me that he thought Paul was having a stroke or was about to have one. He told me he would call the doctors from the neurological and surgical departments and they would come and take Paul to the Christian Medical College by ambulance.

I got Paul into bed and called our good friends Augustin and Valsa who lived fairly close to the guesthouse where we were staying. (Augustin is now the hospital administrator and his wife Valsa is a social worker.) When I told them about the situation, Augustin said, "We were going to go over to CMC to listen to Dr. Brand, but somehow we knew that we should not go." If they had gone, there would have been nobody around for me to call, since everyone at Karigiri had gone to hear Paul speak!

Augustin and Valsa came to the house and prayed with me. It was a terribly difficult time for me as my mind filled with questions: *What am I going to do if Paul dies? How am I going to contact all the family?* Paul and I had often talked about how much extensive, supportive medical care we would want, and he had said, "I *don't* want to have any support system. I *don't* want to be on tubes and so forth. Let me go when there doesn't seem to be any hope of a normal life after recovery." Those words also were in my thoughts.

When we finished praying, Augustin said, "He's going to be all right. I know he's going to get better." I instantly believed him and felt a sense of relief.

The ambulance arrived, along with about eight doctors, who started examining Paul and asking me questions. He had a temperature of about 102, which was not insignificant for a person of his age. "We must get him into the ambulance," they said. "It's just outside the door now, waiting. We'll take care of him."

We were scheduled to leave Karigiri the next day for Madras, and then on to England, but if Paul were hospitalized, we might be in Vellore for the next two weeks because of the difficulty of getting flights booked at that short notice. I also knew Paul had an appointment the next day with an attorney about the Mother Brand Trust, created to support and continue his mother's work in the hills.

Paul looked at me rather helplessly as if to say, "You know what I want and don't want." The doctors said to me, "We'll all sleep much better if we know he's under watch in Intensive Care," and I answered, "But I don't think he'll sleep at all!"

Paul had been working late and not sleeping well. He had probably picked up a viral infection, judging from his fever. He was exhausted, and I decided that, more than anything, sleep was what he needed. So I decided not to let them take him to the hospital. One of the other Karigiri doctors said, "I, too, think he needs sleep." She was living in the apartment right upstairs from us, and if I had trouble with Paul during the night, she said, I could just bang on the ceiling and she would come down. She was an experienced doctor and a good ally. The eight physicians respected my decision, and they and the ambulance departed.

That night Paul slept well, and in the morning his speech was back to normal. He still felt poorly but was able to go the attorney's office, accompanied by Ernest Fritschi. (The night before, Ernest had given Paul's speech at the dinner, and we later heard that it was a real triumph. The audience was told why Paul wasn't delivering the address, and many present prayed for Paul's healing.)

I still had to give my students their final exam and mark their papers and sign their certificates. Then I had to pack our belongings. It was becoming apparent that we both had some sort of flu, and the three-hour car ride to Madras was terrible, as we both had bad headaches. We were to stay overnight at a hotel near the airport, but the driver didn't know where the hotel was and kept driving us all around Madras. When we finally got to our room, the air-conditioning was freezing cold, and we couldn't turn it down. We put on all the clothing we had and huddled in the bed, but we couldn't sleep because we were so cold. We got up much earlier than we needed to, but we felt we would be warmer at the airport.

Connie's husband, David, met us in London at Heathrow Airport and took us to their home, where we could sleep in a normal bed at a normal temperature. Later we went on to Jean's and then to Pauline's before returning home to Seattle. After we got home, Paul and I took turns making pots of tea so that we were each forced to get up and in turn help the other. I eventually developed pneumonia from all of this. Mary remembers talking to us by phone and asking if we had any cough syrup, to which Paul replied, in a sad and pathetic voice, "Yes, but we can't get the cap off!"

In October 1997, Margaret and Paul once again traveled to India for their yearly visit. For a seventy-eight-year-old, Dr. Margaret had been given a rather hectic schedule of responsibilities. She taught a three-week eye course to paramedics, followed by an additional two-week course for physicians. She was to have been assisted by a co-instructor, but that person had been called away and not replaced. After the exhausting time in India, they traveled to England, where they first went to Leeds to visit Pauline, her husband, Mark, and their children. They then went to Southampton on the southern coast for a week with Jean before they returned to Seattle. Two days before their departure, however, Margaret awoke in the middle of the night with chest pain.

On the morning of October 4 I woke up feeling quite poorly. I was nauseous, so I went to the loo, but my legs were so weak I could hardly make it back to bed. I woke Paul and told him I was having severe chest pain. He tried to get a pulse but couldn't find one, and Jean called for an ambulance. As soon as it arrived, the attendants gave me nitroglycerin and oxygen, and I started to feel better. I remember looking at Paul and thinking I had never seen him look so crumpled. I was glad to be able to tell him, "I'm feeling much better now." But that feeling didn't last long, and soon I didn't care how I got to the hospital—I just wanted somebody to give me something for the pain.

When they told me at the hospital that I'd had a heart attack, it was no surprise. They started treatment, and within a few days moved me out of intensive care and into one of the extension wards where they could still monitor my heart.

Then around 10:00 on Sunday evening, October 12, I again started to have severe pain in my chest. The nurse gave me nitroglycerin, but when my blood pressure began falling they moved me back to the intensive care ward. The young doctor said I would have to have an infusion of a drug to dissolve any blood clots in my coronary arteries, but he said, "I've got to tell you this. You could have a stroke with this medication or you could get retinal hemorrhages."

I thought, *Paul is going to come in the morning and I'll either have had a stroke or I'll be blind.* And did I really want this medication? Wasn't this rather like supportive care when there's really no future for you? I said I'd like to call my husband and have him come over. This was about 3:00 in the morning.

Poor Paul. He and Jean were sound asleep, and when he heard the phone ring at that hour he knew it was bad news. I told him I wanted to talk with him because this could be our good-bye. The doctor said he needed to start the clot-dissolving drug and to start it soon, but I asked him to wait for a few minutes. Jean and Paul were coming, and if I had a stroke, I wouldn't be able to talk with him.

When they came in, I told Paul that this drug might help my heart but might spoil other things, and our life might be totally different because of this. Paul said, "Jean, you pray and pray specifically about this." I don't remember what she prayed, but I felt a great sense of resolution and peace following the prayer. They stayed with me while the medicine was given to me—it went in rather slowly—and the doctor stayed with me as well. I didn't stroke and I didn't have a retinal hemorrhage. The pain eased and Jean left. Paul stayed with me and slept in the chair.

Later the doctor told me that I needed an angiogram. After they told Paul and I the risks of this procedure, I called Estelle in Hawaii.

Meanwhile, Mary called, but since I was on a gurney being readied to be transported to OR, she asked the night nurse to tell me to sing "Kept by the Power of God." The nurse gave me Mary's message and said that she knew the hymn and would be happy to sing it with me. So together we sang this wonderfully comforting hymn as I was being pushed down the hallway for my angiogram.

I was feeling quite detached as I watched my heart on the monitor. I had to keep reminding myself that was *me* on the monitor! The cardiologist said that an angioplasty wouldn't work, as the angiogram revealed that there was too much blockage, but that I was a good candidate for bypass surgery and put me on the list for Friday. I asked if perhaps I should go back to the States to have the surgery. I felt I had jumped the queue—there were others in the ward who had been waiting for surgery longer than I had. They told me, "You're not even going out for an afternoon!" I suppose they felt I was unstable and couldn't wait that long, and they monitored me closely.

Pauline and her children came down from Leeds during the week before my surgery, and Mary surprised me by coming over from the States, arriving the day before my operation. I had asked for the hospital chaplain to visit me, and she came and anointed me. Then someone from Jean's church came and anointed me, so I was well prepared. Before I went to sleep on Thursday night, I wrote a letter to our grandchildren describing the peace that I felt in spite of the gravity of the situation, thanks to my faith in the Lord.

In the days before Margaret's surgery, Paul had taken to walking from Jean's house to the hospital—about a mile walk involving hilly residential streets. During these walks he started having pains in his chest, especially after a hill climb. He took this to be "sympathetic" pain, sharing with Margaret what she was experiencing. The evening before her bypass operation, as he, Jean, and Mary sat with Margaret, he mentioned to her that it was amazing how he too had experienced chest pain like she had in the past week. Margaret said he should get this checked out, and he promised that he would when they returned to Seattle. But he awoke at two o'clock the morning of Margaret's surgery with severe chest pain, which clearly was more than just empathy for his beloved wife. Jean and Mary rushed him to the emergency room, where he was diagnosed as having a heart attack and admitted to intensive care. Following the doctors' advice, the girls decided not to tell Margaret about this since it was right before her surgery, so she didn't find out about his "sympathetic heart attack" until later.

> It was great to wake up and find the chest pain gone. There was a new pain from the incision, of course, but that went away fairly quickly, and I only needed some Tylenol for a few days. Then Mary and Jean told me about Paul after I was out of Recovery and back in the ward. I wasn't allowed to visit him on his floor because there was some kind of infectious bug going around. How we rejoiced once we finally were able to see one another!

Paul's heart attack proved to be mild and was successfully treated without the need for an angiogram or any type of surgical intervention. He was discharged the day before Margaret, but since neither of them was to travel for six weeks, they moved into Jean's house to convalesce. Thankfully Jean had space for her parents, and she set aside her own work to help nurse them to health. Jim, Mary's husband, came over from the States, his contribution chiefly being the construction of a gate in the back of Jean's garden fence so that the two patients could stroll directly out into the park beyond for their daily walk. During their time of recovery, a parade of friends and family came to visit. It was as if the Lord had forced them to stop in one place long enough for old companions to see them.

In an outpouring of love, visitors, flowers, and cards filled the house. The mailman was especially taxed during those weeks by the sheer volume of cards and letters he had to carry to Jean's every day. And Paul and Margaret prized every one, more than the senders could have imagined. They read each card and letter with joy—the power of the message and the presence of the person sending it seeming to give both of them a bit more strength, the ability to take one more step.

> When we were able to travel home to Seattle, Trish, Mike, and the children met us at the airport. Four-year-old Madeline and seven-year-old Josh stood there solemnly holding a banner that went right across the room, saying, "Welcome Home, Grammy and Grampy!" Madeline didn't say a word to me. She just kept looking at me as if she wasn't quite sure if I were alive or not. Finally, when we were in the car, she asked sweetly,

"Grammy, why *didn't* you die?" and I couldn't think of an answer. She repeated her question, but I'm still working on the answer to that! If the heart attack had happened two days later on the airplane as we traveled home, I am quite sure I wouldn't have survived.

Evidently the Lord has more for me to do.

Over the course of 1998, Paul and Margaret continued their recovery. Like children being punished, they reluctantly agreed to the admonitions of family members not to commit themselves to a hectic schedule, not to promise their presence at endless conferences. This lasted for a reasonable amount of time, during which they took the opportunity to answer many of the greetings and get well wishes. Paul even briefly consented not to travel out of the Seattle area. But Margaret began feeling well enough to believe that she should keep her commitment to speak in China at a leprosy conference late in 1998. She felt that her strength had returned, and she knew that the Lord would let her know if He didn't want her to go. He did.

Just thirty-six hours before I was to leave for Beijing to teach, I went into a profound arrhythmia (an irregular heartbeat). I went to the emergency room to get it straightened out. Then the next day I had a second bout. The cardiologist said that if the arrhythmia had occurred on the plane, I would probably have had a stroke by the time I landed in China.

Chris Doyle, the CEO for American Leprosy Mission, was going to the conference, and he had not yet left. By overnight delivery we sent him my papers, handouts, and slides, and he took them to Dr. Ebbie Daniel, who read my lecture. I had never before written a lecture out word for word, but I just "happened" to have done it that time.

Sometimes God has to intervene and slow us down before we get ourselves in real trouble.

For the first time in years, Paul and Margaret did not go to Karigiri in October. Nevertheless, following this one setback with the arrhythmia, Margaret's health once again flourished, and at the age of eighty she was feeling quite well as the autumn of 1999 approached. The administrators at Karigiri decided that if she came that year, they would videotape her talks so that in future years these could serve to educate the course attendees without her having to be there in person. So much of her teaching had included hands-on demonstrations on real patients that this concept didn't appeal to her, but for the visit of December 1999 she did agree to the project.

Paul, who long before had forgotten his promise about restricted travel, also planned to return. They traveled first to England, where they stayed for two weeks to see old friends and to meet up with daughter Pauline. She then traveled with them to India—her first visit since she left the country in 1963. At a ceremony in Delhi, Paul relinquished the presidency of the International Leprosy Mission and handed it over to Dr. K. C. Job, who had been one of Paul's favorite students back in the 1940s and was now a world-renowned leprologist. They next flew down to Madras and took the familiar drive to Vellore. Their granddaughter Stephanie (Mary's daughter) had arrived a few weeks before to observe the medical care being provided at Karigiri and Vellore.

While Dr. Margaret stayed behind at Karigiri to leave her legacy of teaching tapes, Paul and Pauline and Stephanie visited the Kolli Hills where Paul had been raised and where his mother had worked for so many decades. One last time Paul walked the old familiar mountain paths of his childhood, this time with part of his own living legacy—daughter and granddaughter.

August of 2000 saw the Department of Surgery at CMC celebrating its fiftieth anniversary while the college as a whole was celebrating its centenary. It had been one hundred years since Dr. Ida Scudder had arrived from America to open her modest clinic for women. Paul and Margaret attended the celebrations. Mary and her husband, Jim, with their close friends Freda and Paul Seward from England, also visited the campus and sites throughout southern India that had been so precious to Mary during her years there. In 2003 Trish and Mike took their children to India for a similar tour. These vistas and people of South India represent the Brand children's childhood, and, like their father, it will always be the place where they feel most at home.

Chapter 26

Arrived Safely

"The time has come for my departure.
I have fought the good fight, I have finished the race,
I have kept the faith."
                    — 2 Timothy, 4:6–7

Margaret's beloved Paul died on July 8, 2003, at the age of eighty-eight. On the very day of their sixtieth wedding anniversary, May 29, 2003, he had suffered a small stroke that had left him with a slight facial weakness. Typical of Drs. Margaret and Paul, they did not allow this to interfere with the anniversary dinner Trish had arranged for that evening. Only a few days later did Paul agree to undergo scans under the direction of son-in-law Mike, and only reluctantly did he agree to see a neurologist that Mike and Trish had contacted. He was put on a second drug besides aspirin in an attempt to prevent future strokes.

In their retirement years, Margaret and Paul had continued with their busy lives. Besides speaking engagements, Paul now was primarily occupied with his correspondence. He had once been impressed to learn that the great Christian author C. S. Lewis answered every letter his readers sent him. Paul vowed to do the same, as over the years the success of the books bearing his name had resulted in an ongoing stream of letters and now e-mails from throughout the world. He also had started writing a series of litanies—contemplative prayers of gratitude for organ systems of the human body. He enjoyed participating in discussion groups at their church, West Side Presbyterian, and working with Margaret on the board of CRISTA headquartered in Seattle. And he and Margaret looked forward to attending granddaughter Margaret's wedding in Hawaii scheduled for late in July, with the entire family planning to return to Seattle afterward for a belated celebration of their parents' sixtieth anniversary.

Margaret was occupied with her own voluminous correspondence as well as speaking engagements and church activities. She played violin with a church group for special occasions and especially enjoyed participating in Vacation Bible School each summer. She was busy with her vegetable garden, managing the mass of berries produced in their yard, and making homemade marmalade—for there was always a demand within her own home!

Their little house overlooking Puget Sound was still "home central" for the extended Brand family, and the Grandparents Brand were in constant communication with their children and grandchildren. If any member of the family called, Paul and Margaret would together be on the phone. Trish and Mike were nearby, and Christopher and his family were frequent guests, now living only an hour's drive away. As had been true throughout their lives, Paul and Margaret's greatest satisfaction came from communicating with their children and grandchildren in whatever way possible.

Almost daily their invaluable assistant, Molly Coyner Cozens, came to the house for a few hours of work. One of Molly's most difficult tasks continued to be trying to limit the commitments Paul and Margaret were all too willing to accept. At the ages of eighty-eight and eighty-three, they still had the next twenty-four calendar months taped up across one wall. There seemed to be no end to the demands placed upon them, yet they relished the work.

Then, on June 19, 2003, Margaret's eighty-fourth birthday, Paul fell down the living room stairs and hit his head. Margaret took him to a hospital in Seattle, where Trish met them. Paul soon lost consciousness and underwent emergency surgery to remove a blood clot on the surface of the brain. Part of the problem was the bleeding caused by the blood-thinning drugs he was taking to prevent stroke. After the surgery the outcome looked successful, but then his condition deteriorated due to a different problem, that of bleeding within the brain itself.

Over the next two weeks a painful, grieving vigil ensued as family members gathered at his bedside. A remarkable number of wonderful friends came to comfort the family, some traveling great distances. Paul had made his wishes clear in the event of such an illness. He did not desire any heroic measures unless he could return to his previous state of health. So the outcome was left in the hands of the Lord, and the Lord took Paul to Himself on July 8, nineteen days after his injury.

Paul's condition gave us time as a family to summon everybody, even though at times tickets looked impossible to obtain. We were able to assemble together around his bed for several days and have a bittersweet but precious family reunion. Pauline and Jean came from England, Estelle from Hawaii, Mary and Jim from Minnesota, Christopher, Kelly, and Evelyn from Olympia, and Trish, Mike, and the children from Seattle.

What a beautiful thing it is to be in the presence of someone who is shortly going to be in the Lord's presence. We reminisced, we wept, we prayed, and we laughed a great deal. At one point Mary and I were standing over Dad's bed, and I commented about how I dreaded the thought of living in our house all alone. Mary said that perhaps I should consider getting a puppy for companionship. I told her that I didn't think I would feel like house-training a new puppy. Mary said, "Well, maybe you could go to the pound and get an older dog whose owner has just died." I have trouble hearing at times, and what I heard Mary say was "get an older dog *who's only just died.*" I stared at her in disbelief, wondering what on earth she was talking about. She was perplexed at the expression on my face, and when I told her what I thought she had said we collapsed in peals of laughter. She went on to say that yes, that might be good too, and the maintenance of such a pet would be inexpensive. We felt that Dad was enjoying this exchange as much as we were, though I'm certain the intensive care staff couldn't imagine what was going on in Paul's room.

We sang songs that Paul loved. And while we sensed that this was the preliminary to the final good-bye, we faced it with a sense of awe. Our dear husband, father, and grandfather was straddling that little border between earth and heaven. I don't remember it being a particularly sad time, although there were moments when I would go away and sob. I think we each sensed that although we were very sad at the prospect of losing him, we also had a great sense of joy and anticipation of getting to see him again. And there was great comfort in knowing that he would be united with the Lord he loved and with the people he had loved who had passed on.

About two days before his final departure, Paul's breathing became more rapid and agitated. The doctors tried increasing his oxygen and morphine to relieve any discomfort he might be feeling, but he continued to breathe rapidly. He was panting, and his face had a troubled, anxious look, as if he were engaged in some really difficult task, climbing a difficult hill, fighting something.

Late on the evening of July 7, we said good night to him. Jean was going to take over the night vigil, as several of us, including two dear friends, Dee Myers and Gayle Reiber, had taken turns on other nights. About 4:00 in the morning, Jean called to say that we should come to the hospital quickly because Dad's breathing had changed, and she felt the end was close. When we got to the hospital room, just two minutes after Paul had taken his last breath, I went immediately to his side and looked down at the face which for the past two days had looked so anxious and troubled with a furrowed frown on his forehead. Now there was absolute peace, even joy, on his face.

It reminded me of days gone by when Paul would make some long journey in situations of dangerous air travel. Knowing that I would be waiting anxiously to hear that he had arrived at his destination, he would send me a telegram with just four words: "Arrived safely. Love, Paul." Now, as I looked down at his peaceful face, I could almost see written across it, "Arrived safely."

Following a quiet graveside service, Paul was laid to rest in a cemetery on Vashon Island, an island within Puget Sound located opposite the shore-line of West Seattle. On July 20 a memorial service was held at West Side Presbyterian Church, and August 2 the CRISTA board, of which Paul and Margaret were members, held a second memorial service, conducted by Jim Gwinn, president of CRISTA Ministries.

This was a celebration of all facets of Paul's life, with speakers including daughter Pauline, West Side pastor Paul W. Smith, and dear friend and author Philip Yancey. Bruce Carman, son of Jack Carman, Paul's first surgeon partner at Vellore, sang a hymn written by his grandfather. Each speaker shared his or her different experiences with this remarkable man. Pauline gave a memorable tribute to the love, strength, and self-confidence her father had imparted to her. It was masterful and overwhelmed the audience with the depth of affection she shared. Pastor Smith discussed Paul's deep and abiding Christian faith and made the audience feel his own joy at Paul's having attained, without question, the kingdom of heaven. Philip movingly recounted Paul's effect on his own spiritual journey, serving as mentor, critic, and loyal friend. In honor of Paul's style, Philip delivered his comments barefooted and began by eating cherries and spitting the pits onto the floor, mimicking the famous opening Paul used in one of his sermons to illustrate how the gospel is attractively sweet so that as it is enjoyed the seed is spread. Molly's son, Adam Cozens, created a PowerPoint presentation of photos for the service, and typical of the range of emotions in the hearts of all present, this brought smiles and laughter as well as tears.

Another memorial service was held in India at CMC, and on October 4 a service was held in London. Mary and Jim were able to accompany Margaret to London for the service.

Among the many wonderful memorials arranged around the world for Paul, three involved my being there with whatever family members could attend. In October 2003 a service for our UK friends was held in London at Bloomsbury Central Baptist Church, which was near the original office of The Leprosy Mission International (TLMI). Trevor Durston and the staff of TLMI arranged this memorial, and the church kindly allowed their facilities to be used. The mission beautifully organized both the service and the buffet lunch that followed. We stayed with dear friends Freda and Paul Seward in Reading. Freda had been one of Mary's best friends at Clarendon.

Various people gave tributes, and some of Paul's favorite hymns were sung, including the one we had sung at the graveside service, "How Good Is the God We Adore," a hymn Paul had often quoted and sung. Paul's sister Connie and her husband David were there, and Connie gave a lovely remembrance of Paul as a boy, the only person who could do that. Andrew Wilmshurst, her son, who is a hand and plastic reconstructive surgeon, spoke of how Paul was one of his heroes and role model.

Eddie Askew, a longtime friend who worked with us in India and was the general director of The Leprosy Mission International for many years, gave an amusing tribute, typical of Eddie and full of love. John Webb, who himself was not well, came from Devonshire and spoke lovingly of the years of friendship that he and Paul had enjoyed. Our daughter Pauline gave the tribute that she had given at the CRISTA memorial in

Seattle, and Jean brought it all to a conclusion, offering final remarks and
singing a song Paul had loved and which Jean had written, "The Foot
Washing Song."

Following the service we enjoyed a relaxing tea party hosted by
the Webbs at a nearby hotel in Bloomsbury. It was marvelous to
spend this time with such old and dear friends and to recount our
days as the "Wends." We next went to the London flat of our niece,
Elizabeth Wilmshurst, where we once again could laugh together over
reminiscences of past times. It was a long day but a happy one and
celebrated not only Paul's life but also the parts played in it by so many
wonderful friends and family.

We spent several more days in England, with Jim driving us to visit
friends and relatives. It was a great blessing for me to see such love and
helped me through those difficult days.

Though all who loved Paul know that he is enjoying his place in heaven
and his reunion with his father and mother, he is and will remain grievously
missed. He represented, throughout his entire life and in everything he did,
the closest to pure goodness an individual may achieve on this earth through
Christ. Such examples are truly rare. He shared himself with hundreds of
thousands of people through his surgical expertise and medical discoveries, through his teaching and speaking, and through his writings. His influence will continue to flow outward forever through those he has touched
and those who read his works. And, God willing, those touched by Paul will
touch others in like fashion. He is one who has left this earth a better place.

When I think about Paul's last day, I remember the words the angels
gave the women who came to the tomb on Easter morning: "He is not
here . . . He is going ahead of you into Galilee . . . (Mark 16:6–7).

Often when Paul and I went for a walk, he tended to walk faster than
I could and would get ahead of me without realizing it. But July 8, 2003,
was the day he stepped out ahead of me for the last time. Now I have to
remember: I have not lost my beloved Paul; he has just gone on ahead of
me, and I will catch up one of these days.

Chapter 27

Great Is Thy Faithfulness

*"No eye has seen, no ear has heard, no mind has conceived,
what God has prepared for those who love Him."*
—*1 Corinthians 2:9*

In the months following Paul's death, loving family and friends helped Margaret. Trish and Mike, who lived nearby, offered comfort and support. Christopher and Kelly, as well as Dee Myers, stayed with Margaret on a regular basis. Christopher was especially appreciated for his assistance with endless legal matters. Molly and her family took care of countless details. Church friends stepped in to help in any way they could. A small greenhouse for the back garden was donated to honor Paul. And messages from around the world flowed in by phone, card, letter, and e-mail to offer both condolences and encouragement. But Margaret's greatest comfort came from her faith and the strength given her by the Lord to get through the darkest days.

I was reading in the book of Isaiah, chapter 54. Suddenly I read verse five, the words almost shouting at me: "Your Maker is your husband." It was like a strong ray of sunshine breaking through dark clouds. My heart rejoiced, and I knew I would be able to cope. My Maker/Husband would never leave me and would see that His angels were on hand to help me every day. They have. I can say with the hymn writer Chisholm, "All I have needed Thy hand hath provided. Great is Thy faithfulness, Lord, unto me."

As was typical of her entire life, Dr. Margaret could not be idle. Her first priority was to try to respond to the correspondence she received after Paul's death—over five hundred written notes of condolence and words of love and support. This seemed an overwhelming task, yet it was a labor of love and something she enjoyed, no matter how much time it required. Also, it helped her to be busy and provided great joy to see the kind of impact she and Paul had had on so many people.

No one expected that she would feel like resuming the commitments and activities that had occupied her time before Paul's death. She herself wasn't certain what she might still wish to do. But as the grace of God eased some of the pain and diminished some of the grief, she began looking forward. She felt that it was the Lord's will to take Paul when He did, but His will had left her behind for the present. Buoyed by the assurance that she would join him when God wished her to do so, she felt a peace and found that she could perhaps return to some of the work she had started.

As it happened, 2004 was extraordinary in the way that so many elements of her life history returned and provided her with joy for the present and gratitude for the past. It all began with a phone call from a special friend, an "adopted granddaughter."

Early in 2004 I received a surprise telephone call from Lily, who had been our interpreter on our China visits in 1989 and 1995. We had kept in close contact with her over the years, speaking to her by phone almost monthly, sending her books. She had quit her work as an interpreter several years ago and had recently started working in Beijing for the Ford Foundation, which offered scholarships to foreign students throughout the world. Lily told me that in March she would be at a conference in Hawaii and that she would be allowed to come to Seattle for a few days. She said that she always wanted "Grandpa Paul" to baptize her but wondered if our pastor, Dr. Paul Smith, whom Paul had loved, would do that.

Pastor Paul Smith said he would interview Lily and make certain that she was serious about her faith. If all was in order, the presbytery would allow him to baptize her. We wanted to have a special celebration for her, and several people offered to organize a Chinese meal for the occasion. Invitations were sent to our small Bible group, our prayer group, the missions committee, the elders, and the deacons.

Lily arrived on a Monday evening and met with Pastor Paul the next day. He had no difficulty accepting her for her baptism. Lily had already shown the determination of her faith; she had risked her own life in order to stay true to her Lord, something few of us ever have had to do. She had already demonstrated that her faith meant more to her than life itself.

The baptism was in the church's little chapel, which had new stained glass windows with the theme "How Great a Cloud of Witnesses." Lily felt that Grandpa Paul was present at her baptism as one of those witnesses. She answered the questions from her heart and gave her testimony of what it meant to her to be a Christian. The reception followed, and next day she had to leave us.

Despite her enjoyment of Lily's visit and baptism, Margaret still felt uncertain about committing to the next event to which she was invited. Medical alumni of the Vellore Christian Medical College were going to have a "GOTC" (Gathering of the Clan) reunion in Charleston, South Carolina, in June 2004, and Margaret was invited as guest of honor. Not only would this be the first time Margaret had seen these old friends without Paul, but the day of the main banquet would be the one-year anniversary of the day he fell and it would rouse painful memories. Some of Margaret's dread at facing such an emotional weekend was alleviated when Mary volunteered to accompany her.

That weekend we were surrounded by people who sorrowed with me at Paul's passing but also shared so many funny stories from their memories of Paul. Their welcome to me was sweet and heartfelt, and, though bittersweet, those few days became very special. I was comforted by the experience, especially to see that some of the alums, who as students expressed no faith, had come to the Lord.

Early in the program at the banquet I was to make a few remarks. I told a story about Molly Abraham, who was in the audience. Molly was one of the students who would often come to our house and who knew our children well. She would bring beautiful gifts, especially at Christmas. One year she brought identical dresses for Mary and Estelle, but a different dress for Trish. Trish adored Molly and the dress.

I told how one night after I had finished reading "Snow White and the Seven Dwarfs" to Trish, she asked me what a stepmother was. So I told her that if a man's wife dies and he marries again, the new wife is the stepmother of his children. "Well, I hope that when you die Daddy will marry Molly," said Trish. Just like that! Not "*if* you die" but "*when* you die"! This brought a roar of laughter from the audience.

This incident showed what a deep affection there was between the women students and our children, and it took me right back to Vellore days. Although I was missing Paul horribly, I sort of asked him, "Paul, did you enjoy this story too?" Somehow I felt him near me.

The GOTC reunion helped Margaret step further out into the world, and as the Lord continued showing her that she could tolerate the demands expected of her and accomplish the work He wanted her to do, her life gradually became busier again with local church work and meetings of the CRISTA and American Leprosy Mission boards. She continued to spend a great deal of time on correspondence, and her prayer list was extensive as new concerns were brought to her attention.

The next invitation she received was far more challenging than the weekend in Charleston: to visit India in late August of 2004 for a series of events. She had last been to India in 2000 for the celebration of CMC's centenary year. The first event this time would be a celebration of the fiftieth anniversary of the founding of Schieffelin, which would include an international scientific meeting on leprosy where she would make the opening remarks. The second event for Margaret was to lay the foundation stone for a new outpatient clinic to be named "The Paul W. Brand Integrated Health Centre" in the nearby town of Katpadi, as an outreach facility for Schieffelin. The third event was the dedication of a new wing, which would include a beautiful little chapel—"The Margaret and Paul Brand Extension"—being added to the spinal rehabilitation center near the CMC campus. Finally, besides attending a flag-raising ceremony on Indian Independence Day, she was asked to address a group of visiting Vellore alumni. Mixed with all these scheduled commitments would be time spent in the Ophthalmology Department, the unpredictable arrival of old friends and patients, along with invitations to meals in various staff homes.

In the end, however, after much prayer, Margaret felt that the Lord wanted her to go and was certain that He would help her. She invited Estelle, who had not been back to India since leaving in 1963, to accompany her. And when Mary heard of the trip, she signed on as well. Excitement and anticipation soon replaced doubts or concerns.

In June of 2004, Margaret had signed a contract with Discovery House Publishers to publish her biography. Shortly before she was to leave for India, RBC Ministries, with which Discovery House is affiliated, asked her permission to send a film crew to India while she was there to take footage for a *Day of Discovery* television program. Hence there would be one more project to add to the others. She was undaunted.

The final plan for this complex odyssey involved Margaret and Estelle flying to England, where they would meet up with Mary and her husband Jim, who was accompanying her to England. The foursome would visit Jean in southern England, Pauline and her family in northern England, and then Margaret and her two daughters would leave for India. An accident during the England visit suddenly made the India plans even more challenging.

> By the time we left, I wasn't fearful about the trip. Decisions can be so difficult to make, but once made you begin to organize around them. Estelle flew from Hawaii to Seattle and off we went, meeting up with Jean, Mary, and Jim in London. Immediately I knew that this was going to be fun.
>
> The first thing we did was to drive past our old house on Colebrooke Avenue in Ealing. I was so glad to see how lived in and well cared for it looked. During our brief few days we visited family and old friends. We were scheduled to have afternoon tea at Connie and David's near London and decided to visit Winchester Cathedral that morning, since it is near Jean's where we were staying. As we left the cathedral and were walking along a paved pathway, I stumbled on an uneven stone. I fell forward and felt a searing pain in my upper left arm. My first thought as I lay there, afraid to move, was, *Am I going to die here?* No. Then, *Am I going to India?* I'm not sure. Then, oddly, the third thought was, *Will I play my violin again?* I only play it for the Easter and Christmas services at church, yet this seemed important.
>
> The kids helped me to roll over and sit on the ground, leaning against Jean. Jim went off to the cathedral gift shop and came back with a canvas apron, which he fashioned into a sling and which he called my "souvenir sling." This at least allowed me to stand.
>
> We drove to the casualty department (emergency room) at Southampton General, where an X-ray confirmed a fracture of my upper arm near the shoulder joint. I was provided with a professional sling, pain

medications, and an appointment the next day in the Fracture Clinic with an orthopedic consultant. He advised that my fracture could be treated without surgery, and after the appointment we stopped at a shop where the girls helped me find new tops. (I hadn't packed any clothes suited for slings!)

We visited with Connie and David and drove up to Pauline's in Leeds. And by the day of our flight I felt confident that I could travel and was getting better at sleeping sitting up, which was the most healing position for my arm.

Estelle, Mary, and I arrived in Chennai at 5:00 a.m. Sunday morning, where we were greeted by Dr. Abraham Joseph, the director of Schieffelin. I could tell by his face how much I was welcomed and how concerned he was for my welfare.

Dr. Joseph cancelled some of Margaret's lesser commitments, allowing her time to rest and to work on the addresses she was to deliver once the weekend came. She was examined by orthopedic consultants from both Schieffelin and CMC, who agreed that the sling treatment was working satisfactorily, though she did develop a skin infection during the second week from an elbow abrasion suffered at the time of her fall. With antibiotics and a change in her sleeping position which allowed her to sleep lying down, her arm steadily improved.

By the end of the week she was able to attend a tea hosted in the eye department at Schieffelin by Dr. Ebenezer Daniel, a well-loved colleague who was now chief of her old section. After the tea, the entire group visited the small village of Shanthigramam near the Schieffelin grounds where elderly leprosy patients from the old days now reside. Everyone, including Estelle and Mary, were somewhat shocked when one gentleman proudly removed his artificial inner nose support, something that Dr. Paul had helped him obtain. The newly arrived film crew from RBC Ministries had been given a bold introduction into the world of leprosy.

On Friday the group toured the spinal rehabilitation center project, had lunch with Susie Koshi, a friend for over forty years going back to Paul's New Life Centre, and at teatime Margaret had an emotional reunion with Ernest Fritschi. This was the first time Ernest had seen Margaret since the death of Paul and the death of his wife Mano. He welcomed Margaret with roses, and the two friends wept together over their mutual losses. The day ended with the visit of a group of men who had been patients at Paul's New Life Centre when they were boys.

The weekend schedule included the Saturday morning alumni meeting where Margaret received the "Alumnus of the Year" award, an afternoon visit with the Brands' cook and ayah, Aruldoss and Manomani, and an evening banquet with the medical student alums. Margaret and her two daughters were resplendent in their saris. Then on Sunday, following the worship service in St. Luke's chapel, she gave the keynote address to the scientific assembly for the start of their meetings.

After spending some time at the meetings on Monday, she and the girls participated in the "laying of the foundation stone" ceremony for the "Paul Brand Integrated Medical Centre" in Katpadi. Fittingly, the organizers had Margaret use the very same trowel that Dr. Ida Scudder had used for a similar ceremony fifty years earlier when construction began on the Schieffelin Leprosy Research and Training Centre. On Tuesday she met with an Indian couple, Paul Stephen and his wife Deborah, currently continuing Granny Brand's work in the Kalarayan Hills. During breakfast with them, a former leprosy patient of Paul's, Subalakshmi, appeared. Subalakshmi's life had been intertwined with the Brands in a remarkable way.

As a young woman Subalakshmi had been photographed as Paul examined her hands, and this photo was subsequently used in Dorothy Clarke Wilson's book *Ten Fingers for God,* a book about Paul's life and work. Subalakshmi announced that she wanted Margaret to arrange her admission to the hospital for a badly infected foot. She agreed to be taken to the hospital at Vellore. At the end of the afternoon, after several other visitors had descended upon Margaret, Subalakshmi reappeared, having been denied admission at Vellore. Margaret's last task in India was helping arrange Subalakshmi's admission to Schieffelin—as if Dr. Margaret, some forty years later, was still on duty at Karigiri.

On Wednesday morning at 2:00 a.m., the Brand women left for Madras. Although tired from the hectic schedule and the brevity of their night's rest, all three felt invigorated rather than fatigued. It had been a joyous trip in spite of the difficult start. The grief Margaret felt over Paul's absence had abated somewhat as she was able to relive their wonderful years together in India and the work they had accomplished.

One month after her return from India, Margaret traveled to Kansas City to attend a banquet program honoring the lives and contributions of Paul and Dr. Dave Robinson. Dr. Robinson had been one of the American plastic surgeons who had spent several weeks at Vellore. He was internationally famous in the areas of burn treatment and wound healing. He and Paul had remained close friends throughout the remainder of their lives and had died within one month of each other. His successor at the University of Kansas Burn Center, Dr. Mani, was a Vellore graduate and another close friend of Paul's.

Dr. Mani was now retired, but in his decades of patient care he had embraced not only the medical teachings of these two giants but also their spirituality and ethics. He wished to celebrate these teachers and to honor their legacy by creating a fund that would sponsor health care students wishing to study abroad. Besides Dr. Mani, several other Vellore grads working in the Kansas City area participated, including Dr. Vimala Seshumurty, Margaret's original assistant years before at Schieffelin. As the guest of honor surrounded by such love, Margaret could see the legacy she and Paul had created, and thanked the Lord for the opportunities He had given the two of them.

The Lord appeared to have used these special events of 2004 not only to show Margaret how dearly she and Paul were loved by so many but also to infuse enthusiasm back into her life, reinvigorating her so that she would be able to continue the tasks God wished her to do. By giving her these opportunities to re-trace her steps through the lives of so many people, places, and past efforts, it was as if God were braiding hundreds of bright strands from Margaret's life into a stout rope and using this to pull her along through the difficult months and years following Paul's death.

The most important strand God wove into the rope was the strand of love, for it is this element, bestowed upon Margaret in abundance, that has restored her health. The love of God reflected in the love of family—both biological and church families—friends, colleagues, and countless others gives her the vigor to continue on. The energy she brings to her day is fueled by the affection she has received. The twinkle that has returned to her eyes is from the love she feels from God and which she wants to share with everyone around her.

Until Dr. Margaret is called into the Lord's presence, she is content to do His work for as long as He has tasks to give her. She is an active member of the board of trustees for CRISTA Ministries, which includes her special interest in the work of World Concern. She serves on the board of the American Leprosy Mission as medical advisor and attends their meetings in South Carolina. In her church she serves on the Missions Committee and, as an elder, is involved in the work of the Outreach Committee for West Side Presbyterian Church and participates in Bible study and small group discussions. She is honorary co-chairperson of a fund-raising committee created by the Vellore CMC Board–USA to raise money for a new school of nursing at CMC. She has also joined an effort to raise funds for the Paul Brand Integrated Health Centre in Katpadi.

In recent years she has become involved with ophthalmology mission work in China and is on the Board of Advisors of Operation Eyesight, a group of Chinese Christian doctors who bring cataract surgery to a poor province of China. She has become involved with the Chinese Christian community in Seattle and elsewhere and has given several talks to their assemblies in Cincinnati.

At home she keeps the birdfeeders in the garden stocked with seed, as Paul once did. She picks the berries in her yard to make fruit sauces and makes Indian dishes for dinner parties with friends. She praises the Lord for wonderful mobility in her shoulder—and she once again enjoys playing the violin!

How often the words of the note that Dr. Carol Jameson sent me in November 1948 have come to mind! "You'll learn. Please start on Monday." We have to make a choice: Am I willing to do so-and-so, or do I dig my heels in and say "I can't. I won't." One thing I have learned: God never asks us to do something without supplying the needed "tools" for the job, be they physical, intellectual, or spiritual. You just begin with trust and let Him stay in charge.

"All I have needed Thy hand hath provided. Great is Thy faithfulness, Lord, unto me."

The Brand Children

Christopher Brand

Christopher graduated from Louisiana State University in Natchitoches in 1968 with a degree in zoology. He then decided to pursue marine biology, which combined his science interests and his love of underwater exploration. He entered a master's degree program at the University of Kingston, Jamaica, which was affiliated with Birmingham University in England, and while there he became certified in scuba diving. He then chose to leave his academic pursuits for a time.

In 1969, with the Vietnam War at its height, and despite his being a British citizen, Christopher enlisted in the United States Army. Through promotion he reached the highest level a resident alien could achieve. After he completed his military service, and using benefits of the G.I. Bill, he entered LSU in Baton Rouge and attained a master's degree in aquaculture. In 1974 he took a position with the Environmental Research Laboratory, affiliated with the University of Arizona–Tucson. His work began in Mexico, which allowed him the opportunity to learn Spanish. Later his research took him to Hawaii, then Singapore, back to Hawaii, and ultimately to Tucson where he had started.

In Hawaii, Christopher met Kelly Oakley, and on March 6, 1982, they were married in Haleiwa on Oahu. Christopher and Kelly's daughter, Evelyn, was born in Hawaii in 1984. She was named after Christopher's grandmother, Evelyn Brand. In 2000 the family moved to Olympia, Washington. Evelyn completed high school in 2002 and is now a graduate student in veterinary school at Washington State University in Pullman. Christopher took further training to become a certified teacher and now teaches science in a public high school in Olympia.

Jean Brand

In 1971 Jean applied to a missionary organization and also submitted an application for a visa from the Indian government. But India in the 1970s had become increasingly hostile to westerners. In 1974, however, she was able to go to India and spent the years from 1974 through 1979 in Bombay, working in Bible teaching and theological training.

In 1979 Jean returned to England and settled in the port city of Southampton on the southern coast. She supported herself for some months with various nursing jobs while working with a rapidly expanding church. Subsequently she moved to London to work with her church group there. She used her interest and skill in interior decorating and remodeling work to develop a business that for some years became her main source of income.

In 1992 she enrolled in Denver Baptist Seminary in Denver, Colorado, and graduated with a master's degree (with honors) in Christian Counseling. She then returned to Southampton, England, where she counsels, trains Christian counselors, and writes training manuals. She is the author of a book on the role of women from a Christian perspective, *A Woman's Privilege*, and is now working on a second book, which explores the themes of Galatians.

Mary (Brand) Jost

While attending the LSU nursing program in New Orleans, Mary met Jim Jost, a young man from St. Louis who was a medical student at Tulane University. They were married in the Protestant chapel at Carville on July 17, 1971.

In June of 1972 they moved to Minneapolis, Minnesota, where Jim did his six-year surgery residency. Their first child, Daniel, was born in 1972, followed by Rachael in 1974, Stephanie in 1976, and Alexandra in 1979.

Jim continues to practice surgery in central Minnesota, while Mary has recently renewed her nursing license to return to her professional career. She has been a group leader in Bible Study Fellowship for many years. Daniel is a manager in a large corporation in the Twin Cities and married Julie Rodriguez in September of 2005. Rachael lives in St. Paul, Minnesota, and works in medical information system management for a large health system. Stephanie has started a residency in Internal Medicine at the same hospital in Minneapolis where her father trained. Alex, having graduated from college with an interest in counseling, has become a licensed beautician and works in a salon in Duluth, Minnesota, as she considers possible graduate school in the future.

Estelle (Brand) Pauelua

In 1971, while living at Carville and attending classes at LSU, Estelle met a young man in the Protestant chapel choir who was a patient from Hawaii. Sylvester (Syl) Pauelua, had come to Carville to stabilize his leprosy disease and to have corrective surgery on his hands. Syl later returned to Hawaii, and upon completing her master's degree in 1974, Estelle decided to visit Hawaii. She returned from that visit and announced that Syl had proposed to her—and that she had accepted.

Estelle and Syl were married in Honolulu on May 28, 1977, with the entire Brand family along with Sylvester's extended clan in attendance. The couple eventually moved from the island of Oahu to the big island of Hawaii, where they built a home outside of the main city of Hilo. Estelle took a position as a preschool teacher, while Syl worked at developing their land for fruit and macadamia nut farming. Their daughter Margaret—named for her grandmother—was born in 1981 and their son Stephen in 1985.

In 2003, Margaret graduated from Northlands Bible College in Wisconsin and in July of that year married Matthew Summer. They now live in South Carolina, where they both hope eventually to enter teaching careers. Their daughter, and Dr. Margaret's first great-grandchild, Kylie Ipolani, was born on October 1, 2004, with a second child, Brandon Kupuno, born to the Summers on May 29, 2006 (Paul and Margaret's wedding anniversary date).

Estelle and Syl's son, Stephen, began studying engineering at the University of Hawaii, Honolulu, in the fall of 2003.

Patricia (Brand) Peters

Upon completing her A Level exams at Clarendon in 1972, Trish decided upon a career in medicine and was accepted at her parents' alma mater, University College and Hospital, London. Following her graduation from medical school, she took an anesthesiology residency at the University of Washington in Seattle.

During her first year of practice, she met Michael Peters, and they were married in Seattle in August of 1984. Mike completed a residency in radiology and began his practice, while Trish continued working in anesthesia. In 1991 they adopted Joshua Michael, and in 1994 they adopted Madeline Marie.

Today they live on Mercer Island in Seattle, and Trish continues to work part-time in anesthesia while Mike is now the head of his radiology group.

Pauline (Brand) Nelson

Pauline completed her high school education at Clarendon School in England and then returned to the States to attend Wheaton College in Wheaton, Illinois. After graduating with a degree in English in 1980, she returned to London, where she worked as a production studio assistant with BBC Television in their London studios.

On December 28, 1985, she married a fellow Wheaton graduate, Mark Nelson. Mark had obtained a PhD in Philosophy from Notre Dame and had accepted an appointment on the faculty of Hampden-Sydney College, an all-men's college in Farmville, Virginia, where Pauline found a position as a reporter for the local newspaper. She later went on to teach classes in writing at Longwood College in Farmville.

Pauline and Mark's first daughter, Eleanor, was born in 1988, and their second daughter, Isabel, in 1990. In 1994, Mark accepted a position in the Department of Philosophy at the University of Leeds in north-central England, and the family moved to the UK. Their third daughter, Lydia, was born in Leeds in 1994.

Pauline now works in healthcare research, and a new appointment for Mark will bring the family back to the States in 2006.

Note to the Reader

The publisher invites you to share your response to the message of this book by writing Discovery House Publishers, P.O. Box 3566, Grand Rapids, MI 49501, U.S.A. For information about other Discovery House books, music, videos, or DVDs, contact us at the same address or call 1-800-653-8333. Find us on the Internet at http://www.dhp.org/ or send e-mail to books@dhp.org.